EVERY HOUR - ON THE HOUR

A Baltimore Limited at dusk in the 1920's by Howard Fogg. King collection.

EVERY HOUR - ON THE HOUR

A CHRONICLE OF THE
WASHINGTON BALTIMORE & ANNAPOLIS
ELECTRIC RAILROAD

BY

JOHN E. MERRIKEN

LEROY O. KING, JR

EDITOR

Bulletin 130 of the Central Electric Railfans' Association

To Richard C. Meyer

Bulletin 130
Central Electric Railfans' Association
A special edition of *Every Hour on the Hour*

Publisher
LeRoy O. King, Jr.
4815 Allencrest
Dallas, TX 75244

Manufactured in the United States of America by
Taylor Publishing Company, Dallas

Library of Congress Catalogue Card Number 92-97149
ISBN 0 - 9600938 - 3 - 4

CONTENTS

LIST OF MAPS

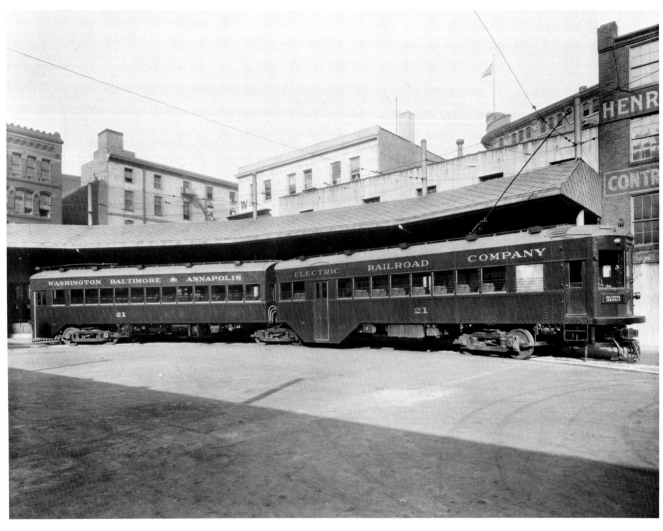

The legendary articulated cars make their debut, March 1927. Author's collection.

INTRODUCTION

The growth of nineteenth century America is a saga of the railroads building westward. This, however, is a story of westerners who turned east to build their tracks; a story that happened ere the twentieth century was barely a decade old, when the men from Cleveland came to Maryland, there to perceive the likelihood of heavy travel within a tight triangle of three cities rising to prominence, each according to its separate renown. They dreamed of a Washington Baltimore and Annapolis Electric Line; and, in the ways of free enterprise, an indomitable faith, and diligent pursuit—it came to be.

The city dweller then discovered the suburbs, the commuter became of age, and for the first time an inter-urban community of interest prospered on the promise of departures EVERY HOUR ON THE HOUR! It was a reassuring phrase which somehow lessened the time and shortened the distance to the far away city. But the service soon surpassed the slogan, until half-hourly schedules became the rule. From the very start, the Overland Electric outdid itself. It was perhaps typical of The W B & A whose record is often measured in superlatives.

The hour is yet early to pronounce a final judgement on the reasons for its rather short existence, for already the notion is advanced that a modern megalopolis served by "corridors" of high-speed electric trains is an innovation of the Great Society. The automobile of today is no more like Mr. Ford's Model T than the latest jetliner resembles the first trials at Kitty Hawk. Each of these pioneer efforts was perfected apace with advancing technology. Thus, any distinction between the visionary bullet trains of tomorrow and an "updated" interurban is purely one of semantics.

As was observed long ago—history does repeat.

J. E. M.

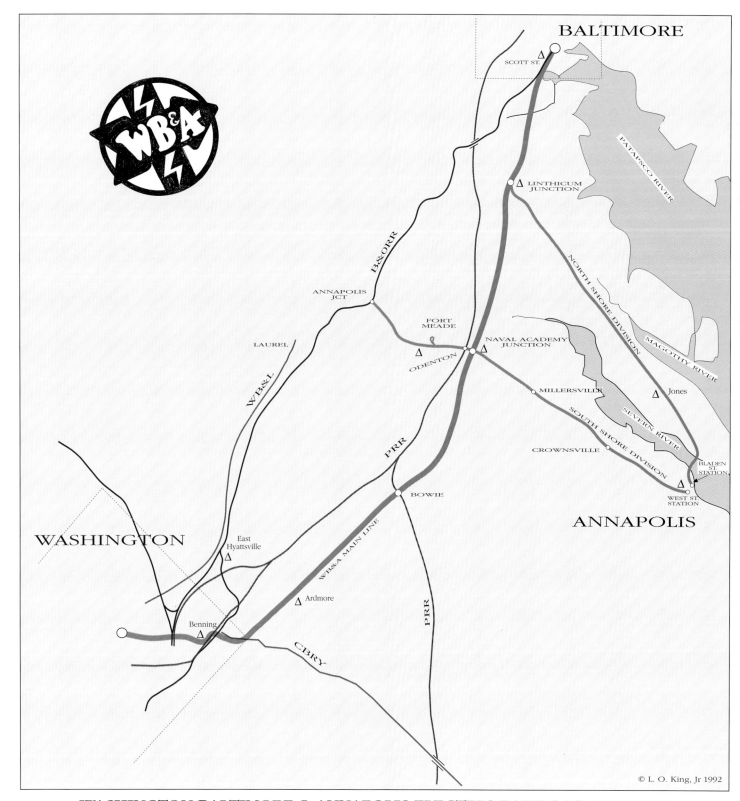

BALTIMORE

SCOTT ST. △

PATAPSCO RIVER

△ LINTHICUM JUNCTION

B&ORR

ANNAPOLIS JCT

LAUREL

WB&L

FORT MEADE

△ ODENTON

NORTH SHORE DIVISION

MAGOTHY RIVER

NAVAL ACADEMY JUNCTION △

△ Jones

MILLERSVILLE

SEVERN RIVER

PRR

CROWNSVILLE

SOUTH SHORE DIVISION

BLADEN ST. STATION

△ WEST ST STATION

BOWIE

ANNAPOLIS

WASHINGTON

East Hyattsville △

WB&A MAIN LINE

PRR

△ Ardmore

Benning △

CBRY

© L. O. King, Jr 1992

WASHINGTON BALTIMORE & ANNAPOLIS ELECTRIC RAILROAD COMPANY SYSTEM MAP

LEGEND

WB&A DOUBLE TRACK	WASHINGTON BERWYN & LAUREL
SINGLE TRACK	CHESAPEAKE BEACH
PENNSYLVANIA RAILROAD	POLITICAL BOUNDARIES
BALTIMORE & OHIO RAILROAD	SUB-STATIONS △

1

THE BUILDERS

A railroad is more than just cars and track. To the extent that it is an asset to its community, it is in turn a reflection of the people and industries that are its patrons. Its engineering achievements represent man's conquest of its natural obstacles; its service proclaims the efficiency of the men who make it run, and finally, its very existence is a tribute to the faith and foresight of those who built it. They were courageous men, these builders, who despite their speculative motives, must have believed in the future of the Interurban. Certainly, there was something of trust in the unfettered system of private initiative, where (with no thought of government help) the builders could envision an enterprise of such scope that might flourish or falter based upon their wisdom, ambition, and the size of their investments which were often as unrestricted as they were unguaranteed.

Such were the men from Cleveland, headed by W. H. Lamprecht, F. N. Wilcox, and James Christy, Jr. who, in May 1901, purchased the rights for a line which had been chartered two years before (May 22, 1899) as the Potomac & Severn Electric Railway Paraphrasing the first name, it was renamed the Washington and Annapolis Electric Railway under changes outlined in Chapter 307, Maryland General Assembly, Acts of 1900. That act had conferred certain additional powers which, despite the corporate name (Washington and Annapolis), had authorized the company to proceed with plans for a route to Baltimore*. In fact, by the summer of 1901 surveyors had already established the alignment, a remarkably straight course, from the easternmost corner of the District of Columbia to Westport at the southwestern limits of Baltimore; and negotiations with the United Railways & Electric Company had reached a tenta-

tive agreement for the use of city streetcar tracks from there into downtown Baltimore. These plans for city trackage rights were, however, subsequently defeated by rival interests associated with another interurban (via Catonsville) which had been partially built some years before.

These were years of "laying claim" to a given territory. It was an emulous era of acquiring routes that could forestall later competition, wherein the railroad builders, in their zeal, sometimes foresaw a need more imagined than real. Although the Washington & Annapolis Company in 1901 had yet to begin its own construction, there was an opportunity presented by successors to the ill-fated Columbia & Maryland Railway which secured for it still another line. On June 14, 1901, Henry A. Everett, on behalf of the Washington & Annapolis Electric Railway, purchased 8.96 miles of a completed double-track roadbed from Berwyn to Laurel.

In the course of negotiations with the Western Reserve Trust Company to underwrite construction funds for both projects, the promoters' goals and official titles were considerably enlarged when, on April 8, 1902, there appears for the first time the corporate entity called the Washington Baltimore and Annapolis Electric Railway; which in turn guaranteed the bonds and completion of the Washington Berwyn & Laurel Electric Railroad. Within six months a substation was built at

_____

* Article 6, Chapter 307 of the Maryland Acts of 1900 had empowered the Company to construct, maintain, and operate branch lines of electric railways to such distant cities, towns, and other points, etc; provided, that no extension built pursuant to this article would be longer than 25 miles, unless—etc. So the Baltimore end, originally called the branch line, very soon became the main line. Students of local history will recall a similar legal pretense of the Baltimore & Potomac Railroad's so-called "branch line" to Washington

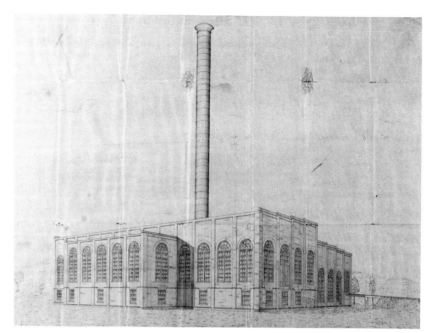

Construction of this massive power plant began in 1902 at Hyattsville, Maryland. The coal trestle ramp would have been from the Baltimore and Ohio Railroad's Alexandria Branch. The 1903 receivership caused the project to be abandoned. Author's collection.

Ammendale and a single track completed between Berwyn and Laurel. It was opened for service on September 21, 1902 under an operating agreement which provided for the cars and crews to be furnished by the City & Suburban Railway of Washington.

Meanwhile, the prime contract for design and construction of the main line was awarded on May 7, 1902 to the Cleveland Construction Company of Akron, Ohio. In the course of their preliminary study to recommend: "the nature of system best suited to local conditions, location of the generating plant, character of steam and electric machinery, etc.", the engineers planned a power house to be located on the banks of the Little Patuxent River. Without positive identification, there are clues to suggest that this first power house was designed for a site near the old iron foundry below Welch's Bridge on the county road leading to Portland Station (AW&B Railroad). Although land had been acquired, this plan was soon abandoned in favor of a much larger plant that was built in East Hyattsville. Strangely, that power house was not located along the interurban right-of-way, but rather beside the Alexandria Branch of the Baltimore & Ohio Railroad where that line crossed the upper reaches of the Anacostia River*. During the

summer of 1902, a tract of four acres had been purchased, and no less than seven major contracts were awarded for the building and equipment. Specifications for this project had envisioned a capacity sufficient for power requirements not only of the entire WB&A System and their Berwyn & Laurel Line, but also for a partial electrification of the Chesapeake Beach Railway, then being planned.

The building itself, a rather imposing pile, with some of the bases for the heaviest machinery, was estimated as two-thirds complete before work was suspended a year later. The receivership of 1903 was to force abandonment of the power house project, but to this day (1993) the extent of its foundations illustrates significantly the scope and hope of new railway planning in that halcyon age of Electric Traction.

During the initial stages, a supplemental contract with the supervising engineers dated August 1902 called for design of the cars, including: "specifications for trucks, motors, heaters, trolley poles and/or track conductor devices, and other appliances pertaining thereto". Although orders were awarded to G.C. Kuhlman Car Company and the Peckham Truck Company, the

_____
* See page 171 for more information.

The *Severn* built in 1875 by Rogers Locomotive Works. Author's collection.

nominal cost of these agreements suggests that preliminary work had not advanced very far.

Throughout the summer and fall of 1902, the new line took form with workmen starting the main power house, and sub-contractors engaged in massive grading and concrete work representing the abutments for some thirty-five bridges and major culverts. Because the road traversed countryside involving extensive cuts and fills, it would entail some 1.6 million cubic yards of excavation for the 30.74 miles of 66 foot right-of-way. Little trains of dump cars, mule drawn scoops and wagons, crude dynamite, and steam driven cement mixers were the tools of the day. And these were manned by construction gangs composed largely of immigrant laborers billeted in tent camps.

For engineering reference, the right-of-way was outlined by surveyors' "stations" which were designated by 100-foot chords numbered consecutively from the District Line northward, so that the 31 miles to Westport were represented by 1640 such stations. Though for convenience, the construction crews often used somewhat more descriptive references, such as Magruder Cut; Chinquapin (Cherry Grove); Horsepen (Lloyds); Dark Wood; Meyers' Farm; January Road (Waugh Chapel), Voltage (nearest the

substation near Mayfield); or Wheat Place; some of which bore only faint resemblance to later names that eventually made up the timetable. At a place in the woods where the surveyors crossed the Annapolis Washington & Baltimore (Elk Ridge) Railroad, their profile noted "Station No. 954 + 87.3", or a point 18.082 miles from milepost zero, which would one day become the railroad's center of operations. They called it Naval Academy Junction!

For the Annapolis division, the steam road known as the AW&B Railroad was acquired on February 26, 1903 by purchase of its entire capital stock from the Baltimore & Annapolis Short Line Railroad Co. It afforded an existing east-west road 20.13 miles in length, intersecting the north-south main line near Odenton. The AW&B line was a reorganization (April 1886) of the original Annapolis & Elk Ridge Rail Road which dated from an early charter granted in March 1837, and because of its pioneer beginnings, that had envisioned an extremely irregular, and in places very narrow, right-of-way, it was (even when electrified) to remain always a single-track operation. The AW&B Railroad was later deeded to the WB&A Electric Railway by formal purchase on December 16, 1908.

But construction was costly with little more

than grading and concrete work along the main line as tangible evidence to justify expenditures which, by the summer of 1903, had reached nearly $1,000,000. When the underwriters failed to respond with additional funds, bankruptcy ensued, and the work stopped.

A year and a half passed until what must have seemed the long-awaited benefactor appeared in the person of one Albert E. Green who had subscribed to a substantial 65 percent of the total stock then authorized, for which he had paid a cash deposit of $260,000. As the facts evolved, Green was merely the so-called "straw man" acting on behalf of a Cleveland syndicate organized by George T. Bishop and John Sherwin. In the expanding world of railway empires, those names were no strangers. Bold ventures in finance and imaginative planning had long been the hallmark of George T. Bishop whose name, before and since, has appeared throughout an impressive list of interurban and electric utilities projects. On February 8, 1905, an agreement was drafted wherein the syndicate, as purchasers, would acquire certain bonds, claims, and other liabilities incurred during construction of the WB&A main line, and completion of the Washington Berwyn & Laurel Electric Railroad, as well as the entire capital stock of the Annapolis Washington & Baltimore Railroad then valued at $358,000 for which the original underwriters would be paid in underlying securities of the new company. The new securities would be certified under two bond issues (totaling $4,000,000) which would be secured by first and second mortgages given to the Cleveland Trust Company.

On May 1, 1905 the stockholders met at the old Second Street depot in Annapolis to ratify the arrangement. Next day the Board of Directors, meeting in Baltimore, elected Mr. Bishop as their new president, with John Sherwin as vice president. And within days both mortgages were signed to raise funds needed to pay off the debts and resume work. Under new management, the Cleveland Construction Company was replaced by Roberts & Abbott Company who would handle engineering design and general supervision. In all aspects of their planning, the foremost consideration was *speed*. In fact, the entire route, in bypassing all intermediate villages, was taking the most direct line between Washington and the limits of Baltimore, wherein its advantages of the shorter distance, reduced running time, and frequency of interurban schedules propounded a certain preeminence over service already offered by two existing steam railroads. Though undaunted by any thought of competition, the interurban backers were reassured by a rather obvious distinction. for in those days the very name *Electric Railway* implied a modern concept which was synonymous with progress and speed.

Back in 1902, the Westinghouse Electric & Manufacturing Company had announced a completely new system of electric traction made possible by utilizing single-phase alternating current (AC) from a high-voltage trolley. After long experiment, Benjamin G. Lamme, the Chief Engineer at Westinghouse, had designed an AC single-phase series commutator-type motor, which held promise of decided benefits for railway use, in that it could reduce the number and initial costs of substations along the line. The merits of his invention , when compared with the more conventional type of direct current (DC) railway apparatus, attracted wide attention in scientific debates, the technical press, and even in foreign trade journals. Moreover, it was announced that the WB&A Electric Railway would be the first full scale commercial operation to demonstrate the advantages of this new system.* But the receivership of 1903 had interrupted all that. Although the Westinghouse system, meanwhile, had been adopted by other interurban lines with varying degrees of success, it was of interest that the WB&A project, as it was resumed under new owners with a completely different staff of engi-

---

* A paper by Benjamin G. Lamme of Westinghouse read before the American Institute of Electrical Engineers on September 26, 1902, and reprinted in Street Railway Journal of October 4, 1902.

George T. Bishop (1864-1940). Western Reserve Historical Society.

Three young men whose futures were to frame an adventure in railroading beyond dreams of even the most ardent interurban enthusiast. Carson Schumacher who would become the Superintendent of Transportation; Eber W. Weinland, future Chief Engineer; and James J. Doyle, destined to be General Manager, and eventually President. Author's collection.

neers, was still to adopt an AC single-phase electrification; but to be built this time by the General Electric Company.

As construction work again got underway, the immediate task, to the exclusion of city terminal arrangements, was to complete the cross-country (interurban) section in accordance with profiles already established by the previous builders. In this, a certain urgency was involved.

The WB&A countryside was always sparsely settled, and passengers of a later period were to remember the undulating fields of corn and tobacco, and especially the lush forests of scrub pine that bordered the line for miles. But the aftermath of the early construction had left its scars. As a new motorman was to remark during the first days of operation: "All stops look alike. It's all red clay." Such was the scene in 1905. The previous builders had made a venturous start—and left. In various cases, farmland had been

split, rural access roads had been severed, and drainage problems created by cuts and fills of the unfinished work from 1903; so that some real and tangible progress was now essential to keep faith with those who had sold land or granted easements in consideration of benefits to be derived from completion of the promised railroad.

By mid-summer of 1905 the place was again alive with bustling activity, as the Fidelity Construction Company of Detroit took over the contract for grading, pipe culverts, track laying, and ballasting of 29.4 route miles, or 58.8 track miles, with fourteen sidings, and all special work for the yards and shop to be established near Odenton, about midway of the line. The line was divided into three construction camps known as "residencies", whose supervisors would coordinate the advance of their roadbed, with delivery of rail as needed, with output from the gravel pits, with 60 days prior notice for shipment of specific bridge-work when ready. And in an age still innocent of rubber tires, practically all forms of machinery and material moved via rail, which required that roadbed and river crossings be usable as the line progressed.

An inventory of the Fidelity Construction Company affords a unique insight into the methods employed. Among other items, it lists:

3 Standard gauge 40 ton locomotives, with tenders
1 Engine on loan from the A. W. & B. Railroad
24 Standard gauge flat cars
36 Narrow gauge dump cars (of 4 cubic yard capacity)
1 Gasoline motor car
1 Spreader car
2 Steam shovels, Vulcan type Giant-D
1 Complete camp outfit at Odenton Farm
5 Tents, with cots and bedding
6 Farm wagons and 1 Buggy
4 Mules
2 Sorrel horses named "Dandy" and "Dan"
1 Spotted pony named "Dolly"

Standard cross ties of chestnut or white oak were specified to be placed twenty-four inches apart, or to number not less than 2640 to the mile. And while the railway's permanent track materials could be used for construction purposes (that permitted the contractor to spike ties for one narrow gauge track), it was agreed that all spike holes would be filled with chestnut plugs when the finished track was laid for standard gauge. The abundance of good grade ballast, which was readily obtained from various gravel pits along the line, had overridden any consideration of treated ties.

Eighty pound rail and other track materials furnished by the Carnegie Steel Company, Cambria Steel Company, and the Pennsylvania Steel Company were received at Odenton Junction, as well as through a temporary connection with the B&O at Clifford. On May 9, 1906, a contract with Kaltenbach & Griess (Interstate Engineering Company) of Bedford, Ohio ordered prefabricated steelwork for the following bridges:

Pope's Creek Viaduct (High Bridge)
3 x 64-foot spans for Big Patuxent River
3 x 64-foot spans for Little Patuxent River
1 x 64 foot span for Holly Run Cove (North of Pumphreys)
5 x 64-foot spans for Patapsco River
"I" Beams for various solid-floor bridges
All trolley poles attached to bridges (structures for the Baltimore Terminal Company not included)

Some measure of the magnitude of all this may be gleaned from a latter-day accounting of the project that itemizes:

Gross tons of steel rail & fittings	13,412
Gross tons of steel bridges	2,337
Number of overhead timber bridges	22
Number of cross ties	240,675
Overhead linework, including:	
Number of poles	4,498
Aluminum wire(pounds)	99,054
Copper wire(pounds)	1,037,557
(Concrete bridges and culverts, inseparable from real estate, not included)	

The engineering firm of Roberts & Abbott was based in Cleveland, so it was hardly surprising that much of their supervisory talent had been recruited from the ranks of several of their previous projects throughout Ohio and Indiana. One employee was a young surveyor from West Baltimore*, Ohio who had worked on various location surveys for

_____
* West Baltimore was later renamed Verona, Ohio

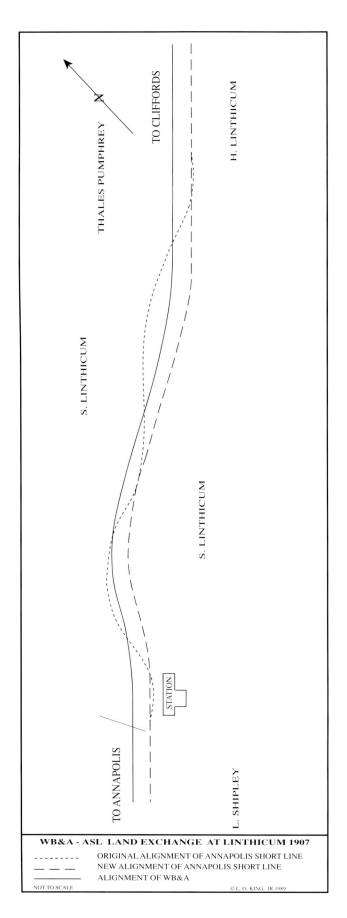

THALES PUMPHREY

TO CLIFFORDS

H. LINTHICUM

S. LINTHICUM

S. LINTHICUM

STATION

TO ANNAPOLIS

L. SHIPLEY

WB&A - ASL LAND EXCHANGE AT LINTHICUM 1907

· · · · · · · · ORIGINAL ALIGNMENT OF ANNAPOLIS SHORT LINE
— — — NEW ALIGNMENT OF ANNAPOLIS SHORT LINE
——— ALIGNMENT OF WB&A

NOT TO SCALE   © L. O. KING, JR 1989

the interurban routes out of Dayton. In 1906, Eber W. Weinland, who was then only twenty-seven, had been sent to Maryland as chief of the party supervising trackwork of the southern residency (District Line to Bowie Road). A year later he returned as resident engineer to complete the northern section as far as Cliffords; and afterwards was to remain as Chief of Maintenance-of-Way throughout the entire life of The WB&A. There was nothing about real estate, roadbed, signals, track, or bridges that couldn't be answered by E. W. Weinland. Thus, from the reputable word of some of his reports and fragmentary notes are a few of the builder's problems vaguely seen.

With one exception, the main line had been held to minimum grades not exceeding two percent; a built-in advantage that would have to be exploited. But considerations of easy grades and highway grade separations were not the only prerequisites to fast schedules. As a case in point, the projected route as laid out through Linthicum involved crossing and recrossing the more sinuous path of the original Baltimore & Annapolis Short Line Railroad which then ran somewhat to the *west* of the new line. In order to avoid these crossings, and at the same time adhere to the straighter alignment, the WB&A Company arranged for an exchange of the respective rights-of-way; and relocated the Short Line tracks on a new parallel roadbed to the *east*.

In the days before big yellow earth movers with huge rubber tires, railroad embankments were built up by means of timber falsework that enabled little dirt trains to reach out over the lowlands, depositing their loads of earth and rock into a loose fill which was often very unstable. Without efficient means of compacting the spoil, it required months for such fills to stabilize; and in cases of sub-strata of mud or marsh, it often seemed they never would.

At the site of the Patapsco crossing, the builders had envisioned the south approach as a long fill across the wide mud flats leading to the river. Over the years, an accumulation of alluvial silt had formed a sand bar, or small island, which separated the main stream from the mouth of a tributary known as Holly Run Cove. By utilizing this center island, protected by a kind of counter-fort reinforcing the abutments, it was planned to cross the river on two bridges, comprised of one span at Holly Run and five spans over the Patapsco. Indeed, much of the concrete had been poured and steelwork had been ordered according to such a plan. But man has not always reckoned with the vagaries of Mother Nature. One evening the workforce had built up the earthen back-fill to a height of nineteen feet. By next morning it had disappeared completely— swept away by the current. Several nights later, to a lesser extent, the same thing happened again.

Less than eighty feet downstream, the Baltimore & Annapolis Short Line crossed the same water on a long timber trestle, but as the river carried away large amounts of mud, rock, boulders, etc. from the new construction (upstream), it lodged against the parallel trestle so as to seriously threaten its alignment. So great was the force of this rising tide that retaining guy cables, stretched between the two bridges, gave way as several of the concrete piers sunk out of sight. The Short Line Company filed for an injunction to halt the work, until large timber fenders were built upstream to divert the river's torrent away from the foundations. In the course of solving this problem, the WB&A Company was to abandon its plans for the first bridge to reach the mutable island of sand, which was covered over with an even larger fill. And to this day the concrete outlines of Holly Run bridge lie buried deep beneath the south embankment, which may someday yield a puzzle for future archaeologists.

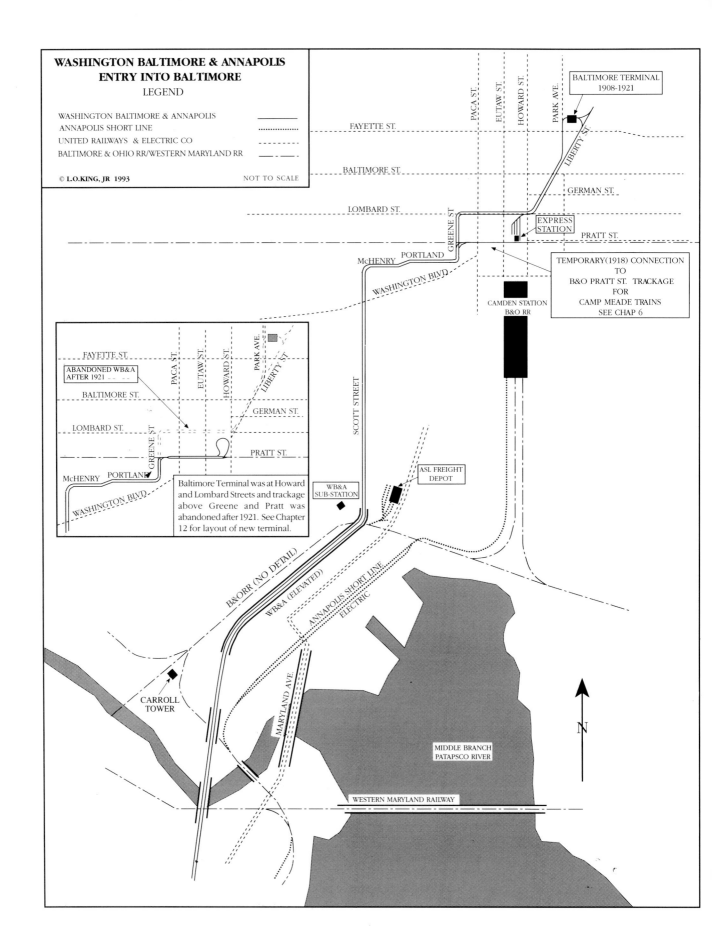

WASHINGTON BALTIMORE & ANNAPOLIS
ENTRY INTO BALTIMORE
LEGEND

WASHINGTON BALTIMORE & ANNAPOLIS
ANNAPOLIS SHORT LINE
UNITED RAILWAYS & ELECTRIC CO
BALTIMORE & OHIO RR/WESTERN MARYLAND RR

© L.O.KING, JR 1993   NOT TO SCALE

PACA ST.
EUTAW ST.
HOWARD ST.
PARK AVE.
LIBERTY ST.

BALTIMORE TERMINAL
1908-1921

FAYETTE ST.

BALTIMORE ST.

GERMAN ST.

LOMBARD ST.

GREENE ST.

EXPRESS
STATION

PRATT ST.

McHENRY   PORTLAND

WASHINGTON BLVD.

TEMPORARY(1918) CONNECTION
TO
B&O PRATT ST. TRACKAGE
FOR
CAMP MEADE TRAINS
SEE CHAP 6

CAMDEN STATION
B&O RR

FAYETTE ST.
PACA ST.
EUTAW ST.
HOWARD ST.
PARK AVE.
LIBERTY ST.

ABANDONED WB&A
AFTER 1921

BALTIMORE ST.

GERMAN ST.

LOMBARD ST.

GREENE ST.

PRATT ST.

McHENRY   PORTLAND

WASHINGTON BLVD.

SCOTT STREET

Baltimore Terminal was at Howard
and Lombard Streets and trackage
above Greene and Pratt was
abandoned after 1921. See Chapter
12 for layout of new terminal.

WB&A
SUB-STATION

ASL FREIGHT
DEPOT

B&ORR (NO DETAIL)

WB&A (ELEVATED)

ANNAPOLIS SHORT LINE
ELECTRIC

CARROLL
TOWER

MARYLAND AVE.

N

MIDDLE BRANCH
PATAPSCO RIVER

WESTERN MARYLAND RAILWAY

2

THE BALTIMORE TERMINAL COMPANY

As mentioned, the Washington and Annapolis Company's right-of-way ended at Westport. There the original builders had purchased a tract of 1.865 acres for the car barn which was to have been located west of the line at Fish House Road (Waterview Avenue). In those days the right-of-way ran closely beside (to the west of) the B&O South Baltimore Branch which was an extension of Kloman Street. By 1907, however, both railroads had been relocated: the B&O to the east and the WB&A on a more northerly alignment to the west, leaving the old car barn site then to the *east* of the established line.* In the Baltimore papers of January 18, 1902 it was even announced that a trackage agreement had been concluded, granting the interurban an entry into town via the Westport Branch of United Railways & Electric Company, an arrangement that was promptly denied by the street car management. Whatever the accord, or lack thereof, the concept of that Westport hilltop as an important railway junction is totally at odds with the current-day spectacle of a seething mass of traffic that slices squarely through the middle of the hill, with its disjoined halves east and west. In fact, the first partition of Westport coincides roughly with the revised plans which followed the railroad's reorganization of 1905.

Among other business concluded at the stockholders' meeting of May 1, 1905, they had voted:

> "RESOLVED: To extend the branch line.**
> from its present terminus at Westport
> near the city limits of Baltimore to some
> convenient point in the City of Baltimore

---

* Land records of Baltimore County, Libre N.M.B. 257 Folio 118 recorded 4 Nov 1901.

** Dating from the original charter of the W & A Railway Company, the Baltimore end was still called the branch line, which very soon became the main line.

either by building an electric railway, or by acquiring rights over lines owned by others."

Little did they realize the futility of this last phrase of their resolution which would hardly conform to some definite opinions of the new president, who was a shrewd and farsighted pragmatist. Under his direction, the WB&A, theretofore cast in the mold of a rural trolley line, had now advanced to the status of a high-speed railroad. Encouraged by his recent success in building the Northern Texas Traction Company (Fort Worth to Dallas), Mr. Bishop was determined that no expense should be spared to complete his Maryland road in keeping with the highest standards of modern interurban construction. The main line would be double tracked throughout, and over a million dollars would be committed solely for the bridges and underpasses that would eliminate practically all public grade crossings. Then to what avail were these investments in a high-speed operation if only to be sacrificed to joint running with a city streetcar line? Moreover, the route of the Shore Line (Westport) trolley crossed three steam railroads at grade—another penalty in any attempt at precise scheduling. It was perhaps typical of George T. Bishop that the problem should be met head on. His railroad would go over the obstacles.

On June 5, 1905, he organized the Baltimore Terminal Company Inc., which would finance and build an independent approach to a downtown passenger station. After first acquiring a site for the mid-city terminal, Mr. Bishop negotiated the terms of a city franchise for his line to reach it. However, access to the center of town was not without a minor compromise in which less than a mile of dual-gauge track was to be shared with the city cars. Though most important, the Terminal Company

What was to become the Westport Tunnels began in 1906 with an excavation forty feet deep that sliced squarely through the hill at Waterview Avenue. Author's collection.

planned a rather unique rapid transit route across the various obstacles of South Baltimore which, with the tunnels, bridges, viaduct structures, and city tracks, ultimately evolved as one of the most costly ventures of its kind.

Under provisions of the Maryland Acts ratified on March 30, 1906, the Baltimore Terminal Company extended its domain from Westport to Clifford, a mere 1.31 mile which, technically, reduced the WB&A mileage correspondingly. Although little more than a legal distinction, this exchange of boundaries had enabled the Terminal Company to reach a point of connection with the Baltimore & Annapolis Short Line Railroad; and, providing that steam road would convert to electric passenger operations, to have both companies assume the downtown terminal project as a joint undertaking. A contract to that effect was signed on January 17, 1906. Here, it might be recalled that this agreement was just prior to a merger that would provide financial infusion from the Maryland Electric Railways syndicate which did, indeed, bring about the Short Line's eventual electrification. But that was still in the future. There is ample evidence to verify a brief period of combined planning between the Short Line and the Terminal Company. Though despite subsequent default which left it without the conjoined backing, Mr. Bishop still affirmed that the original project would nevertheless prevail.

On October 27, 1905, the Traction Construction Company was chartered as a Delaware corporation , later licensed in Maryland, as a contracting agency for most of the work to be awarded on behalf of the Terminal Company. As a subsidiary, the construction company served as a legal device to protect the parent corporation against lawsuits and claims arising from the acquisition of land, construction disputes, and to enforce each contractor's compliance with technical specifications outlined by the supervising engineers. While the engineering residency (or region of responsibility) was restricted to Baltimore City and County, that short segment was by far the most complex of the entire line.

In the present age of feverish land development on all sides it takes great effort now to summon back the excitement, the awe even, which attended the big construction events of 1906. Kestler's farm, located on Annapolis Road near Grave Yard Lane, was soon the scene of two steam shovels starting a long and very deep cut, which prompted one engineer to observe that this chasm (over 46 feet at its deepest) looked like the Panama Canal coming through Westport. Within the trench, sidewalls and

North portal of the Westport tunnels. Author's collection.

a ceiling of reinforced concrete were placed to form a bore 18 feet x 24 feet, which was then backfilled to create two tunnels of a total length of 461 feet, connected by high retaining walls.

Next came the bridges, thirteen in all, including an agreement for two not yet required:

> Three timber bridges for private road crossings vicinity of English Consul
> Curtis Bay Branch, B&O RR underpass
> First Street (Maisel St.) Westport underpass
> Kent Street Westport
> Gwynns Falls and Western Maryland Rwy
> Putnam Street, B&O Passenger underpass (future covenant)
> South Baltimore Branch, B&O Railroad temporary trestle
> Clare Street, B&O Freight Line (future covenant)
> Elk Street elevated
> Bush Street elevated
> Scott Street, B&O Railroad Main Line

From 1884 until the first years of this century, the Baltimore & Ohio Railroad had formulated some rather grandiose designs for rerouting its main line through Baltimore. There was the proposed Pratt Street/Eastern Avenue viaduct extending from Camden Station to Patterson Park*. There was the Howard Street Belt Line, an underground route which was, indeed, built; and a few years later, under the dynamic reign of Leonor F. Loree as president, there was an elaborate project for changing (straightening) the southwest approaches to Camden Station via a four-track passenger high line, separate from a revised alignment of the freight tracks, Carroll Junction to Bailey**. Thus, in securing a right-of-way, the Baltimore Terminal Company found itself deeply involved not only in that which was—but in that which was to be. In these negotiations, the Terminal Company had agreed, when required at a future date, to lower its tracks by some thirteen feet in order to pass under

---

* Municipal Acts of 1884, Chapter 233

** 81st and 82nd Annual Reports, B&O RR, 1907-1908

During the fall of 1907, piers and abutments for the Gwynns Falls Bridge were placed by the Henry N. Hooper Company for a three-span viaduct crossing Manokin Street, the Western Maryland tracks, and the stream. The high fill seen here behind the north abutment was soon removed in favor of the revised design as shown below. Author's collection.

In 1906, the contractor had just placed the footings for the new interurban viaduct parallel to the B&O main line at Bayard Street. Author's collection.

A train from Annapolis crossing the B&O Main Line at Scott Street. A Brill car and the two tone paint of the rebuilt trailer indicate the standard consist of the North Shore Division during the period of 1925 -1929. B&O Museum.

the B&O's proposed four-track passenger line at Putnam Street and *over* a new four-track freight route that would intersect near Clare Street. Needless to say, these plans never came to pass; and as force of circumstances were ultimately to prove, the Electric Line's timber trestle, always called the "temporary" crossing, would become as permanent as everything else.

In order to satisfy requirements of the B&O Railroad's Department of Bridges, the underpass at the Curtis Bay Line (until then a timber trestle) and a thru-truss superstructure at Scott Street were ordered from the Baltimore Bridge Works (a subsidiary of the railroad). All other steel work was fabricated by the Inter-state Engineering Company of Bedford, Ohio who were the general bridge contractors for the entire railroad.

Of particular interest was the crossing at Gwynns Falls which was designed as a three-span thru plate girder bridge on concrete piers and abutments. After eighteen months of construction, the project was essentially finished before it was determined that the north approach, an earthen embankment over thirty-eight feet high, would not stabilize and settle sufficiently to support the tracks. Accordingly, a new contract was hastily awarded on March 27, 1908 to Lauer and Harper Company for reconstruction of the north abutment, with two additional bridge spans to rest on a steel bent supported by steel towers and pedestals, replacing the dirt fill. This last-minute revision was to delay the opening of the Baltimore end by some two months after the Washington service had begun.

The eighth floor suite of the Maryland Trust Building in Baltimore was a busy place. As local headquarters for the supervising engineers, it was a consultation room where prospective bidders came to review specifications, data sheets, and a veritable library of blueprints. It was a real estate office with all the legal implications that that involved. As business offices for the railway, the terminal company, and its contracting agency, the eighth floor housed a variety of administrative functions whose records and files generated voluminous paperwork. And in the final months, it was also a meeting place—a conference room where negotiations were held for the contracts and working agreements that would govern a railroad about to begin.

The introductory stage of any large enterprise also demands a bid for public acceptance; an effort in public relations with its press releases, advertising, and a bit of splurge and splash for general inspection. Months before the line was operational, the Company had sponsored tours for local businessmen, civic groups, politicians, and the press. One reporter described his trip from Baltimore, starting on the Westport street car, to view the elevated construction still in progress; of scrambling down the loose dirt embankment for a better look at the Patapsco bridge; of his ride on one of the new Niles cars which was coupled behind a steam engine; and of his visit to see the big turbines at Benning. No doubt it was impressive and the newspapers frequently carried glowing accounts under ebullient captions, such as: "Route of the Electric Pullmans" or "To Washington by Trolley" or "High-Speed Service on the Dot" or "New Electric Line Soon Ready". It was, to be sure, a time of "Great Expectations!"

A LIST OF ESSENTIAL TERMINAL CONTRACTS AND OPERATING
AGREEMENTS COMPLETED PRIOR TO THE OPENING OF THE LINE

• Baltimore City Ordinance No 123 approved April 27, 1906 which authorized the use of certain streets.

• Contracts with United Railways & Electric Company to build certain city trackwork, and with Smethurst & Allen Company (August, 1906) to construct the overhead lines on the streets of Baltimore.

• Trackage rights with United Railways & Electric Company as outlined in a joint operating agreement concluded December 28, 1906.

• Contract with United Railways & Electric Company (November 18, 1907) for purchase of current from overhead used jointly with street cars.

• Contract with J. Henry Miller (May 18, 1907) to build the Terminal Station in Baltimore.

• Contract with Potomac Electric Power Company (January 18, 1907) for all electric power, except for the November 18, 1907 agreement with the United Railways and Electric Company. The power house in Hyattsville was retained, unused, until it was sold on December 21, 1912.

• Trackage rights with Washington Railway & Electric Company for joint operations within District of Columbia concluded by agreement signed April 15, 1907.

• Contract with Washington Railway & Electric Company (October, 1907) to build the White House Station and terminal yards in Washington.

• A contract with the Chesapeake Beach Railway Company. In order to cross the District Line at Seat Pleasant, the interurban's alignment would have cut across multiple yard tracks of the Chesapeake Beach Railway. To simplify this layout, the station building and yards of the steam road were relocated to the east to make way for a new junction where the Electric Line's double tracks crossed only one track of the Chesapeake Beach Line at grade.

• Franchises approved June 23 and July 2, 1907 by the Mayor and Aldermen of Annapolis for the use of certain streets.

• Contract with E. D. Skipper & Company (January, 1908) to build a new West Street Station in Annapolis.

• A formal lease of all passenger cars. As of 1907, the WB&A Company owned only two forty-six-ton electric freight motors, twenty-five flat cars, and one caboose. In addition to several steam locomotives borrowed from the AW&B Railroad (controlled though not yet owned by the Cleveland management), this was the extent of rolling stock then available to the Railway Company. Over the next four years, all passenger equipment, comprising some sixty cars of four different types, would be acquired by the Baltimore Terminal Company for lease to the operating company. For the opening of the line, there were at first nineteen limited cars and four local combination types, purchased at a cost of $460,000 fully equipped. Within Baltimore City, these were licensed at the rather risible rate of $ 0.41$^{2/3}$ per car per month, payable to the Collector of Water Rents and Licenses.

Right: This view looks east at Chesapeake Junction. The WB&A's District Line station shelter is straight ahead while the terminal of the WRY&ECO's Columbia Line and the Chesapeake Beach Railway station are to the right. King collection.

Below: The right of way just as the line left the District of Columbia. The bridge in the background carries Addison Chapel Road over the railroad. Author's collection.

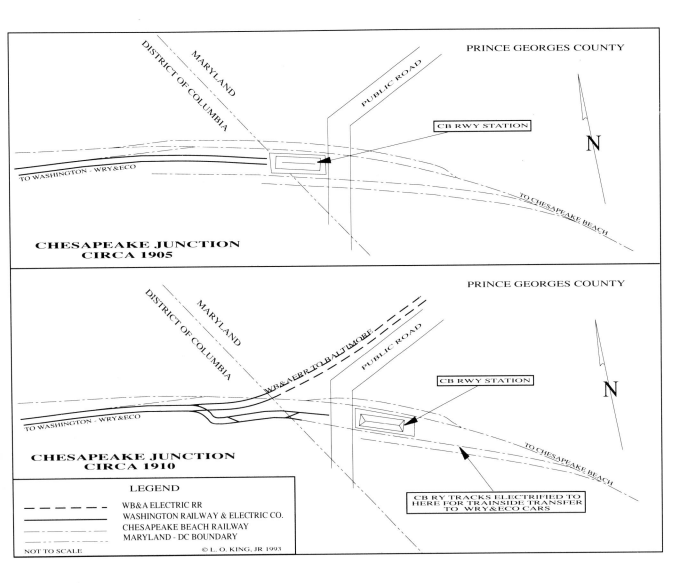

PRINCE GEORGES COUNTY

MARYLAND

DISTRICT OF COLUMBIA

PUBLIC ROAD

CB RWY STATION

N

TO WASHINGTON - WRY&ECO

TO CHESAPEAKE BEACH

**CHESAPEAKE JUNCTION
CIRCA 1905**

PRINCE GEORGES COUNTY

MARYLAND

DISTRICT OF COLUMBIA

WB&A ER R TO BALTIMORE

PUBLIC ROAD

CB RWY STATION

N

TO WASHINGTON - WRY&ECO

TO CHESAPEAKE BEACH

**CHESAPEAKE JUNCTION
CIRCA 1910**

CB RY TRACKS ELECTRIFIED TO
HERE FOR TRAINSIDE TRANSFER
TO WRY&ECO CARS

LEGEND

— — — — —   WB&A ELECTRIC RR
————————   WASHINGTON RAILWAY & ELECTRIC CO.
————————   CHESAPEAKE BEACH RAILWAY
—·—·—·—·—   MARYLAND - DC BOUNDARY

NOT TO SCALE   © L. O. KING, JR 1993

A Baltimore Limited made up of two of the original "Electric Pullmans" makes ready to leave from White House Station at 15th & H Streets N. E. in Washington. The shopman, motorman (in traditional striped overalls), and the conductor are all equally proud of their handsome charge. King collection.

3

A TIME TO REJOICE

Viewed through the optimistic gates of newness, the prospects gleamed! Merchants of both cities hailed the new line as a means of bringing more customers. The chambers of commerce saw it in terms of convention and excursion possibilities. The New Era Amusement Company announced plans for another "Electric Park" to be built at Naval Academy Junction. The Lincoln Heights Land Improvement Company published a handsome brochure describing its new subdivision (later Seabrook) just eleven minutes from the District Line; while the New Respess City Industrial Colony Company of Baltimore advertised over 5,000 homesites sold for a completely new city on the site that would one day become Camp Meade. Such were the hopeful horizons created through the magic of modern transportation.

February 7, 1908 is the date frequently given for the opening of the line, and in fact it did mark the beginning of a limited trial operation between Washington and Annapolis. That schedule was maintained by one car on a two hour headway, inasmuch as there were, as yet, no signals to regulate opposing runs; and because the entire distance, even the main line, was still restricted to a single track; the second track being constantly occupied by construction trains.

There are dates hardly recognized in the conventional understanding of school book history—dates which, lacking the glaring overtones of famous birthdays, heroic battles, or politics, nevertheless were to become those epic portents of the interurban era then unfolding. Such a date for Baltimore was March 25, 1908; and 'tis a great loss to history that there had not been present on that occasion all the modern instruments of sight and sound to record exactly how it happened. Next best, however, are the old newspapers whose accounts gave it form.

The Washington - Annapolis Divisions had been running for almost two months, tentatively, as it were, awaiting only their third component to proclaim the *Finis Coronat Opus*. Wednesday the 25th turned up unseasonably mild. A fairer day could not have been chosen. On either side of the Baltimore Terminal, huge banners bearing the Company emblem were hung across the middle of each street. Up and down Liberty and Lexington Streets, flags snapped in the March breeze, while many of the downtown merchants featured festive red white and blue bunting draped across the store fronts, with a large sign of congratulations or other special display in their windows. Hochschild Kohn & Company ran a half page newspaper ad in all three cities: "Baltimore's Best Store greets The WB&A" with a stylized sketch of the new trains bringing new customers from all around . The station waiting room was banked with flowers; beautiful lithographed timetables were there for the taking; and tin lapel buttons, green and white, imprinted with "The Electric Line" were distributed to the curious onlookers who, as it turned out, would not have a ride for another nine days.

In the Directors' meeting room on the second floor, refreshments were being served to company officials and distinguished guests, including George T. Bishop, President; John Sherwin, Vice President; James N. Shannahan, General Manager; George Weems Williams, Vice President & General Counsel; George A. Craig, President of the Traction Construction Company; E.P. Roberts, M.A. Munn, J.C. Gillette, and Bret Harter of the Supervising Engineers; C.E. Eveleth and T.M. Childs from the General Electric Company; George W. Fisher of the Fidelity Construction Company; Charles E. Gladfelter of the AW&B. Railroad who was also Secretary of The WB&A Co.; John Wilson Brown and other officials of The Annapolis Short Line; Waldo H.

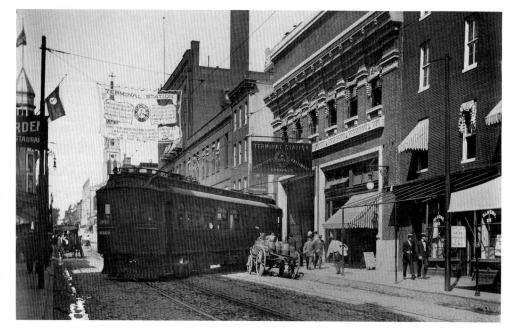

Shortly after the official opening, one of the inaugural banners is still displayed across Park Avenue as the Washington Limited leaves the station. Note dual gauge of the southbound track. Author's collection.

Sawin, soon to become Superintendent of the Maryland Electric Railways; Officials from the street car companies; the B&O and Pennsylvania Railroads; as well as prominent members from the banking circles of Cleveland and Baltimore.

As the General Manager called "All Aboard!" it was 10:15 a.m.. when he signaled the motorman, and the big Niles car rolled out into Park Avenue with its vibrating gong clattering, the white markers

fluttering, and the sidewalk crowd cheering. It was the culmination of seven years; and on that day at least, the Monumental City's greatest monument was neither bronze statue nor marble shrine, but a practical work of bare utility—an Electric Railway.

As the big car left town it picked up speed, and at times, seemingly effortless, reeled off a mile a minute until the party reached Naval Academy Junction. There they were shown the impressive

An early scene shows one of the Limited cars as it left the Baltimore terminal on Park Ave., southbound. Norton D. Clark collection

Opening the line into Annapolis, March 25, 1908. The group posed here at Church Circle includes the President George T. Bishop (to the right of the car's retriever) and, second from his left, James J. Doyle then Superintendent of Track and Overhead, later to become the President. M. E. Warren Studio.

transformers, and a demonstration of the high-speed capabilities attained through flexibility of the catenary overhead. In the shops, they were shown a performance by the big traveling crane, the wheel press, and other modern facilities for car repairs; and, of course, they inspected the long lines of shiny new cars still undergoing final tests of their equipment being installed in these shops. Next the party was taken to Washington to see White House Station, with its dispatcher's tower overlooking the yard, and the landscaped front lawn encircled by a loop track for the city cars to meet the trains.

Then on to Annapolis where another crowd had gathered at the old depot opposite Second Street. Although electric trains had been arriving there for some weeks, this was to be the first time that a railway car of any kind had invaded the narrow streets for operation through the town By happy coincidence, it was a holiday (Maryland Day), school was out, and small fry of every description waved and pranced and danced beside the big car as it rumbled into West Street and up to Church Circle. There, joined by the Mayor of Annapolis, Mrs. Emma Abbott Gage of "The Evening Capital", Dr. Elihu S. Riley, the local historian, and others, everybody posed for the official photograph to commemorate: "an event which will go down in history as the greatest Maryland Day Celebration that ever happened in Annapolis". Apparently overcome by the auspiciousness of the moment, one reporter lapsed into a haze of hyperbole that goes:

> "Eureka!" some exclaimed, "I have found it, found at last a modern way to arouse interest from the outside world in a great old town teeming with antiquity and culture, but still clinging to the moldy past.* The first boat on the Mississippi did not cause as much excitement as the first trolley in Annapolis, as its party all agog sped through the streets in the Private Electric Car."

At the foot of Main Street people from the market and the wharves joined the jovial throng, waving and cheering the procession. At Lutz's Saloon the customers lined the curb, mugs in hand, to toast The New WB&A. The official party then went to Carvel Hall for an elaborate dinner and the necessary speeches, echoing such acclaim that all were convinced that here at last was the embodiment of

_____
* "Still clinging to the moldy past" alludes to a dramatic scene in the Town Council several months previously led by opponents of the railroad, and a fiery oration delivered by (Judge) Robert Moss in defense of progress.

intercity commerce such as had never before been known.

On a larger scale, the three cities had become beneficiaries of an endowment——a public asset wrought by finance, technical talent, and labor of the private sector. Relatively speaking, the creative tasks of this construction had been somewhat lightened by conditions of that day. The open countryside was then more open and available; matters of environmental impact were as yet unknown; public opinion was more receptive to public works; and free enterprise more free. Still and all, for the common good of *The Free State* it was indeed free.

Afterwards, the special car returned to Naval Academy Junction, to be taken by a locomotive to Annapolis Junction, where the distinguished guests boarded B&O trains for their respective cities. Three days later, another inspection trip was held for Mayor Mahool of Baltimore, his

Board of Estimates, members of the City Council, and a delegation of present and former politicians who were the Company's guests at a luncheon given at the New Willard in Washington. The line was opened to the public on April 3, 1908, and by that Friday night, several thousand citizens had given it their personal approval.

But jubilation and marvel over the new service was tempered all too soon by an ominous reality that haunts every railroad. In its haste to begin operations as early as possible, and to meet certain deadlines specified in its franchise, the road had sustained two wrecks in barely three months. Each of them on the single-track Annapolis Division, had resulted from an inadequate signal system; and although properly functioning signals were soon completed, public confidence had suffered as had any earnings that had to be diverted toward the settlement of claims from the accidents.

Inasmuch as the AW&B Railroad west of Odenton had not yet been electrified, the Annapolis Division was at first a joint steam/electric operation for both passenger and freight schedules. The main line was a passenger only timetable aimed primarily at capturing that business which had previously gone to the competing roads. Though, from a revenue standpoint, business began slowly. Not that patronage was lacking, initially, but rather that an unforeseen ratio of operating costs to gross receipts was mounting too fast to maintain a reasonable margin of safety. A glimmer of hope, as well as a crucial test, came over a year later during the presidential inauguration of March 4, 1909, which was also the occasion of a blizzard unparalleled in recent memory. Transportation everywhere was paralyzed—though to the interurban's credit, it performed remarkably throughout the storm, and was among the very first to clear the tracks and resume service for the crowds that had been stranded in Washington. A contingent of midshipmen from the Naval Academy which was to have marched in the parade, got as far as Odenton where it was to have taken the Pennsylvania Railroad to Washington. But when there was no longer any hope of reaching the festivities in time, the midshipmen returned to Annapolis—round trip via The Electric Line. For once at least, the weight and horsepower of those massive cars was an advantage.

55, one of the original Niles cars at the White House Station at the edge of Washington. It was taken by the photograph owner's father. Joseph Canfield collection

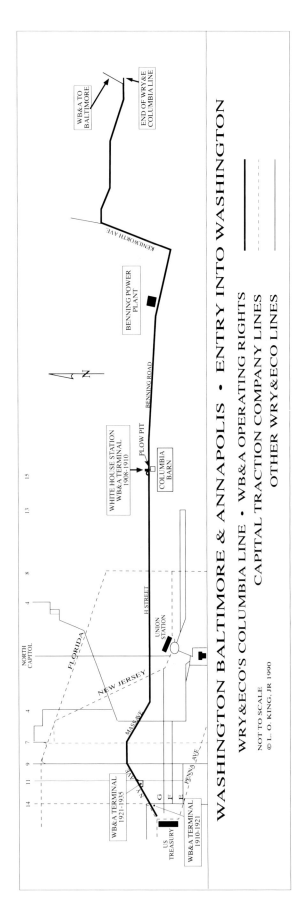

WASHINGTON BALTIMORE & ANNAPOLIS • ENTRY INTO WASHINGTON

WRY&ECO'S COLUMBIA LINE • WB&A OPERATING RIGHTS

CAPITAL TRACTION COMPANY LINES

OTHER WRY&ECO LINES

NOT TO SCALE
© L. O. KING, JR 1990

SPARKS

FROM

THE ELECTRIC LINE

A Weekly Magazine issued to inform the Public of interesting

events in

Washington, Baltimore and Annapolis

Free Distribution from Ticket Offices of The Electric Line

VOLUME 2	Week of February 15th, 1909	NUMBER 7

For Advertising Space in this Magazine apply to B. R. JOHNSON, Agent, Piper Building, Baltimore, Md.

Through to the Treasury

Announcement has already been made of the successful conclusion of negotiations between the Washington, Baltimore and Annapolis Electric Railway Company and the Washington Railway and Electric Company, by which an agreement has been reached to so rebuild the tracks of the Columbia line on H street and Massachusetts and New York avenues, that they will carry the interurban cars from Baltimore and Annapolis to the Treasury building at 15th street and New York avenue, northwest.

The proposition to extend the W., B. & A. line to the center of Washington met with universal support from all patrons of the road. Such representative Maryland people as Governor Crothers, Mayor Mahool, Mayor Claude, Cardinal Gibbons, James W. Owens and many others lent their active support to accomplish the result.

It is now expected that the tracks will have been rebuilt and the cars will be running without change from the centers of Baltimore and Annapolis to the very doors of the Treasury building in Washington by the first of the year. The inconvenience of changing to and from city cars at the edge of town will be entirely done away.

The arrangement means a long step forward in transportation facilities for Washington.

Author's collection

Washington, Baltimore and Annapolis Electric Railway Co.

THE ELECTRIC LINE

RATES OF FARE.

	ONE WAY	ROUND TRIP
Baltimore-Washington	$ .75	$1.25
Baltimore-Annapolis	.60	1.00
Washington-Annapolis	.75	1.25

TICKETS GOOD UNTIL USED.

COMMUTATION AND PARTY RATES WILL BE FURNISHED ON APPLICATION.

TICKET OFFICES.

WASHINGTON—1424 New York Ave. Northwest and White House Station, Fifteenth and H Sts. Northeast.

BALTIMORE—Terminal Station, Park Ave. and Liberty St., between Fayette and Lexington Sts. and Albaugh's, 109 N. Charles St.

ANNAPOLIS—West St. Station, Maryland Hotel, Carvel Hall, Green's Drug Store, W. H. Moss, opp. Governor's Mansion, and U. S. Naval Academy P. O. (for Naval officers only.)

BUY TICKETS FROM AGENTS.   NONE SOLD ON CARS.

BAGGAGE CHECKED

Direct connections with city cars in Washington with free transfers to all points in the District of Columbia on the lines of the Washington Railway and Electric Co. The only line between Baltimore and Annapolis whose cars reach the centers of both cities, connect in Baltimore with all principal street car lines and reach the gate of the famous United States Naval Academy at Annapolis.

GENERAL OFFICES
TERMINAL STATION BUILDING
PARK AVE. AND LIBERTY ST.
BET. FAYETTE & LEXINGTON STS.
BALTIMORE, MD.

CAMP PAROLE.

IN EFFECT SEPTEMBER 1, 1909.

WASHINGTON BALTIMORE & ANNAPOLIS ELECTRIC RY.

NOTICE—Passengers from Washington should in all cases ask the conductor of the street car for transfer checks to the W., B. & A. cars for presentation to W., B. & A. conductor, unless tickets are purchased at White House Station.

These time tables supersede all others previously issued and are subject to change and correction without notice. The Company will not be responsible for consequences arising from errors in these printed schedules.

For tickets and information, apply at City Ticket Offices or address General Passenger Agent, Baltimore, Md.

ANNE ARUNDEL FARM,
EXCHANGE,
PAROLE, - MD.

CAMP PAROLE.
DAILY
BALTIMORE AND ANNAPOLIS

Cars leave Baltimore from Terminal Station, Park Ave. and Liberty St., near Lexington. The Annapolis time indicates West St. Station, but all cars leave U. S. Naval Academy ten minutes earlier and Governor's Mansion seven minutes earlier and arrive at these points five and three minutes later respectively than arriving time here given.

Leave Baltimore.	Arrive Annapolis.	Leave Annapolis.	Arrive Baltimore.
6.45 A. M.	7.45 A. M.	5.30 A. M.	6.30 A. M.
7.45 "	8.45 "	6.30 "	7.30 "
8.45 "	9.45 "	7.30 "	8.30 "
9.45 "	10.45 "	8.30 "	9.30 "
10.45 "	11.45 "	9.30 "	10.30 "
11.45 "	12.45 P. M.	10.30 "	11.30 "
12.45 P. M.	1.45 "	11.30 "	12.30 P. M.
1.45 "	2.45 "	12.30 P. M.	1.30 "
2.45 "	3.45 "	1.30 "	2.30 "
3.45 H	4.45 "	2.30 "	3.30 "
4.45 "	5.45 "	3.30 "	4.30 "
5.45 "	6.45 "	4.30 "	5.30 "
6.45 "	7.45 "	5.30 "	6.30 "
7.45 "	8.45 "	6.30m "	7.30 "
8.30s "	9.37 "	7.45s "	8.45 "
9.45 "	10.45 "	8.30 "	9.30 "
11.55 "	12.55 A. M.	10.30 "	11.30 "

EXPLANATION OF SIGNS: H Local Baltimore to Naval Academy Jct. to discharge passengers only, except Saturdays and Sundays. s Transfer at Naval Academy Jct. m Will stop on signal to receive passengers at Linthicum. Cars run local Naval Academy Jct. and Annapolis.

CAMP PAROLE.
WASHINGTON AND ANNAPOLIS

(REQUIRING CHANGE AT NAVAL ACADEMY JUNCTION.)

Cars leave Washington from White House Station, 15th and H Sts., N. E. The Annapolis time indicates West St. Station, but all cars leave U. S. Naval Academy ten minutes earlier, and Governor's Mansion seven minutes earlier and arrive at these points five and three minutes later respectively than arriving time here given.

Leave Washington.	Arrive Annapolis.	Leave Annapolis.	Arrive Washington.
6.30 A. M.	7.45 A. M.	5.30 A. M.	6.45 A. M.
7.30 "	8.45 "	6.30 "	7.45 "
8.30 "	9.45 "	7.30 "	8.45 "
9.30 "	10.45 "	8.30 "	9.45 "
10.30 "	11.45 "	9.30 "	10.45 "
11.30 "	12.45 P. M.	10.30 "	11.45 "
12.30 P. M.	1.45 "	11.30 "	12.45 P. M.
1.30 "	2.45 "	12.30 P. M.	1.45 "
2.30 "	3.45 "	1.30 "	2.45 "
3.30 "	4.45 "	2.30 "	3.45 "
4.30 "	5.45 "	3.30 "	4.45 "
5.30 "	6.45 "	4.30 "	5.45 "
6.30 "	7.45 "	5.30 "	6.45 "
7.30 "	8.45 "	6.30 "	7.45 "
8.30 "	9.37 "	7.45 "	8.45 "
9.30 "	10.45 "	8.30 "	9.45 "
11.48 "	12.55 A. M.	10.30 "	11.45 "

DAILY
WASHINGTON AND BALTIMORE. LIMITED CARS.

Leave Baltimore.	Arrive Washington.	Leave Washington.	Arrive Baltimore.
* 6 00 A. M.	7.10 A. M.	* 6.00 A. M.	7.15 A. M.
6.30 "	7.45 "	6.30x "	7.45 "
* 7.20x "	8.30 "	7.30 "	8.45 "
7.30 "	8.45 "	* 8.00 "	9.10 "
8.00 "	9.10 "	8.30 "	9.45 "
8.30 "	9.45 "	* 9.00 "	10.10 "
* 9.00 "	10.10 "	*10.00 "	11.10 "
9.30 "	10.45 "	10.30 "	11.45 "
10.00 "	11.10 "	11.30 "	12.45 P. M.
10.30 "	11.45 "	*12.00 Noon	1.10 "
11.30 "	12.45 P. M.	12.30 P. M.	1.45 "
*12.00 Noon	1.10 "	1.30 "	2.45 "
12.30 P. M.	1.45 "	* 2.00 "	3.10 "
1.30 "	2.45 "	2.30 "	3.45 "
* 2.00 "	3.10 "	* 4.00 "	4.45 "
2.30 "	3.45 "	* 4.50x "	5.20 "
3.30 "	4.45 "	* 5.00 "	6.10 "
* 4.00 "	5.10 "	5.30 "	6.45 "
4.50x "	5.30 "	* 6.00 "	7.10 "
5.30 "	6.45 "	6.30 "	7.45 "
6.00m "	7.15 "	7.30 "	8.45 "
7.30 "	8.45 "	8.30m "	9.45 "
8.30m "	9.45 "	9.30 "	10.45 "
9.30 "	10.45 "	10.30 "	11.45 "
10.30 "	11.45 "	11.48 "	1.03 A. M.
12.00 "	1.15 A. M.		

EXPLANATION OF SIGNS: * Makes no stop between Baltimore and District Line; other cars make stop at Naval Academy Jct. s Will stop on signal at High Bridge to receive passengers. m Will stop on notice to Conductor to discharge passengers at Dodge Park. N Local from Naval Academy Jct. x Except Sunday.

WASHINGTON AND BALTIMORE
ACCOMMODATION CARS. (Making Local Stops.)

Leave Baltimore.	Arrive Washington.	Leave Washington.	Arrive Baltimore.
6.50 A. M.	8.25 A. M.	6 00 A. M.	7.15 A. M.
9.05 "	10.40 "	6.55 "	8.30 "
11.05 "	12.40 P. M.	9.05 "	10.40 "
1.05 P. M.	2.40 "	11.05 "	12.40 P. M.
3.05 "	4.40 "	1.05 P. M.	2.40 "
5.05 "	6.40 "	3.05 "	4.40 "
6.00N "	7.15 "	5.05 "	6.40 "
6.15 "	To N. A. Jct. Only	5.35x "	To N. A. Jct. Only
7.05 "	To N. A. Jct. Only	7.05 "	8.40 "
8.00 "	9.45 P. M.	7.35x "	To N. A. Jct. Only
8.30N "	9.45 P. M.	8.40N "	9.40 "
8.45 "	To N. A. Jct. Only	8.35 "	To N. A. Jct. Only
11.00 "	11.45 P. M.	10.30 "	11.45 P. M.
12.00 "	1.15 A. M.	11.48 "	1.03 A. M.

EXPLANATION OF SIGNS: N Local from Naval Academy Jct.

NAVAL ACADEMY JUNCTION TO WASHINGTON & BALTIMORE.
ACCOMMODATION CARS. (Making Local Stops.)

Leave Naval Academy Jct.	Arrive Baltimore.	Leave Naval Academy Jct.	Arrive Washington.
5.45 A. M.	6.20 A. M.	5.45 A. M.	6.35 A. M.
6.10 "	6.45 "	6.40 "	7.30 "
7.15 "	7.50 "	7.15 "	8.05 "
8.15 "	8 50 "		

NAVAL ACADEMY JCT. AND ANNAPOLIS JCT.

READ DOWN			Heavy Figures denote P. M.			READ UP
7.05	11.05	3.05	7.05	Lv. Naval Acad. Jct. Ar.	8.10	12.10	4.10	8.10
7.09	11.09	3.09	7.09	Odenton	8.09	12.09	4.09	8.09
7.18	11.18	3.18	7.18	Portland	7.57	11.57	3.57	7.57
7.23	11.23	3.23	7.23	Ar. Annapolis Jct. Lv.	7.50	11.50	3.50	7.50

George Krambles collection.

Brand-new combination car 23 at the Naval Academy Junction yard on February 8, 1908. LeRoy O. King, Sr. photograph.

During the spring of 1908 work trains were still engaged in ballasting the main line, as seen here near Buena Vista, later Defense Highway. Author's collection

Operation into downtown Washington required the cars to be equipped for 600-volt operation with both double trolley poles and underground conduit plows and, for a time, portable fenders. These requirements made the new cars among the most complex of all interurbans. This scene is at the end of track at 15th and New York Avenue, N. W. George Krambles collection.

4

A TIME OF UNCERTAINTY

But any advantage presented by the high-speed "Electric Pullmans" was soon outweighed by the daily problems and expense of running them. In addition to excessive power consumption and frequent mechanical failures, the cars (provided with massive transformers and intricate control apparatus) had evolved in weight far above the forty ton limit imposed by the city authorities in Washington. And being unable to reach a mid-city terminal, passengers disliked the inconvenience of transferring to street cars, which was reflected in a gradual decline in patronage. Moreover, the city operations in Baltimore and Annapolis had necessitated that single-phase motor generator sets be installed in local substations just to supply the 600 volt overhead for short stretches of street trackage. Now, that which had all looked so reasonable on paper was turning out to be quite a different matter in practice; and it was all too clear that the unproven single phase system had been a mistake.

In April 1909, a new contract was awarded to the Cleveland Construction Company for specifications and supervision to convert to a 1200 volt direct current installation; and another contract was negotiated with General Electric Company for the required apparatus, including all car equipments. J.N. Shannahan of the railway company and W.E. Davis of the construction company were sent immediately to Schenectady for the purpose of getting out plans for the new work. Under terms of the original contract, two and a half years earlier, General Electric Company had agreed, should the AC single-phase plant prove to be unsatisfactory, to replace it with all equipment for a direct current operation, upon payment of the difference in cost between the two systems. Even so, it was a misfortune of major consequence!

Somewhere in that heyday of bullish railroad investments the sun was shining, but there was no joy in Baltimore or Cleveland. From the perspective of October 1909, it almost seemed that the grand design had gone awry. As a result of formidable debts outstanding that were being compounded daily by the mounting costs for routine operations, the Company had defaulted on its bond interest which was payable May 1st, which in turn had weakened market confidence in the value of its other securities. And now, another semi-annual interest coupon was due on November 1, 1909. It was at this moment of ebb that the Directors, meeting in Cleveland on October 25th voted to sell all interest in their Washington Berwyn & Laurel Electric Railroad in order to raise urgently needed cash. Mr. Bishop took the evening train for Washington where he had arranged to meet with the president of Washington Railway & Electric Railway Company as the most likely buyer. But when they failed to come to terms, there was little else left to protect the stockholders but to file for receivership, which was decreed on October 28, 1909. President Bishop, ever a pillar of steadfast confidence in times of trouble, was to issue a receiver's statement in which he explained:

> "Under the receivership which should not be of long duration, all of the reconstruction work can be continued and the cost thereof which has not already been paid can be provided for. A plan for funding accrued interest and other indebtedness will soon be submitted to the security holders, but it is the belief of company officials that no drastic action will be necessary.
> "The company has no question of expiring franchises to bother it, its rights are secure, its property is intact, and its railway is in first-class physical condition.

One of the five major trestles along the main line, High Bridge is located ten miles north of the District Line where the electric line's double tracks cross the Pope's Creek Branch of the Pennsylvania Railroad. Henry Rinn collection.

A group of operating employees pose beside one of the DC cars at White House Station, Washington. Author's Collection.

"The cause of the present condition can be summed up by stating that the amount of the company's present liabilities, for which it has not been able to issue securities, is made up entirely of the amount which it has been required to put into its construction account, and the deficit caused by the large percentage of operating expenses under the alternating current system."*

In other words, there was nothing wrong with The WB&A that could not be resolved by the present conversion project. In broad terms, the unanticipated construction account might be summarized as follows:

Re-equipping five substations (complete)
Purchase of thirty-eight new cars (complete)
Re-equipping (with new trucks & motors) five of the existing cars
Installation of the new apparatus in stations & cars
Construction of additional transmission lines not theretofore required under the AC system
Construction of an additional substation building at Ardmore, not theretofore required under the AC system
Acquisition of a new carbarn and express depot in Baltimore
Rebuilding the conduit tracks in Washington ($175,676) to permit operation of interurban trains over city streets
Engineering expenses of the Cleveland Construction Company covering specifications & supervision of the project;

all of which, after allowances for various cars and AC equipment returned to the manufacturers, brought the total project to approximately $880,000.

The autumn of 1909 was a time of feverish activity. Apart from the cheerless state of affairs in

* Washington Evening Star, October 29, 1909, page 16.

the board room, others responsible for management and engineering were busy as never before. New transformers, rotary converters, reactance coils, oil circuit breakers, and big marble-faced switch panels, all reckoned in terms of gross tonnage, had to be received at each substation according to a rigid schedule. To avoid unnecessary handling and shifting, the heaviest pieces had to be positioned directly on existing foundations and erected in place; all without interruption to normal service. Meanwhile, the single-phase equipment, of equally massive bulk and burden (which was still running the system), had been shifted onto temporary settings beside each station.

In late October, Mr. Gladfelter reported on his visit to the Niles Car & Manufacturing Company where he had inspected the first of the new cars being painted and otherwise readied for shipment. At Naval Academy Junction, there were row upon row of traction motors and crates of control equipment waiting to be installed. Insofar as possible, the trucks arrived first to have their motors mounted by G.E. mechanics before the car body, delivered on board a flat car, was pushed into the shop to be hoisted by the big overhead crane. As Mr. Henry L. Erb the foreman later remarked: "It was a pretty fair assembly line. After all, there were 66 trucks (initially) and twice that number of motors". By the first of the year, various testing had begun, the retraining of all personnel was underway, and a precise plan was drawn of the innumerable details—jumpers and leads to be connected and disconnected at the exact time of changeover. It occurred during the early hours of February 15, 1910 without a hitch. Two weeks later, on March 1, the Company announced direct service from downtown Baltimore all the way through to the Treasury building in Washington. At this time, each car was lettered in gold leaf with a small by-line, MID-CITY TERMINALS, Among the competitors, no one else could make that claim.

Although the new cars were smaller and not as fast, their quicker rate of acceleration enabled them to maintain the same overall schedules which had been set with the original single-phase equipment;

CHARTER HISTORY
WASHINGTON, BALTIMORE & ANNAPOLIS ELECTRIC RAILROAD COMPANY

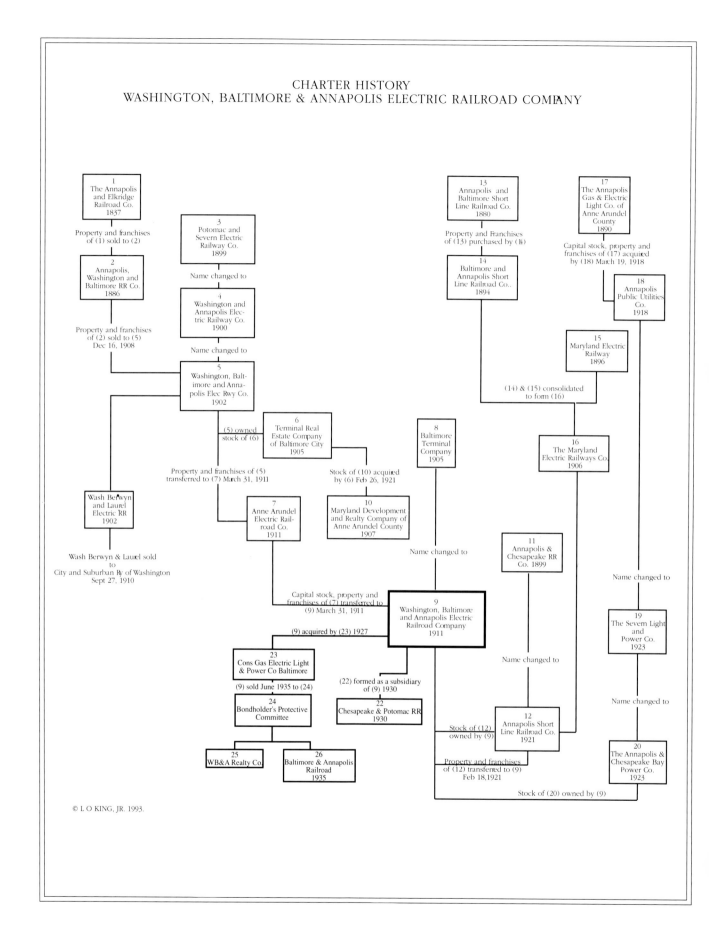

© L O KING, JR. 1993.

The first of the new 1200V Niles cars was delivered about November 1, 1909. Two more of the series had arrived on December 31, 1909 and are seen here awaiting round pilots, destination signs and other accessories for regular service which began six weeks later. Author's collection.

a fact made even more noteworthy considering that the new terminal in Washington had now added 2.82 miles to an already disproportionate amount of street operations. With the more efficient motors, a saving of approximately forty percent in power consumption was realized, the number of shop employees was cut in half, and detentions caused by mechanical failures were greatly reduced. Be it noted, however, that the commendable performance reflected under the new system also resulted from an exceptionally high standard of periodic inspection and maintenance of the whole plant.

As net earnings gradually increased, a plan of reorganization was formulated to terminate the receivership. From its inception, the Washington & Annapolis Railway Company (later The WB&A) had controlled the Washington Berwyn & Laurel Electric Railroad, and had guaranteed its bonds. For more than eight years, plans were frequently announced that had envisioned a connection of only 4.8 miles to be built from Annapolis Junction to Laurel, and thus prepare the way for an alternate route to Washington serving the far more populous territories of Laurel, College Park, Hyattsville, and others. But the little line's revenues were barely enough to cover operating accounts, much less to

meet the interest on its bonds, that had been paid regularly by the parent company. And the parent management, itself then at the brink of bankruptcy (brought on by the failure of its AC single-phase electric system), had been compelled to rule against further subsidies to the Laurel Line. On October 20, 1908 there was an adjustment of accounts between the two companies, after which the Washington Berwyn & Laurel Electric Railroad Company defaulted on its obligations. More recently, however, personal loans from certain of the Cleveland directors had rescued the situation, enabling those bonds to be called in and various other debts to be paid off, thus removing obstacles that had prevented the sale just nine months before. In July 1910, a Trustee was appointed for the Laurel Line, and two months later the road was sold under foreclosure proceedings (on September 1, 1910) to George T. Bishop, who on September 27, 1910 sold it back to the City & Suburban Railway of Washington. Through successive owners the suburban trolley line via Berwyn was, in ever-diminishing form, to survive until September 1958. Although grander designs of its founders were comparatively short-lived, the idea of a second interurban route to Washington was sufficiently plausible, persistent, and publicized to have been well charted in maps and narrative of the official record.

On October 30, 1908, George A. Craig with John Sherwin and Mrs. Anna L. Bishop had advanced a personal loan to the W B & A Company, payable on demand. A year later Craig filed suit to recover, which action then triggered proceedings brought by the Cleveland Trust Company to foreclose on their first and second mortgages of 1905. In due course, all assets of the railway company (excepting 30,000 shares of capital stock in the Baltimore Terminal Company) were sold on March 20, 1911 to George A. Craig, representing The W B & A Reorganization Committee. Eleven days later, and before the results were ratified by court action, the Trustee, the Receivers, the Railway Company, and Mr. Craig, acting jointly, substituted the name of George Winship Taylor as their assignee for the purchase. Taylor, and four of his associates of Catonsville and Walbrook, then formed a corporation known as the Anne Arundel Electric Railroad Company; and for one day only (March 31, 1911) received and conveyed all stock, real estate, franchises, railway property, etc. over to the Baltimore Terminal Company which, by amendment to its charter on the same day, changed its name to the Washington Baltimore & Annapolis Electric Railroad Company. Next, in order to fund obligations incurred by this acquisition, the new and solvent W

Washington, Baltimore & Annapolis Electric Railway Co.
and
Baltimore Terminal Co. Reorganization Committee
1000 Schofield Bldg.
Cleveland, O.

COMMITTEE
JOHN L. SEVERANCE
HINSDILL PARSONS
GEORGE A. CRAIG
JOHN SHERWIN
JOHN J. NELLIGAN
GEORGE T. BISHOP
CHAIRMAN

April 20th, 1911.

McKenney & Flannery,

Hibbs Building,

Washington, D.C.

Gentlemen:

Enclosed you will find check to your order for $30.48, to reimburse you for cash expenditures made by you for account of Washington, Baltimore and Annapolis Electric Railway Company from February 5th, 1909, to March 12th, 1910. Please sign the enclosed assignment of the amount to the Committee, and return same to me with receipted bill, and oblige,

Very truly yours,

CHAIRMAN

Author's collection

B & A Company gave a new mortgage to the same Cleveland Trust Company, which in turn authorized the issuance of five percent thirty year gold bonds up to an aggregate amount of $7.5 million.

Thus, by a rather deft financial maneuver, the former Railway and Terminal Companies had been consolidated. Their combined capitalization, previously outstanding at $13.4 million, had been reduced to $9.6 million; and their bonded indebtedness was also reduced under a single mortgage which was materially strengthened by the valuable terminal properties, city real estate, and rolling

J. J. DOYLE
General Manager Washington, Baltimore & Annapolis Electric Railroad

Author's collection

stock previously owned separately by the Terminal Company. Heading the new WB&A Electric *Railroad*, as it was now called, Mr. Bishop continued as President, surrounded by several of the biggest names in Cleveland financial circles.

For the inevitable legal maneuvers that were to ensue, Mr. Bishop formed a close personal and business association with George Weems Williams, an eminent lawyer and noted civic leader of Baltimore, who became the railroad's General Counsel. In this position he was to serve for more than twenty-eight years, throughout good times and bad. Mr. Williams was also to become a Vice President, and three times, the court-appointed receiver for the company. Another Maryland attorney, Thomas P. Littlepage, was to gain prominence as The Electric Line's spokesman for the Railroad's affairs in Washington, with the War Department and the Naval Academy. The first General Manager was James N. Shannahan, who left the W B & A at

an early date to join the railway consultant firm of Peck Shannahan & Cherry Inc. They were closely associated with management of the Maryland Electric Railways Company; and in time Mr. Shannahan became President of their Annapolis Short Line.

Meanwhile, the down-to-earth business of track and overhead was handled by a promising young man from Cleveland. James J. Doyle began his career in 1889 as an employee in the Maintenance of Way Department of the Pennsylvania Railroad. Later he worked for the old Connotton Valley (narrow gauge) Railroad, and still later earned his reputation as a construction engineer for the Eastern Ohio Traction Company. His success with that company attracted the notice of the Cleveland promoters which, in turn, led to his position with the WB&A. One year after the new line opened in 1908, J. J. Doyle was promoted to the job of General Superintendent. In 1911, at the age of thirty-five, he was made Vice President and General Manager, and later President, in which capacities he served with distinction until his untimely death in January 1929. Over the relatively brief span of those eighteen years, the incredible rise and fall of the Electric Railway Industry was an uncharted course that demanded the utmost in bold venture, ingenuity, and sound business judgement. Whether it was Inauguration Day in Washington; June Week at the Academy; or the racing season at Bowie—whether they were extending the line to Camp Meade; or building the new terminals in each city; or designing the first articulated train; it was a rather extraordinary chapter in the short story of "Electric Traction"—with J. J. Doyle as its central figure!

Everything about the Electric Line reflected a high degree of operational efficiency. It was a regnant tradition that extended from the training and discipline of employees to a willingness of management to spend wherever necessary to al-

Author's collection.

OFFICIALS OF THE WB&A ELECTRIC RAILROAD

FRONT ROW:

WILLIAM L. SCHULTZ	GENERAL CLAIMS AGENT
ALAN P. NORRIS	TRAINMASTER & DISPATCHER
EDWARD BALLARD	FREIGHT AGENT

SEATED SECOND ROW:

ARNOLD S. OSBELT	GENERAL SUPERINTENDENT
JAMES J. DOYLE	GENERAL MANAGER
JAMES N. SHANNAHAN	VICE PRESIDENT & GENERAL MANAGER
WILLIAM STEWART	SECRETARY & PURCHASING AGENT
CARSON SCHUMACHER	TRAINMASTER

STANDING BACK ROW:

W. H. WRIGHT	AUDITOR
EDWARD A. GANNON	GENERAL PASSENGER AGENT
MARION A. TATUM	TRAFFIC AGENT
RAY TOWNES	PASSENGER AGENT
MILTON E. HARDING	SUPERINTENDENT OF TRACK & OVERHEAD
E. W. WEINLAND	ENGINEER FOR MAINTENANCE OF WAY

ways insure the best in safety, service, and upkeep. Part of this efficiency was a Traffic Department, ever alert to the possibilities of places and events of interest which might stimulate increased patronage. And regions of the Chesapeake and Potomac abounded in attractions of such possibilities.

In addition to these diurnal schedules that were advertised for specific events, the Company was to exert a much more lasting influence in the location along its lines of several permanent institutions of Maryland, which survive to this day.

In 1913, the Government sought to establish an independent source of milk and garden produce for the Naval Academy. With the railroad's assistance, a tract of 797 acres of farmland was purchased at Gambrills, and a short spur line was laid directly to the barns and silos, which enabled a regular express service between the US Government Dairy Farm and the Academy at Annapolis. In addition to the daily "milk run", the railroad also delivered carload coal for the boilers which fired the pasteurization plant.

A year later, the Southern Maryland Agricultural Fair Association announced plans to build a race track. And again the railroad proposed a site, with options to buy the land through its real estate subsidiary. As approved, the area comprised at first 125 acres located just east of the main tracks at Bowie Road. With pardonable pride, the Company noted that instead of using the region adjacent to the Pennsylvania Railroad tracks, where it might have been accessible from either side, the new arena was situated east of the interurban's main line where it could be served by The Electric Line, exclusively. During the first week of October 1914, the electric trains carried 15,722 passengers direct to the stands for the first season at Prince Georges Race Track. In time, the big "wye" trackage there was extended to include a total of 1.827 miles of siding to accommodate as many as seventy-five cars that waited on the bigger racing events. In addition to crowds drawn from the nearby cities, The Electric Line also ran five and six car trains between Bowie and Odenton, where connections were made for Philadelphia and New York. In fact, the traffic was sufficiently encouraging that by the following spring, the company had purchased eight new cars.

No Supplement to This Tariff Will be Issued Except for the Purpose of Cancelling the Tariff.

P. S. C. Md. No. 99
Cancels P. S. C. Md. No. 49

Washington, Baltimore & Annapolis Electric Railroad Company

JOINT PASSENGER TARIFF

OF

One Way and Round Trip Fares

BETWEEN

Annapolis, Md. - Baltimore, Md.

AND

All Stations

ON THE

Chesapeake Beach Railway
(VIA DISTRICT LINE, MD.)

As Named Herein

ADVANCE IN ALL FARES

Rules and Regulations Governing this Tariff are shown on Page No. 2

ISSUED JUNE 1, 1920   EFFECTIVE JULY 1, 1920

By:

J. J. DOYLE,   I. E. BALLARD,
Vice President & General Manager,   Tariff Agent,
Baltimore, Md.   Baltimore, Md.

FILE INDEX No. 282   1

Larry Hampton collection.

PARTICIPATING CARRIERS.

Initial and Terminal Lines.

CHESAPEAKE BEACH RAILWAY CO. (P. Md. 5-No. 1)

ABBREVIATIONS

Co.—Company
Md.—Maryland
Lbs.—Pounds.

RULES AND REGULATIONS

1. BAGGAGE:
   (a) Free Allowance—One hundred and fifty (150) pounds of baggage will be checked free on each whole ticket and seventy-five (75) pounds on each half ticket.
   (b) Excess Baggage—Baggage weighing in excess of the free allowance authorized in Rule 1 (a) will be charged for as excess baggage, and the rates will be based on the first-class one-way unlimited fares published in this tariff at the rates as shown on this page.
   (c) Minimum Collections—The minimum collection for any shipment of baggage of excess weight will be twenty-five (25) cents.
   (d) Maximum Weight—The weight of single pieces of baggage will be limited to two hundred and fifty (250) pounds.

2. BICYCLES, Etc.
   Bicycles, tricycles, baby carriages, go-carts, baby sleighs and children's velocipedes or similar vehicles, will not be checked through to destinations published in this tariff.

4. CHILDREN under five (5) years of age, when accompanied by parents or guardian, free; five (5) years of age and under twelve (12), half fare, adding sufficient to make even cents when half fare is a fraction.

5. CORPSES will not be checked through to destinations published in this tariff.

6. DOGS will not be checked through to destinations published in this tariff.

7. LIMITATION OF TICKETS. One way tickets are unlimited. Round trip tickets are valid for return passage within 30 days from date of sale.

8. SALE OF TICKETS. No tickets for the fares published in this tariff, or through tickets will be sold on trains.

TABLE OF EXCESS BAGGAGE RATES

When one way passenger fare is:		Excess baggage rate per 100 lbs. will be:
From	To	
$ .91	$1.20	$ .20
1.21	1.50	.25
1.51	1.80	.30

JOINT ONE WAY AND ROUND TRIP FARES

Between Annapolis, Md.		and Stations on the Chesapeake Beach Railway (Geographically Arranged)		Between Baltimore, Md.	
One Way	Round Trip			One Way	Round Trip
$1.05	$2.00	Brooks	Md.	$1.05	$2.00
1.07	2.04	Behrend	Md.	1.07	2.04
1.12	2.14	Ritchie	Md.	1.12	2.14
1.18	2.26	Marr	Md.	1.18	2.26
1.21	2.32	Brown	Md.	1.21	2.32
1.24	2.38	Hills	Md.	1.24	2.38
1.26	2.42	Claggett	Md.	1.26	2.42
1.32	2.54	Marlboro	Md.	1.32	2.54
1.36	2.62	Penna. Junction	Md.	1.36	2.62
1.41	2.72	Mt. Calvert	Md.	1.41	2.72
1.47	2.84	Pindell	Md.	1.47	2.84
1.52	2.94	Fischer	Md.	1.52	2.94
1.56	3.02	Chaney	Md.	1.56	3.02
1.60	3.10	Wilson	Md.	1.60	3.10
1.66	3.22	Owings	Md.	1.66	3.22
1.70	3.30	Mt. Harmony	Md.	1.70	3.30
1.80	3.50	Chesapeake Beach	Md.	1.80	3.50

2

1200V DC car at Naval Academy Junction. Author's collection.

Parlor car 100 was the site of the meeting between the Army and representatives of the B&O RR, the Pennsylvania Railroad and the WB&A which led to the establishment of Camp Meade during World War I. This handsome car was also the site of the founding of the National Railway Historical Society on August 18, 1935. The photo was taken in 1935. George Krambles collection.

5

THEN CAME THE WAR

By the spring of 1917 the hour was overdue, indeed it was downright late, for mobilizing the home front to support the fighting in Europe, which had suddenly become America's war. Shortly after the United States declared war, an Army Camp Site Board had been appointed to select suitable cantonment areas for training the new National Army. Mr. Bishop was an astute businessman and quick to recognize that such a site held possibilities for his railroad. At his invitation a meeting was arranged for Major General J. Franklin Bell and his staff from Headquarters, Eastern Department of the Army, along with Vice Presidents W. W. Atterbury of the Pennsylvania, and A. W. Thompson of the Baltimore & Ohio Railroads, to inspect a large tract of land just west of Odenton. On May 25, 1917, the delegation arrived aboard the B&O president's private car which was set out at Annapolis Junction. From there the party was taken in Mr. Bishop's parlor car No 100 to several wayside stations called Portland, Disney, and Admiral, there, amid the rural farmland and woods, to visualize a divisional training camp that was destined to accommodate over 53,000 troops.

To insure the availability of this land they were seeing, Mr. Bishop had been to Washington a week earlier where he was authorized to negotiate, conditionally, for the lease or outright purchase of some 115 farms, totalling 7,500 acres (eventually increased to 9,600 acres) which he would sublet to the government. Under that agreement, the War Department had agreed to a scale of rental ranging up to $25 per acre per year for farmland on which the spring crops had already been planted; and thereafter at the rate of $7.50 per acre per year for the duration of the war and one year longer. There had not been a moment to lose, and next morning three old touring cars went bouncing through the back roads with company agents, oft times bearing

cash in hand, to meet the farmers. They bargained in the name of the Terminal Real Estate Company, a subsidiary of The WB&A Railroad; according to surveys platted by J. Spence Howard, a civil engineer of Baltimore. It was a task somewhat complicated by an unsuccessful real estate promoter who, back in 1907, had subdivided much of that region into numerous small parcels. Though, undaunted by the magnitude of his project, Mr. Bishop not only assured the Camp Site Board that he would obtain clear title to the property, but convinced them of its desirability from viewpoint of its vastness for maneuver and target practice, the convenient access to three railroads, available water supply, and electricity furnished directly from his railroad's own transmission lines. Indeed, were the advocacy of this site to be ascribed to one name, above others, the greatest single influence for its selection was George T. Bishop.

But all the bustle and scurry of those first weeks was, as yet, just that: an advocacy, or proposition, and (relatively) a secret which they had managed to keep from the press for almost a month. The whole affair was contingent upon yet another crucial agreement. It was Sunday morning, June 17th, as the private car number 100 again stopped in the woods near Admiral for a meeting between Colonel W. H. Lawton, QMC., for the government and officials from each of the railroads to negotiate more specifically what became—or did not become—a logistical outline for the enormous construction project about to begin, namely, trackage.

It was agreed that, except for certain large-scale troop movements, The WB&A would handle passengers. For that, the Electric Line had previously contracted to build up to six miles of new track which was envisioned, originally, as a belt line practically encircling the reservation. At issue, actually, was the extent to which the steam rail-

Looking east from Kelly's crossing, the Pennsylvania tracks (left) parallel the WB&A line leaving Camp Meade. Author's collection.

roads were willing to construct, at their own expense, some six miles of parallel access lines into camp—including extensive warehouse sidings for freight. When it is recalled that this hitherto lightly-used part of the WB&A was then only a single track laid with the original fifty-six pound rail, it will be seen that the anticipated heavy traffic arriving east and west towards a center, concurrent with troop movements, plus the daily travel of some 4,000 workmen to and from camp, had contemplated a considerable amount of new trackwork. Everything would, of course, go by rail!

At the meeting that day, the survey party had returned to the parlor car table where they began to outline all the supply yards and rail sidings. The railroad people maintained that new tracks serving the warehouses were a short-term (war emergency) investment on behalf of the Army, and were therefore a government obligation. The War Department, on the other hand, was unwilling to give any assurance of a longer use, claiming that profits to be derived from the greatly increased traffic were an advantage to the railroads. In fact, at that moment, Colonel Lawton was carrying written instructions from The Adjutant General which read in part as follows:

> "It has recently come to the attention of the War Department in connection with the selection of sites for divisional training camps that certain railways have expected to charge the Government cost

plus 10 percent for constructing railway tracks and switches connecting suitable points of their lines with proposed camp sites—No authority has been given to anyone to offer or to give compensation to railways for said service. You will without delay make the contents of this message known to the controlling officials of all railways concerned in your department, informing them that no authority has been or will be, given contemplating payment for such facilities in any case whatever. Where such payment is demanded you will proceed to hunt for suitable camp sites having other railway facilities and make no agreement to pay for facilities of the above type."

The discussion lasted nearly three hours. When an impasse seemed inevitable, Colonel Lawton, somewhat irritated, gathered his blueprints and prepared to leave. It was by no means a foregone conclusion that the camp had to be located there, or for that matter, even in Maryland. He would, as instructed, hunt elsewhere. A moment of decision, however fragile at the time, can have diffuse consequences of extreme duration. Certainly no one at that table could have imagined just then that the fate of the state's biggest source of employment for another seventy years swayed in the balance. Colonel Lawton was persuaded to remain, and a compromise was reached whereby the B&O and Penn-

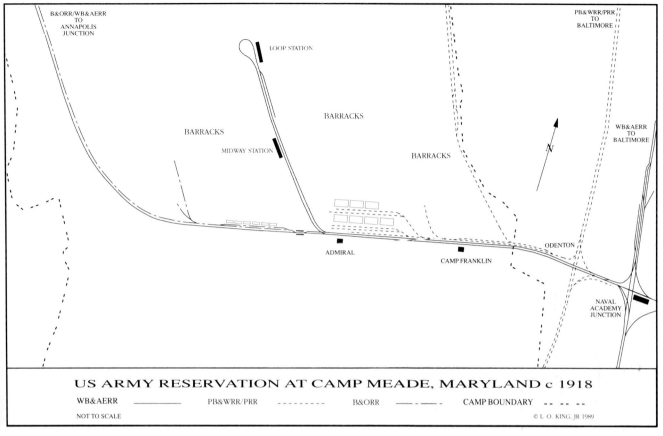

US ARMY RESERVATION AT CAMP MEADE, MARYLAND c 1918

WB&AERR _____ PB&WRR/PRR - - - - - - - - B&ORR — - — - CAMP BOUNDARY -- -- --

NOT TO SCALE   © L. O. KING, JR 1989

sylvania Railroads would, if necessary, provide up to two miles of sidings and switches adjoining their main connecting lines; the total work in no case to exceed eight miles of new tracks. Anything in addition to that amount would have to be built at government expense. Two days later, the Secretary of War telegraphed approval for the U.S. Army Cantonment, Admiral, Maryland. As time would eventually confirm, the founding of an army post was but one of several historic declarations conceived at the conference aboard private car 100.

Within ten days, and before the railroads were ready for it, construction erupted with the impact of an explosion—almost literally. In the early morning of July 2, 1917, Major Ralph F. Proctor, the Constructing Quartermaster, fired his weapon as a symbolic gesture to signal the start of a long race. Smith, Hauser & McIsaac, who were the general contractors, had previously contracted throughout various parts of the country for over 100 carloads of building material, which were suddenly released to converge on a congested segment of single track at

someplace called Admiral, Maryland. And more kept coming! Within weeks, whole trains of loaded cars were backed up at Potomac Yards, Brunswick, Baltimore, and as far away as Harrisburg, waiting for track space at destination.

Almost immediately The WB&A started work from the eastern end to provide double electrified tracks from Naval Academy Junction into Admiral, which line was, for a time, shared with the Pennsylvania Railroad's steam trains arriving via Odenton. Meanwhile, at the western end the B&O officials appear to have underestimated the volume of their traffic, having chosen at first a joint operation over The Electric Line's single track, which would be upgraded while in use. This entailed not only replacing the entire track with heavier eighty-five pound rail (under traffic day and night), but renewal of seventy percent of the ties, and reinforcing several wooden bridges to accommodate the much larger B&O locomotives. The congestion was intolerable, and after a few weeks it was conceded that a second track would have to be laid. This was

A group of soldiers evidently anticipating a pleasant time away from camp, line up to board an approaching WB&A train at Midway Station at Camp Meade. National Archives.

started as a long siding from the wye interchange at Annapolis Junction, graded for one mile along the north side of the existing right-of-way, then crossing over, parallel to the south side for the remaining three miles to the center of camp.*

In the haste of this rebuilding along both sides of the right- of-way, the original alignment was changed wherein the track no longer conformed to the line of trolley poles, so that the overhead was rendered useless. It was a frantic emergency modi-

---

* By an agreement between the three railroads, B&O tracks terminated approximately 1500 feet west of Admiral, while Pennsylvania tracks from the east ended at the station; leaving a gap of some 1000 feet connected only by the WB&A's single track trestle over Rogue Harbor Run, which was used by all classes of service from all three lines. All trackage occupied WB&A right-of-way which was excluded from the government reservation.

fication that would eventually cost $56,138. as the B&O Railroad's obligation to restore the line to its original condition. And more's the pity, considering that ere the second track was finished, the camp's construction boom had passed its peak, with an estimated 90 percent of the housing completed, that had represented the greatest tonnage in building supplies already delivered. But there were now logistics of another kind. On September 15, 1917 the first draftees arrived. Some of them moved into the new barracks even as the roof was being nailed down. In less than three weeks there were 25,000 troops to be fed, clothed, hospitalized, trained, and provided with the endless impedimenta necessary to make a soldier. Among the first units was the celebrated 79th Division, and because so many of its conscripts came from Pennsylvania, the place was named Camp Meade, in honor

A train, headed by one of the 10-17 series motors, waits at loop Station, Camp Meade. Wartime schedules listed no less than eighty-four daily departures to accommodate troops on leave, civilian visitors, and the daily ebb and flow of some 4,000 construction workers. Author's collection.

of the Union general of Gettysburg fame. After the troops, came the visitors—families and friends who, on occasion, numbered over 23,000 in a single week end. At the same time, there was an ever larger exodus from the camp to the cities on week end pass.

Although the interurban had been compelled to suspend electrified service west of Disney (Nov. 23, 1917), it was imperative that regular schedules be maintained from the east for the increasing number of passenger trains arriving and leaving via Naval Academy Junction. And with those runs interspersed with the Pennsylvania's freight traffic over the same tracks, access through Odenton was, to put it mildly, somewhat snarled.

In October 1917, the Philadelphia Baltimore & Washington Railroad Company (i.e. Pennsyl-

vania Railroad) purchased a right-of-way parallel to the WB&A Electric Line where it constructed a double-track line of 1.68 miles from Odenton to Admiral. At Kelly's Crossing, where these tracks entered the camp, a sizeable industrial complex sprang up that housed a railroad labor camp and train facilities, including an engine coaling platform, water tank, ash pit, sand box, and even an old schoolhouse which had been moved across the tracks and enlarged as a less-than-carload freight house. Branching off at this point, there was also a double-track spur line that followed the eastern boundary line (parallel to Chamberlin Street) as far north as Mapes Road. By November 1918 the Signal Corps School known as Camp Franklin had been opened, and a small station, reached via a long boardwalk or pedestrian bridge was erected

CAR STATION AT ADMIRAL AT CAMP MEADE. MD.

Niles car and Long Island trailer at Admiral station, Camp Meade. Frank Tosh collection.

Derailment at Camp Meade Loop, about June 1922. Richard C. Meyer collection.

Postcard view of WB&A's Loop Station at Camp Meade. Frank Tosh collection.

along the embankment near the corner of Chisholm and Rock Avenues. Camp Franklin is no more. Though not far from where the station stood is a small plaque which marks the site of the Army quarters of a then young Captain named Dwight D. Eisenhower.

The hourglass of the whole layout was at Rogue Harbor Run where all movements were constricted through the single track across a small wooden trestle. Because this was also the interchange between two steam roads, it was desirable from a safety standpoint to divert the passenger crowds away from heavy operations centered around the freight yards. During September, The WB&A built a branch line which ran northwesterly along the Rogue Harbor stream to a loop terminal at Mapes Road. Using old rail salvaged from the B&O Railroad's track renewal, the loop line was laid with double tracks to include a 1300 foot siding for the layovers. At the principal stops the company erected two large and commodious buildings known as Midway and Loop Sta-

tions, whose grounds were attractively landscaped and maintained by a gardener hired by the railroad. By 1918, these stations were handling, in addition to special moves ordered by the Army, 32 daily departures for Baltimore, 30 leaving for Washington, 22 for Annapolis, and an equal number of arrivals.

But the founding of Camp Meade was laced with a tragedy that generated traffic of a different kind. Within three months during that fall of 1918 an epidemic of Spanish influenza, worldwide, would rank among the worst plagues in the annals of modern medicine. It was a disease with no known cause and no known cure. In the United States alone, the number of Americans who died of influenza at home would exceed five times their battle casualties overseas. And the fatalities were especially devastating under conditions of large troop concentrations such as those at Camp Meade. At the height of this contagion, carloads of coffins arriving were matched by car-loads of the spectral specials leaving, usually at night.

Photographed in the yard at Naval Academy Junction, this train was typical of the motors and trailers rebuilt in the Company's shops for the wartime expansion. Author's collection

6

ALL THOSE TRAILERS

And the uncommon business of war had created abnormal demands for rolling stock. At that time, new cars could not be had at any price; though by prompt and persistent effort the management, within less than eighteen months, had acquired and rebuilt a total of seventy-four additional cars. Performed in the company shops, this project of major car rebuilding eventually reached a total cost of $332,624. The guiding force in all of this was a salty and resourceful character, one Arnold S. Osbelt who had arrived ten years before with a party from General Electric that installed the original electrification. "Joe" Osbelt had remained to become Master Mechanic and later General Superintendent, although his sphere of endeavors on behalf of the Electric Line was by no means limited to the equipment or operations implied by those titles. Through his interest in local real estate, Mr. Osbelt negotiated the purchase of rural farmland that had determined the location of the US Dairy Farm at Gambrills, and Bowie Race Track is where it is because of his influence in procuring a site favorable to the railroad. Years later, his loyalty to management throughout a difficult siege of strike and labor negotiations was to prove his perseverance in yet another field. Now, as an entire army post burst upon the scene, the company was suddenly confronted with immediate expansion involving more tracks into camp, a new substation, and, of course, more trains to handle it. So it was their able emissary who set out in quest of cars.

In the New York Jamaica Yards of the Long Island Rail Road, he found a fleet of that company's class T-39 wooden trailers which had operated with steam trains in suburban commuter service. The series consisted of fifty-five cars (LIRR 852-906) which had been built in 1898 by the Pullman Palace Car Company, and in 1899 by the Wason Manufacturing Company. These open-platform coaches were 46 feet overall, equipped with center doors that were designed to expedite mass loading and unloading at the Sands Street Terminal of the Brooklyn Bridge, and although wired for operations over the Brooklyn Elevated Lines, they were now restricted as a result of a recent ordinance requiring all-steel equipment in the New York tunnels.

Many of them had not been used for years, and in the course of inspections and bargaining over price, Mr. Osbelt's negotiations had dragged on for a couple of days. Finally, the home office could stand the suspense no longer and on July 10th wired instructions for him to purchase the lot at any cost. The onslaught at Camp Meade had already begun!

The Long Island company was to retain one car (876) which had previously been modified as their baggage car 977. By mid-July, all others began arriving daily at the Pennsylvania's interchange in Odenton. It was an impressive lineup, and there seemed to be red cars everywhere. Tuscan Red was then standard livery for all Long Island equipment and because of this, the farm-oriented Marylanders always spoke of them as *Rhode Island Reds*.

Since their original wiring for heaters could not accommodate the 1200 volt circuits, the center doors were permanently closed and the space was used for a Peter Smith coal stove on one side, opposite two additional seats on the other side. For lighting, train lines were laid on the roof and fitted with receptacles for bus jumpers. The lightweight Van Dorn couplers soon proved no match for train operation with the heavier interurban cars, and in September an expenditure averaging $275 per car provided for reinforcing the drawbars to be equipped with regular MCB automatic couplers. As part of the remodeling, they were painted in the standard green and numbered 301-354. In terms of style and comfort, their Spartan interi-

The 300 class cars were open platform trailers which had been built in 1898-99 by the Pullman's Palace Car Company and Wason Manufacturing Company. They were the only WB&A cars equipped with rattan seats. The center door was never used. The space was occupied by a coal stove of Peter Smith forced draft patent. Author's collection.

ors of rattan upholstery, plain light bulbs, bare wooden floors, and now the necessity for coal stoves, were certainly not to be compared with any of the larger interurbans which, traditionally, had set the standard for passenger comfort; but this was war, and the Rhode Island Reds fulfilled a need when the need was greatest.

Mr. Osbelt next returned to his old haunts near Schenectady where he obtained two cars from the Albany Southern Railroad. These were long 53 foot 6 inch motor cars equipped for trolley/third rail operations, that had been built in 1907 by the Wason Manufacturing Company. Upon arrival at Naval Academy Junction, they were also refitted with the heavier MCB couplers, and remodeled with end train doors to become WB&A trailers 355-356.

By 1921, there were two more cars added to "All Those Trailers". Through merger with the Annapolis Short Line, two of their coaches (14 &16) dating from the days of steam trains, were renumbered as WB&A trailers 357-358.

As motive power for so many trailers, the Company in June 1917 had awarded contracts for eighteen complete sets of Westinghouse brakes and electrical equipment. Eight of these sets were installed in so-called "locomotives" which had been converted from heavy passenger cars purchased from the Maryland Electric Railways Company. Another five sets were used to re-equip the combine cars which had been General Electric equipment formerly owned by the Wilkes Barre and Hazleton Railway; while the remaining sets completed five partially-built interurban bodies acquired from the St. Louis Car Company. Although differing in outward appearance, these three types were mechanically identical, i.e. in motors, gear ratio, and the standard Westinghouse 15-D-9 controls. Unlike all previous WB&A cars furnished with General Electric control designed to run as high-speed MU cars, these larger wartime motors of higher gear reduction were intended for slower trains of motor cars and trailers.

This was the Company's first venture into a

No. 322.

An ordinance granting the right of the Washington, Baltimore & Annapolis Electric Railroad Company, its successors or assigns, to construct and maintain connections between its two present tracks at or near the intersection of Greene and Pratt Streets, in Baltimore City, with the single track of the Baltimore & Ohio Railroad Company on Pratt Street, and likewise to construct and maintain connections and switches with or from said Baltimore & Ohio Railroad Company's track on Pratt Street, into the property of the Washington, Baltimore & Annapolis Railroad Company, located on the north side of Pratt Street, between Eutaw and Howard Streets, and to construct and maintain the necessary pole and wires over and along said connections, and over and along said Baltimore & Ohio track on Pratt Street, from a point at or near the west side of Green Street, to a point at or near the west side of Howard Street, and to operate and maintain an electric railway thereon, the right to use said Baltimore & Ohio track on Pratt Street, between the points above named, to be subject to an agreement between the Baltimore & Ohio Railroad Company and the said Washington, Baltimore & Annapolis Electric Railroad Company, and providing for the conditions upon which said rights shall be exercised and the compensation to be paid therefor.

Approved February 25, 1918

JAMES H. PRESTON, Mayor.

Baltimore City Ordinance

somewhat different type of service with much longer passenger trains, not to mention the expanded terminal requirements to handle them. Official records refer to trains of four trailers, although there were trainmen who recalled schedules to Camp Meade with as many as six cars hauled by a single freight motor which, itself, offered ample capacity for a standing load as occasion demanded. In Washington, no more than two cars were ever permitted on city streets beyond the White House Station; while in Baltimore the Liberty Street Terminal could not accommodate over two cars on the single track loop. Moreover, even by the measure of traffic for that day, trains of such length could hardly be brought into the very center of town.

In February 1918, an agreement was reached for joint use of the Baltimore and Ohio's single track on Pratt Street; and a switch was installed at Pratt and Greene Streets. As the troop trains arrived eastbound at Pratt and Eutaw Streets, a reserve freight motor,

waiting west of Greene Street, would couple on to the rear to take the train out again; while the lead motor would then go into the reserve position to await the next train. Notwithstanding the B&O freight scheduled between the troop trains, or late at night, that single track was always congested.

During the peak of wartime travel, the Sunday night exodus from Baltimore was an adventure all its own. As the electric trains lined up along Pratt Street, troops returning from pass would converge by the thousands in a frenzied rush to get aboard the cars. Some jumped up between the cars, others stood on the bumpers or swung from the grabrails. A veteran conductor recalled how he once walked the length of a car (on the arm rests) without ever touching the floor, and of a wicker basket in the motorman's cab where he would empty his pockets before returning to collect more fares. Upon leaving the city at the foot of Scott Street, there was a sharp incline where the tracks led out onto a long elevated structure. And since the *Camp Meade Specials* were always so overloaded with passengers riding on the outside, a detail of police had to be stationed at Scott Street to trim the train before it could safely take off for the viaduct.

The Eighteenth Amendment has sometimes been called the Great Experiment. It was a lame attempt to legislate the drinking habits of all citizens. Pending its ratification in January 1919, most of Maryland stayed legally wet, while Washington went theoretically thirsty; causing a newfound interest in the spirits of Baltimore which began to *liquidate* into the capital city via a quaint, and sometimes ingenious, smuggling called bootlegging. Interurban passengers were suddenly carrying more baggage— the fragile kind, and they travelled more frequently in ever increasing numbers. During that arid stretch of October 1918, the WB&A had to put on five extra trains daily, with a sixth added on weekends to handle the happy throng. Tales abound of the *revenuers* riding these trips and of the fatuous cat and mouse tactics used in their efforts to stem the tide. But the tide (more like a torrent) would not be

One of the Pullman built Long Island trailers at Hillside, N. Y. in 1898. The 0-4-4 locomotive is a Rhode Island product of 1894. Author's collection.

Interior of a 300 class trailer. Author's collection

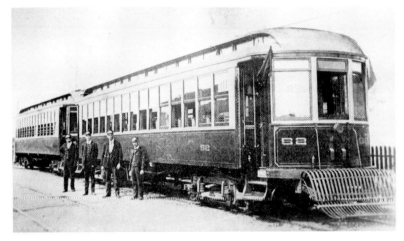

In 1918, Albany and Hudson 30 and 32 from this series were remodeled to become trailers 355 and 356 of the WB&A. Author's collection.

A splendid sketch of 355 by George Krambles.

stemmed. In fact, many a passenger, either out of anxiety or for sheer joy of it, swallowed his evidence before it could get stemmed. The more bibulous were at times less than pleasant company, so to avoid offending regular customers, the management required all those with sloshing luggage to take the Bootlegger's Specials which left from the Pratt Street Station. For all this, the Rhode Island Reds were again pressed into service of a nation at war—this time for a kind of drought relief to circumvent a plight that was self imposed.

In the post war years a diminishing number of the 300's continued in service for the Bowie Race Track Specials, while twelve of them were exten-sively renovated to serve regular assignments on the Annapolis North Shore Division. Although applied in varying degrees to different cars, the improvements of this second project included slack adjusters for smoother starting and stopping, elimination of the center doors, leather seats, refinishing in the brighter cream and orange paint, and in several cases, even the cosmetics of upper window sash of stained glass. At least seven others found their way to such uses as mail cars, a line car, and a tool car equipped with a trolley serving as a wire lubricator. If durability is testimony to the builder's craft, three of the Rhode Island Reds, as work cars, were to survive for fifty two years.

WB&A trailer 354 at Naval Academy Junction car yard March 26, 1935. J. J. Bowman photograph.

Line car 502 in the service of the Baltimore and Annapolis Railroad at Linthicum February 23, 1941. George Krambles collection.

Wire greaser 06 at Annapolis on the Baltimore and Annapolis 1937. King collection.

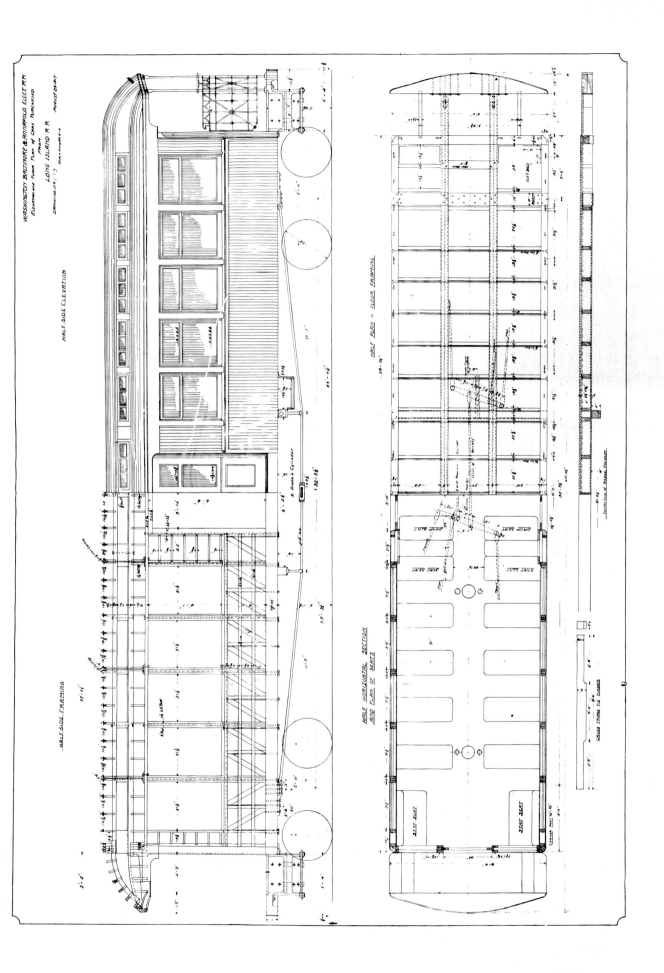

Painters prepare numbers 355 and 356, two of the trailers most used for the Bowie Race Track Specials. In this scene, streetcar number 19 is still stored in the back yard at Naval Academy Junction. George D. Watts collection.

7

AFTERMATH

The saga of Camp Meade and the railroads did not end with the Armistice of 1918. Many of the country's railways, which had been nationalized under the wartime U.S. Railroad Administration, now has to be deregulated and released. Endless claims would involve railroad property to be repaired or replaced. In the course of demobilization, some 96,000 troops were mustered out at Camp Meade; and, except for problems of construction, the whole scenario was replayed in reverse.

So chaotic had been the initial period of mobilzation at Camp Meade, with conflicting directives interposed by the federal Railroad Administration, that informal consent of the WB&A and B&O Railroads governing their joint traffic from the west end had not been confirmed by written agreement until June 16, 1920. In fact, it would be another year (June 6, 1921) before the WB&A resumed regular service to Annapolis Junction, using one track in both directions for its electric operations, while still permitting the other (north track) for use by B&O trains. As compensation, the WB&A was paid $1.50 per car for each loaded freight or passenger car moving to or thru Camp Meade over the Electric Line's tracks. And it may be of interest that, on rare occasions whenever an accident occurred on either of the principal steam roads, a main line passenger train could be seen detouring through Camp Meade to the other railroad.

For the three years ending with the year 1919, the Electric Line had carried nearly fourteen million passengers. The war had been good for business, but it had demanded a sizable expansion in cars, track, and personnel, which were now surplus. Revenues had been large, but so had been investments to meet the short-term commitments of a national emergency, which was now past. In June 1922, the U.S. Treasury filed claim against the WB&A for $698,347 in additional federal taxes alleged due on excess profits earned during the war years. After a year of arduous bargaining the tax deficiency was substantially reduced; but it had emphasized clearly that the railroad's stake in wartime facilities had suddenly become a recurring and burdensome liability. Moreover, the future of Camp Meade was at best uncertain. This was an era of Army-Navy surplus, of post-war retrenchment, of world disarmament— it was a period of indecision about the proposed use, or non-use, of all those temporary training camps. Under the circumstances, the railroad's Board of Directors, more as a matter of self defense, had ruled that certain wartime assets be amortized and abandoned as soon as possible.

Their decision had been confirmed by a War Department announcement on July 27, 1921 that six of the east coast cantonments, including Camp Meade, were to be closed down "at the earliest practical date." As an afterthought, the 12th Infantry Division Training Center Detachment would be kept at Camp Meade for the summer training of reserve units.* As the amortization period expired on December 31, 1924, the railroad served notice that its tracks would be removed. However, the War Department, somewhat at odds with the tax people, was insistent that rail service be retained; whereupon, it was extended for two years, then for six months more. During this period additional federal taxes, amounting to approximately $110,000 for track, overhead and excess cars, were again due on a branch line that now operated little more than several franchise trips each day. From a business standpoint, some relief was imperative.

On May 15, 1927, the wartime trackage comprising two miles of second track from Naval Academy Junction to Admiral, and one and seven tenths mile

---

* Washington Evening Star, 7/27/21, p12

In August, 1921, Citizen's Military Training Corps recruits arrive at Admiral Station, Camp Meade. National Archives.

of the so-called loop line, was technically abandoned. But it was only a legal maneuver. The tracks located within the military reservation were deeded, free, to the U.S. Government; thus constituting abandonment to the satisfaction of the tax collector. Some months later, this arrangement was confirmed by an operating agreement of January 30, 1928, under which the WB&A would provide service, even at a loss, on behalf of the War Department. By then Congress had reversed its earlier decision and designated the post as a permanent installation to be known as Fort Leonard Wood, for one year until February 1929, when the name was changed to Fort George G. Meade.

Across the broad sweep of almost seven decades, certain place names were to become synonymous with established institutions of Maryland. They were sites whose selection had been greatly influenced, if not determined, by the Electric Line. And in the age before rubber

tires, they survived because their locations were accessible, again by the Electric Line. Thus, while the founding of the state hospital, the government dairy, the race track, and the Army post are counted among the railway's endorsements that succeeded, there was yet another one that didn't.

For more than fifty years the State of Maryland had sponsored the building of a railroad to Drum Point on the lower peninsula of Calvert County. Encouraged by prospects of the excellent natural harbor there, as well as the abundant truck farms and seafood trade from southern Maryland, the railroad project was actively pursued on and off (in 1887; 1898; 1911) until over three quarters of a million dollars had been spent for sixty two miles of roadbed graded, bridged, and ready for track. And with each revival of the Drum Point Railroad, its route—which would have crossed the Annapolis Division just west of Millersville—held promise that the AW&B (later WB&A) might yet prosper

63 between runs March 27, 1920. The truck beside it is a Ford Model T. Author's collection..

through a feeder railroad from the potentially rich Tidewater region. When, in 1924, the plans were again revived, Mr. Bishop offered the technical and executive organization of the WB&A Railroad, without cost, to supervise completion and operation of the Drum Point line.

But this time the financing was contingent upon willingness of the two counties involved to approve a bond issue of some $500,000 with the balance to be raised by the state. At public hearings held February 19, 1924, Calvert County approved, while Anne Arundel County opposed the cost; a decision that would this time spell the end of the Drum Point dream for all time.

Until 1908, the company owned seven 4-4-0 locomotives which had been built by Baldwin and a 4-6-0 from the New York Locomotive Works. Number 10 is seen here about to leave Camden Station. Smithsonian collection.

8

ANNAPOLIS SHORT LINE - THE GENEROUS YEARS

The governor's plans to rebuild the long-abandoned suburban tracks were inspired by a need to curb the insatiable automobile with its attending quandaries of commuter traffic, pollution, and ever-increasing fuel demands; which problems previously arose from a lack of adequate public transit, whose deteriorating service had been aggravated by losses in riders and revenues, that had resulted from the railroad abandonment in the first place. I'm sure they'd be proud, the builders of that railroad, to know that their vision of one hundred years ago is now and again reaffirmed by plans for a modern rapid transit route that will recreate a portion of "The Short Line to Annapolis".

In its original version, the railroad was conceived by a group of New Englanders, businessmen from Portland and Boston, who in 1880 organized the Annapolis & Baltimore Short Line Railroad Company. During the first years, their main efforts involved acquisition of property for a right-of-way that had been surveyed by their civil engineer, C. D. Banks. Commencing at Clifford Station on the Curtis Bay Branch of the Baltimore & Ohio Railroad, the proposed road followed a southerly line beyond the Patapsco River as far as Shipley's Farm, where it then struck a more southeasterly course through Wellham, Cromwell, Myrtle Creek (later Glen Burnie), Elvaton, and Boone (later Severna Park), following the peninsula to a point opposite Annapolis. Along the way, there were various twists and curves which, one can only surmise, were the engineer's way of exploiting terrain features in order to minimize the construction problems of excavation and bridges. The heaviest grades would be encountered on both sides of a summit near Shipley and opposite Annapolis, where some descent from the tableland of the Severn north shore would necessitate a forty-foot cut and long fill to reach the river.

By the summer of 1885, the railroad's advance party were exploring both banks of the Severn for a suitable approach to the site of a long bridge which would span the river from the farm of Horace Winchester on the north shore to the property of Elizabeth Gedding on the south bank, known as Wardour Bluffs. R.G.Kenley, a young rodman with the surveyors, kept a diary whose brief entries afford just a glimpse of the adventure of plotting a course through the wilderness which then existed. He recalls various obstacles of bush and stream, the discomfort of ferocious mosquitoes, and an all-day errand via row boat to purchase provisions in Annapolis; mingled with the off-duty pleasures of swimming, fishing, and a feast of fresh oysters to be had for forty cents per bushel.

From the Annapolis side of the river the survey ascended almost due south to a sweeping curve around Geddings Station, through the lands of Charles Reese, then crossed Dorsey Creek to a terminal site on Bladen Street near College Avenue. Near Geddings Station (later West Annapolis), the alignment had unavoidably encroached upon a very small corner of the US Government Farm. When Congress failed to act to cede a matter of a few feet for railroad use, the Secretary of the Navy summarily gave permission for construction to proceed.

After five years of surveys and negotiations, it was announced in September 1885 that some twenty-two miles of right-of-way had been secured and the necessary capital subscribed, to commence actual construction. It was a clear autumn morning at Winchester Point, across the river from Annapolis, where a dozen workmen had cleared the underbrush, and a burly laborer was still hacking away at an ancient apple tree. As a small steamer put in, the official party came ashore; and at noon on October 12, 1885, ground was broken with ceremonies attended by Colonel H. P. Underhill, President, and W.D. Janney, Chief Engineer for the Railroad, W. Wheeler, Secretary of the Bay Ridge Company, T.E. Martin, former mayor of Annapolis, Thomas H. Arnold, a nearby landowner, and other guests. Afterwards, they adjourned to the surveyor's tent for refreshments. The importance of many a lesser event has been emblazoned in statues, bronze plaques, or roadside markers. But if aught else survives to impress a reminder of that historic place and date, perhaps a tribute as fitting as any, are the beautiful lawns of Manresa-on-the-Severn which mark the spot today.

Within days, the North Shore was invaded by an army of workmen. Stretching as far as the eye could see, there were gangs of laborers with pick and shovel, mule teams dragging scrapers, little dump carts loaded with earth, and stone masons building the culverts. At one point, the Chief Engineer reported 800 men engaged in clearing and grading the roadbed.

In a later era, that phenomenon of the garish amusement park evolved as a suburban place of hilarious fun and razzledazzle noise and excitement. Invariably, it was owned by the railroad or traction company as a means of generating traffic to and from the city. Its forerunner, however, which was developed for the same reason, was a more subdued country location usually chosen for its natural beauty, where family groups might enjoy an outing of picnics, boating, or swimming. Always, there was a large rambling hotel that offered modest accommodations, elegant dining, and endless rows of rocking chairs on the porch. As an attempted safeguard against the inevitable, their signs proclaimed an atmosphere of genteel propriety, polite entertainment, and a ban against all forms of gambling and intoxicating drinks.

In the time and prime of that vogue, the builders of the Short Line had also envisioned such a resort, even as they planned the railroad itself. For this, they selected a scenic promontory at Round Bay on the Severn where, in December 1885, a tract of nearly 210 acres was purchased and cleared for the pavilion and hotel; including a spur track five-tenths of a mile in length, which was later laid from a "wye" layout on the main line to the hotel at the water's edge.

On January 13, contracts for three timber-pile bridges, to cross the Patapsco, the Severn, and Dorsey Creek (later called College Creek), were awarded to Ross & Sanford Company of Baltimore. They were also the Contractors for an independent railroad then being built from West Annapolis to Bay Ridge. When the steamer *Empire State* ran aground while trying to dock at Bay Ridge, the pile driver and bridge crews were hurriedly transferred from the Severn railroad bridge to construct a wharf to receive subsequent passengers and supplies at Bay Ridge, pending completion of that railroad. Actual track laying along the Short Line began in April 1886, with 60 pound rail delivered to Clifford Junction; whence the work proceeded southward, until by September, all but six miles were finished.

Meanwhile, the land had been acquired for a Baltimore station to be built in the triangle formed by Cross, Paca, and Scott Streets. But on January 27, 1887, a contract with the B&O Railroad provided other arrangements for trackage rights over the B&O's lines, and the use of Camden Station as a passenger terminal. This contract, drawn for a period of ten years, specified a rental based upon percentages of gross receipts from passenger, mail, and freight traffic; as well as a responsibility for the maintenance of track and roadway based upon car miles operated. In order to shorten the route into Camden Station, the B&O Railroad, for its part, agreed to build a cut-off from the Curtis Bay division, which was later designated as their South Baltimore Branch. At the location originally planned for the Short Line's Baltimore terminal, a freight depot was erected on a smaller site bounded by Paca and West Streets, Burgundy Alley, and the B&O tracks. The new freight yard there comprised four tracks, and a fifth spur track leading into the engine shed. And as though local toponyms were not confusing enough, the Short Line thereafter served a freight station in Baltimore, while the competitor Elk Ridge Rail Road had a terminal in Annapolis, each known as the West Street Depot.

An Annapolis Short Line steam train crosses the Severn River enroute to Baltimore. Jacques Kelly collection.

So the Annapolis & Baltimore Short Line Railroad would run to Baltimore, although its own tracks ended at Clifford Junction some 3.3 to 5.7 miles short of the city destination; these variations resulting from no less than five major track changes that occurred over the ensuing years.

In granting this original access to Baltimore, including terminal rights at Camden Station, the B&O Railroad had incurred the enmity of a rival company, the Annapolis & Elk Ridge Rail Road (recently renamed the Annapolis Washington & Baltimore Railroad). For many years, they had provided all rail service from Annapolis over a longer route via Annapolis Junction, also using B&O tracks for their through trains to either Washington or Baltimore. The rift came after the B&O Company had failed to renew certain reciprocal fare agreements by March 1, 1887, after which conductors of the AW&B trains refused to honor Annapolis tickets sold at Camden Station. Public indignation was echoed in the newspapers who called it "The Railroad Feud". To resolve this dilemma, the Short Line was obliged to inaugurate service somewhat prematurely; and beginning March 9, 1887, the first trains to arrive at Bladen Street unloaded their passengers onto planks across the mud, weeks before the station was built.

The new Short Line was indeed shorter, both in distance and time; a saving that would soon compel the AW&B to abandon its regular through runs into Baltimore. Thus, by force of circumstances, the Short Line became a closer ally of the B&O Railroad; and as such, obtained the operating franchise for a new B&O subsidiary - the Bay Ridge & Annapolis Railroad. The advantages here were twofold. In addition to summer excursion traffic to the bayside resort, plans were already underway on the far side of the Chesapeake for another railroad which would connect by steamboat with a proposed terminal at Bay Ridge.

In March 1886, the Baltimore & Eastern Shore Railroad was incorporated to build a line northwestward from Salisbury, Maryland via Vienna, Easton, and St. Michaels to the bay, where it would establish a ferry crossing to Thomas Point (Bay Ridge) for connections to Baltimore, thereby opening a route from the Monumental City to Eastern Shore points involving only one half the rail distance theretofore required to circumvent the northern reaches of the Chesapeake.

That promise was fulfilled in September 1890 with opening of the new Baltimore & Eastern Shore Railroad, offering regular service from Camden Station, via Annapolis and Bay Ridge (western shore) and Bay City (eastern shore), all the way to Ocean City on the Atlantic. But the ill-fated venture was plagued by bankruptcy, and shortly thereafter was reorganized as the Baltimore Chesapeake & Atlantic Railway, to eliminate the routing via Annapolis.

For its grand opening on March 9, 1887, the Short Line had received three of the four engines ordered

Number 2 shown just outside Camden Station in Baltimore. For years after the electrification, several of these locomotives continued to haul freight to the Short Line's freight terminal on Burgundy Street. Smithsonian collection.

from the Baldwin Locomotive Works. They were 4-4-0 types handsomely outfitted with brass bands over the boiler, with cylinder heads, pipes, and domes done in burnished copper or brass, and with sixty-two-inch driving wheels painted red. The sixteen passenger cars (two combines & fourteen coaches) were built by the Wason Manufacturing Company of Springfield, Mass., while twenty gondolas, ten box cars, and a caboose came from the Ensign Manufacturing Company of Huntington, West Virginia.

The whole line had been built and equipped at a cost of just over a half million dollars—words whose intensity we may not fully grasp at once. But it was different money of other days in other ways that made it so!

The railroad was barely two years old when operations were suspended for five days while (in the cryptic style of early newspapers): "the serpentine curves are being straightened for improved engines which have been secured". Such are the puzzle pieces that confront our legacy of the nebulous past. For weeks nothing more. But on Saturday night, July 27, 1889, the *Evening Capital* bestowed just one sentence: "The new six-wheel driving engine arrived here (Bladen St.) in charge of Engineer Chaulk". It was locomotive number 4.

The experiences of those early years were at times as adventurous as they were unfortunate. Such as that day when the engineer of the *Afternoon Express*, rounding a curve at Revell Station, saw his rear car leaping, careening, and swaying as though trying to break away. A truck bolster under the tender had jarred loose, throwing out the forward spring, which fell between the rails, bounding along and striking the underside of each coach with frightening noises, until it finally derailed the last car, a combine, which overturned. As it did, a bulkhead of the baggage section gave way, releasing barrels of fresh herring that all but smothered the men in the adjoining smoker.

Or that early morning of May 22, 1918 when a

hopper in the middle of a coal train derailed at the draw of the Severn bridge, leaving officials with no better alternative than to dump forty-odd tons of coal into the river in order to right the car. For weeks thereafter the local watermen with oyster tongs hovered over the spot—but not for oysters.

In accordance with foreclosure proceedings filed in October 1893, the Short Line was sold to George Burnham, Jr. of Portland, Maine, who on January 25, 1894, reorganized the company as the Baltimore & Annapolis Short Line Railroad. That reorganization would entail a fifty year mortgage given on May 1, 1894 to secure a bond issue of $600,000. Then on September 1, 1897, a controlling interest in the Short Line was acquired by certain bankers of Baltimore who also owned the Annapolis Washington & Baltimore Railroad. Although the two companies were jointly managed, they were to remain operationally separate. The new owners apparently wielded greater influence in local financial circles, for a year later, negotiations were completed for a new issue of $400,000 in first mortgage bonds under conditions considerably more favorable, both as to term (twenty-five years) and rate; whereupon the earlier debt of 1894 was cancelled.

In December 1898, $325,000 of the new bonds were issued to provide for a floating debt contracted by the AW&B Railroad, in its purchase of the Short Line. The securities thus acquired, amounting to $357,500 of the capital stock of the AW&B Railroad, were then deposited with the Mercantile Trust & Deposit Company of Baltimore (Trustee) as collateral security for the Baltimore & Annapolis Short Line Railroad Company. At the same time, a new board of directors was elected on December 14, 1898, replacing the directorship of the original New England founders of the Short Line. By this convoluted finance, the AW&B Railroad became a subsidiary of the B & A Short Line Railroad.

Early in 1902, the Lamprecht-Wilcox-Christy Syndicate of Cleveland began construction of an electric interurban line which would intersect the AW&B Railroad near Odenton. As part of their plans for the interurban system, the entire capital stock of the AW&B Company was acquired on February 26, 1903 for a cash purchase of $367,400. But the Cleveland management was itself confronted by bankruptcy (July 12, 1903) which delayed formal transfer of the Annapolis line for another five years, until December 16, 1908.

Meanwhile, proceeds from this sale had enabled the Baltimore & Annapolis Short Line to liquidate that company's funded debt, when all bonds were recalled for redemption on June 1, 1903. Encouraged by its new state of solvency, the Short Line's owners explored several possibilities for expansion. And while these projects never materialized beyond the draftsman's desk, they nevertheless reflected the imaginative thinking of private ownership in a more ascendant age when railroading was still the industry of the future.

Lacking any direct interchange with the Pennsylvania System, the Short Line at one point drew plans for a connecting line three and three-tenths miles long, from Shipley westward to the Philadelphia Baltimore & Washington main line near Stoney Run, but the more favorable freight tariffs offered by the AW&B Railroad via Odenton soon caused the plan to be abandoned. Again in June 1906, an extensive survey was completed for another branch line roughly following Cabin Creek from a point near Woodlawn Heights to the waterfront at Curtis Bay, a route that was revived in more specific terms some twenty-one years later. There was, however, yet another extension which was, in fact, realized. They had secured a monopoly, of freight traffic to and from the Naval Academy via a subsidiary called the Annapolis & Chesapeake Railroad .*

Commencing in 1905, a sequence of events was to influence a series of decisions that would profoundly affect the Short Line for years to come. It was the dawn of "The Electric Interurban" that kindled the desire for change; but more specifically, it was the revival of an old rival, now called the WB&A Electric Railway, that presented a new emulator. Under new ownership, the WB&A (still under construction) had then recently acquired the former Annapolis & Elk Ridge line, which it would

* See page 144

electrify as part of a new high-speed interurban route to Baltimore.

This new WB&A management had applied for a charter to operate electric trains through the streets of Annapolis to the town wharves, making direct connection with steamboats of the bay, an advantage obviously denied to steam trains of the Short Line. Moreover, the WB&A, through its subsidiary the Baltimore Terminal Company, was already planning a convenient mid-city station in Baltimore, to be reached via an elaborate rapid transit approach and operations over downtown streets; again, a unique leverage that would preclude steam trains of the Short Line. The rapid transit (viaduct) route through South Baltimore was a costly venture, involving the crossing of four (potentially five) major railroads, the boring of two tunnels, and extensive elevated track construction. To share in this undertaking, the Short Line was invited to participate, on the condition that its lines be equipped for electric operations, either exclusively or concurrently with steam trains. On January 17, 1906, an agreement to that effect was signed between the Baltimore Terminal Company, the Traction Construction Company, United Railways & Electric Company, and the Baltimore & Annapolis Short Line Railroad Company. So, from both ends, pressure mounted for the Short Line to remain competitive by also becoming an Electric Interurban. Five months later the Short Line withdrew from its part in the joint terminal project, allegedly because of excessive toll rates to be levied by the builders; whereupon the Baltimore Terminal Company completed it alone. But the Short Line was still committed to a conversion to electric motive power; lacking, for the moment, only the means.

In 1904, the United Railways & Electric Company was faced with the colossal task of repairing wholesale devastation wrought by the great Baltimore fire of February that year. Despite the car company's heroic efforts in meeting the immediate emergencies, the aftermath of that tragedy had afforded a unique chance to build anew with latest fireproof structures, modern rolling stock, track

extensions, and a variety of other capital improvements. But mortgages incurred at the time of the big consolidation several years before provided that all properties then owned, or which might be acquired in the future, were pledged for the security of existing mortgages. Since, under these restrictions, the United Railways & Electric Company was unable, in itself, to borrow additional funds for the much-needed improvements, the only alternative was the creation of an independent holding company that could finance the new facilities, leasing them back to the operating railway.

For that purpose, a charter of the non-operating Maryland Electric Railway Company (dating from 1898) was secured and amended as a medium for the new corporate arrangement; that company however, being then without any tangible property in its own right. So in order to give stability to the proposed bond issue, making those securities an attractive investment, the Maryland Electric Railway needed some good sound utility outside the city system. Where else but the railroad to Annapolis, which was about to undertake some major construction of its own? Accordingly, the Maryland Electric Railway Company offered to guarantee the outstanding capital stock of the Short Line, with a proposed stock split of three for one on its common shares, in return for its partnership in, a new consolidation to be known as the Maryland Electric Railways Company. Of the 24,000 shares authorized by the new company, stockholders of the B & A Short Line Railroad were issued (fully paid), ninety-two percent of the total then outstanding. On August 6, 1906, one day before the merger took effect, the Baltimore & Annapolis Short Line Railroad, in its own name, executed a forty year mortgage deed of trust to secure $1,000,000 for the planned electrification; which debt became a first lien against the interurban line now backed by the full weight of a vast improvement program undertaken by the entire city railway system.

In one of the legal niceties of this transaction, the Maryland Electric Railway Company, as a gesture of good intention, on August 6, 1906, purchased for $25,000 the "branch line of track" extending from

One of the nine original cars built in 1908 by the Southern Car Company. An unusual feature was the motorman's cab at the left side. Trolley poles had been installed for planned operations over city streets that never came to pass. Peale Museum collection.

the Short Line's Round Bay Station to its terminus near the hotel; in all one half mile of track, which twenty-four hours later reverted to the management who had sold it.

The following spring (April 1907), a contract was awarded to J.G. White & Company of New York for supervising the entire project of electrification, as well as to grade new rights-of-way at various places with a view toward easing some of the curves and reducing the grades for faster schedules. One such point was at Linthicum, where an exchange of real estate with the parallel WB&A line worked to their mutual advantage, as shown by the map on page ten. Other segments of right-of-way that involved the realignment of curves were: Shipley through Woodlawn Heights; Oakwood to a point north of Marley Creek; Earleigh Heights to Robinson; and Revell to Joyce. At the same time, six and four-tenth miles of the main line were made double track, and the entire road was relaid with heavier eighty-pound bonded rails.

As mentioned, the approach to Baltimore was changed several times over the years. When opened in 1887, the Short Line operated under agreement with the B&O Railroad using the Curtis Bay Branch from Clifford, via a somewhat roundabout route to

Mount Clare Junction, thence following the main line into Camden station. Later that year the B&O Railroad completed what was called their South Baltimore Branch, as a single track which left the Curtis Bay line just west of Cherry Hill onto a projection of Kloman Street (Westport), turning westward into the approximate line of Putnam Street, to Carroll Tower and the main line. This route was to serve the Short Line's steam trains for twenty years until the electrification project of 1907 raised certain objections by the B&O Railroad to the construction of a 6600-volt overhead along their tracks. In the untried methods of early electrification, the high-tension trolley was regarded as hazardous, as indeed it was.

Accordingly, the Maryland Electric Railways built an independent right-of-way from Clifford Station, which ran through English Consul in a deep clay cut, passing under the Curtis Bay Branch by means of a viaduct parallel with, and in every respect identical to, the WB&A roadbed beside it. Somewhat unusual at that point were three railroads abreast, each in its separate ditch, with the two deeper level (electric) lines constantly plagued by poor drainage and endless shifting of the high banks of red clay. A second phase of this rerouting,

The local press was lavish in its praise of the first new car which was placed on display at Bladen Street. Author's collection.

Shortly after the electrification, a number of the former steam road coaches still served as trailers as shown in this scene at the entrance to the Bladen street yard. Note the old locomotive turntable to the right. George Krambles collection.

For several months, the new electrified service operated only as far as Westport, where the interurban cars were coupled onto steam engines for the remainder of the trip to Baltimore. Smithsonian collection.

which was not completed until later in 1908, entailed a new double-track line along Russell Street from Putnam Street to tne B&O main line at Stockholm Street, leading into the Camden yards. The combined relocations also required three grade crossings with the Westport streetcar line, each protected by a de-rail interlocking plant.

In the technical realm of actual electrification, changes were already underway which would challenge the then prevailing concept of direct current for most forms of Electric Traction. The first major departure from that theory was a contract awarded by the WB&A Electric Railway in 1902 (and renewed in more specific terms, September 1906) for an alternating current single-phase system of power distribution. Following their precedent, the Short Line in April 1907 also adopted a 6600-volt alternating current single-phase electrification to be built and installed by the Westinghouse Electric & Manufacturing Company. The plans were designed and supervised by Dr. John Boswell Whitehead, Professor of Applied Electric-

ity at Johns Hopkins University, and Waldo H. Sawin, Engineer for J. G. White & Company. Several features of their plans, rather novel for that day, involved (in addition to the motor generator sets at the Westport power plant) only one automatic (unattended) substation at Jones Road. Thirty-three miles of high-tension trolley (including all secondary track) were grounded at five points by the use of large copper plates, each nine square feet in area, embedded in coke in damp earth. Since there were no transmission lines, as such, across the Severn River, the trolley circuit was built to by-pass the draw bridge by means of lead-armored submarine cables.

There were to be nine multiple-unit interurban cars equipped by Westinghouse, each with four 100 h.p. motors mounted in trucks especially constructed by the American Locomotive Company. The fifty-six foot car bodies built by the Southern Car Company resulted in a complete car registered at slightly under forty-nine tons, or about two tons heavier than a similar car designed for direct current

One of the three Jewett cars first used on the AC single-phase system in shown here in 1919 shortly after it was re-equipped for 1200-volt DC operations. The wide window post at one end indicates a modification of the former baggage compartment. Author's collection.

motors and controls.

To the casual observer, their most distinguishing feature was a pantograph, which was variously described by the newspapers as:

> "an arrangement of rods and springs which takes the place of the usual trolley pole. When not in use, the device is held in position by clutches, which when released, permit the pantograph to spring upward and contact the wire by means of a broad iron shoe"
>
> or
>
> "an arrangement not unlike a pair of crab claws, reaching up and holding a broad metal shoe against the trolley wire"

Even the railroad's timetables proclaimed: "Safe High-Speed Pantograph Trolley Cars" as if to imply a certain advantage to the public. Conjoined with its high-voltage pantograph, each car was equipped with two standard pole trolleys, seemingly a vestigial trace of earlier plans to reach a downtown terminal over the local street car tracks.

Within a year after the contract had been let, the electrical system was completed and first operated on April 13, 1908. It was several weeks before the electric trains were placed in regular schedules as far as Westport; and not until August 1908 that the new tracks via Russell Street enabled the interurban line to reach Camden Station. But the single-phase electrification proved to be less than satisfactory, and after only five years the Short Line was converted to a 1200-volt direct current system, which involved a completely new substation number 2 (near Jones Road), rebuilding the entire catenary overhead with steel trolley wire attached to the original copper line (which became a feeder), and the addition of twelve new cars.

In the early 1920's a group of co-eds from one of the Baltimore colleges would be escorted each spring to the June Hop at the Naval Academy. After the dance, the last train from Bladen Street was usually held for the party returning to Baltimore. And aboard that late night ride through the Arundel countryside, there unfolded an impromptu jam session by the musicians in their tuxedos and the young ladies in their frilly finery. With every window open, even the motorman was caught up in the spirit of the evening, as the old air whistle hooted its measured blasts above the din of the whole train singing "Three O'clock in the Morn-

During the summer of 1910, a pair of the original Southern coaches are posed with one of the later Jewett combination cars. George Krambles collection.

ing". There are moments of drama and romance in every life; and my childhood memory of having been along, was one of those!

As a holding company, more concerned with its investments, the Maryland Electric Railways Company had never demonstrated a willingness nor talent for managing the day to day affairs of its city or interurban properties. In 1912, the company retained Allen & Peck, Inc. (later Peck, Shannahan & Cherry) as engineers and managers of various public utilities, at a fee of $12,000 per year, to operate the Annapolis Short Line. Under this arrangement, the president, who was also administering another client company, had his office in Hampton, Virginia.

In so many ways, the fate of The Short Line was always linked to the upkeep of its bridges. In fact, many years later a calamity which caused the first serious suspension of service (well nigh a total abandonment) was the bridge damage wrought by a hurricane. Added to that was the burdensome debt of converting the entire electrical plant. Moreover, the lease granting access to Camden Station had expired, and the B&O Railroad had long since served notice that it would not be renewed.

There is a poignant contrast between the earlier years of a viable railroad operation played strictly according to the rules, and the humble destiny of a later period marked by neglect and the hostile circumstances of subsidized competition, government restraints, vandalism, etc., which we might now call "The Not So Generous Years". Such were the conditions that by 1920 made it assailable for takeover.

Twelve new cars for the 1200 volt service were built in 1913 by the Wason Manufacturing Company. An innovation of that day was the center-entrance for greater capacity and a depressed stairwell for quicker interchange of passengers. Author's collection.

9

THE MERGER

Electrification of the Annapolis Short Line had been completed in April 1908 within a month after the opening of the WB&A. From the beginning, both roads had anticipated a brisk commerce between Maryland's largest city and its capital. Indeed, for a brief period, the ancient city on the bay, with its *two* modern electric railroads, seemed destined to become a significant port for the flourishing trade in tobacco, garden produce, seafood and other traffic with the Eastern Shore. But the bustling business of government and commerce was hardly compatible with the quiet charm of colonial tradition, for the inexorable forces of succeeding years were to witness Annapolis abandoned by many of the state offices, the bay steamboats, yes, even the railroads—both of them!

In the days of those two roads to Annapolis, the Short Line enjoyed a slight advantage in that it ran entirely over private right-of-way via a somewhat more direct route that was 3.7 miles shorter than the WB&A Company's South Shore Line by way of Naval Academy Junction. Though despite this leverage, the Maryland Electric Railways' record was fraught with a tremulous theme whose tone and pitch seldom varied. In a word, this theme was financial. In only one year of the decade ending in 1920 had the Short Line shown a profit.

During the immediate post war period, while most railroads were still riding the crest of their wartime profits, The Short Line's problems remained; and in seeking to resolve them, where else to turn but to its prosperous neighbor—The WB&A. To calm possible fears of uncertainty in financial circles, the first accounts of this approach were carefully couched in terms of a joint operating arrangement aimed at resolving the question of a Baltimore terminal. Nothing more! The banking house of Alex Brown & Sons, who were the principal stockholders of The Short Line, were understandably concerned lest news of an outright merger

be released prematurely.

On May 20, 1920, Mr. Bishop, President of The WB&A, outlined a plan of six basic steps for preliminary negotiations; namely:

1. The Maryland Electric Railways to be granted trackage rights, including the use of stations and other facilities of The WB&A, from Shipley into Baltimore.
2. The seven miles of track and right-of-way north of Shipley (which so closely paralleled The WB&A) to be deeded to the Terminal Real Estate Company, a subsidiary of The WB&A Electric Railroad. This transfer included a new substation established only a year before at Linthicum.
3. The railroad south of Shipley (to Annapolis) to be conveyed to the Annapolis and Chesapeake Railroad* which already possessed a state charter and operating rights for such a contract; and to better reflect the facts, to be known henceforth as the Annapolis Short Line Railroad. **
4. The Maryland Electric Railways to secure release from any existing contracts for purchase of power, operating rights over B&O tracks, city franchises, etc., without obligation to the new owners.
5. The Annapolis Short Line Railroad to assume all outstanding indebtedness previously incurred by the Maryland Electric Railways; including a mortgage of 1906

---

* For a description of the Annapolis and Chesapeake Railroad, see page 144.
** Theretofore used only as a trade name, Annapolis Short Line RR, for the first time became a corporate title that lasted approximately six weeks.

Configuration of the coupler and pantograph of this Short Line car indicates Marley Station as it appeared prior to 1921. Courtesy of Mark N. Schatz and Jack Kelbaugh.

for $1 million covering the original electrification; two car trust leases for $240,000 on its fifteen cars; and a new bond issue of $732,000 to be authorized to fund a floating indebtedness of $558,000 from past operating deficits; and another $115,000 to finance the costs of joining the two lines at Shipley, and of adapting cars, signals, etc. for joint operations with the WB&A system.
6. Allowing for certain securities issued at discount, accrued interest, and other adjustments, the foregoing debts, then placed at $1,992,000, to be guaranteed by the WB&A Electric Railroad Company which would acquire the Annapolis Short Line Railroad.

As ratified by both Boards of Directors, the plan was finally approved February 21, 1921.

Although the two lines converged at Shipley, a considerable difference in grades required that the actual track connections be located closer to Linthicum, which thereafter became the principal junction. Combined operations began on March 16, 1921, and until an adequate Baltimore terminal was completed some seven months later, the old Short Line tracks near Baltimore Highlands were to serve as the car storage and service facilities in lieu of the city yards. North of Baltimore Highlands, a three mile segment of the former Short Line (via Clifford and Kloman Street) was retained to serve a freight yard on Russell Street and an eventual interchange with the Western Maryland Railway in Westport.

Upon acquiring The Short Line, The WB&A company promptly undertook an ambitious program of rehabilitation, that included the installa-

Wardour Station in 1950. The plan of block signals included C-14 (foreground) and C-21 (opposite shore) which controlled automatic derails to protect the Severn Bridge. The view looks toward Baltimore. R. A. Truax photograph.

tion of a new block signal system, a rearrangement of the power distribution aimed at providing a more uniform line voltage, and the remodeling of fourteen passenger cars. Though by far its biggest venture was the reconstruction of the Severn River bridge.

In the years just prior to the consolidation, it was generally known that The Short Line had a serious backlog of deferred maintenance, though it is hard to imagine how (as a public carrier) it had continued to use the Severn bridge with impunity. As one of its first priorities, the WB&A in April 1921 negotiated two contracts for extensive repairs to the swing span; the addition of 137 new bents to be

constructed between each pair of existing bents on 376 spliced piles to be driven to a deeper penetration throughout the entire length of the trestle. Even so, submarine inspections by the divers would indicate considerable variations in what was called a *firm bottom*. In this work, some of the new piling had failed to reach bedrock. As E. W. Weinland (who was the Company's expert) would describe it, the Severn Bridge rested on a number of 120 foot *suction* piles, a term which would seem to place the support in question. But as experience elsewhere had shown, strata of sand and stone, sufficiently dense and compact, can provide a footing as solid as rock itself.

Annapolis Short Line freight motor number 300 with train of standard steam road coaches at Bladen Street Station. The Wason center-entrance car on the track to the right establishes this as 1914 or later. King collection.

The work lasted for five months throughout that summer. At Severnside, the railroad owned a large tract (later known as Manresa) where the Empire Engineering Company established a contractor's supply yard and dock for the barges and steam hammers working in the river. One phase of the project necessitated the complete suspension of service, during which time all through schedules were routed via the South Shore Division; while a local shuttle from Winchester to Annapolis was handled by two "Blue Line" busses leased from the United Railways & Electric Company. Toward the end of September, regular bridge traffic was resumed, though the work was by no means finished.

The Public Service Commission was now inspecting the bridge, with a long report of additional renewals amounting to a supplemental estimate equal in scope and cost to the contracts just completed. The second bridge project was awarded in

April 1924 for construction that went on throughout most of 1925.

To distinguish the territories served along both sides of the Severn River, the separate routes to Annapolis were now designated as the North Shore and South Shore Divisions. Although there had always been connecting tracks at Bay Ridge Junction (Cedar Park) for interchange of freight in West Annapolis, the two lines continued to use their separate passenger stations at Bladen Street and West Street. On those occasions of special events at the Naval Academy, extra moves which involved standard railroad equipment with steam locomotives, were invariably routed over the South Shore Line to avoid heavy tonnage crossing the Severn bridge; and at the same time to afford a more direct transfer of trains to either of the steam railroads at Odenton or Annapolis Junction. At such times, the remnant special-work at Bay Ridge Junction pro-

Number 57 arriving at Bladen Street station, Annapolis. King collection.

On August 17, 1935, an articulated train bound for Baltimore crosses the Patapsco River at Pumphrey , Md. The abandoned Annapolis Short Line bridge is to the right. James P. Shuman photograph.

The bridge crossing Crain Highway was built from a locomotive turntable. Since it would also be used by heavier trains of the B&O Railroad, timber bents were added to reinforce the outer ends of the cantilever beams. Special Collections, University of Maryland at College Park Libraries.

vided a convenient turning point for the bigger locomotives.

In 1923 the Robert Crain Highway was built from Baltimore to Upper Marlboro, crossing the WB&A South Shore Line west of Millersville. In order to avoid a grade crossing, the cost of erecting a bridge over a planned highway underpass was to be borne entirely by the railroad company.

Dating from the merger with the Annapolis Short Line just two years before, the railroad had acquired, as part of the Bladen Street Yards, a sixty-ton locomotive turntable which was no longer used. With the need for a bridge at Millersville, it was decided that this turntable (a balanced cantilever weighing twelve and a half tons with a span of nearly fifty five feet) could be moved intact to the bridge site. Commencing on April 8, 1923, the turntable was jacked out of the cylindrical pit to a level that enabled a temporary track and two flat cars to be placed under it. The entire structure, still rigidly connected with all cross-bracing, was then hauled from Annapolis to Millersville where it was unloaded onto tie cribbing beside the exact location. As soon as the last train had passed at midnight on April 10th, the track was broken and a pit was dug in the roadbed where the bridge was to be placed. The turntable was then skidded into position more or less flush with the surrounding terrain; and the track was connected in time for the first regular service at 5:00 AM. Under normal working schedules, pits were then dug under each end for the supporting abutments, while the center section of the cantilever rested on the remaining earth. When all foundation work was finished, the depressed highway approaches were excavated and the earth tunneled away between the abutments to expose a single-track deck-girder bridge whose "fish belly" contours always betrayed its roundhouse origin.

1921 was the mid-point in the short history of The WB&A Electric Line. With consolidation of The Annapolis Short Line, and the opening of completely new terminals in Washington on January 31 and in Baltimore on October 30, that year was to witness the Company's utmost reach in property expansion. And, sadly, it also marked another turning point; for without serious calculation, it was soon evident that the private automobile and subsidized commerce via rubber tires had already asserted their places as new forms of competition.

After the first stage of re-building by the WB&A, one of the Wason cars crosses the Severn River. It is an exceptional view in that the car still retains the original couplers and pilots used prior to its second rebuilding, to WB&A standards, in 1924. Author's collection.

Wason car 105 running as a North Shore Local at Kent Street, Baltimore, August 17. 1935. James P. Shuman photograph.

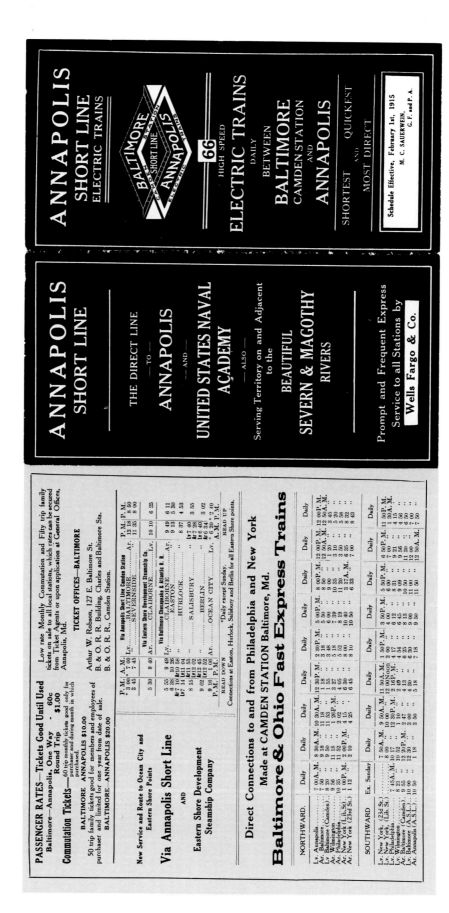

Signal paddles are placed at all stations which should be held in a horizontal position as a signal to Motorman to stop trains to take on passengers.

SOUTH BOUND. BALTIMORE (CAMDEN STATION) TO ANNAPOLIS

STATIONS	Miles
BALTIMORE	0
CALYPSO	3.3
BALTO. HIGHLANDS	4.5
PUMPHREY	5.4
LINTHICUM	6.4
SHIPLEY	6.9
WOODLAWN HEIGHTS	7.4
WELLHAM	8.2
GLEN BURNIE	9.9
SAUNDERS RANGE	10.5
MARLEY	12.
ELVATON	13.5
PASADENA	15.
EARLEIGH HEIGHTS	15.4
ROBINSON	17.
ROUND (Severna Park)	17.5
ROUND BAY	18.1
JONES	19.
REVELL	20.
JOYCE	20.8
ARNOLD	21.4
WINCHESTER	22.4
SEVERNSIDE	23.8
WALDOUR	23.9
WEST ANNAPOLIS	24.6
ANNAPOLIS	25.3

NORTH BOUND. ANNAPOLIS TO BALTIMORE (CAMDEN STATION)

STATIONS	Miles
ANNAPOLIS	0
WEST ANNAPOLIS	1.4
WALDOUR	2.9
SEVERNSIDE	4.0
WINCHESTER	5.3
ARNOLD	7.2
REVELL	8.3
JONES	9.9
ROUND BAY	10.8
ROUND (Severna Park)	14.8
ROBINSON	15.4
EARLEIGH HEIGHTS	18.4
PASADENA	18.9
ELVATON	19.9
MARLEY	20.3
SAUNDERS RANGE	25.3

THE ADVERTISER-REPUBLICAN PRINT

Trains will be stopped at stations at which they are scheduled to stop (on proper signal) or (on notification to Conductor) to let off passengers or to take them on.

North from Bragers Station, freight motor number one waits on the east side spur track circa 1935. Another spur leading to the Little Patuxent gravel pit may be seen to the west (left) background. Author's collection.

10

FAST FREIGHT - SLOW FREIGHT

From its inception, the Washington Baltimore and Annapolis Electric Railway was seen essentially as a passenger carrier. Moreover, considering the sparsely settled countryside between the cities, its first timetables had emphasized high-speed service, terminal to terminal, with only a casual bow to the accommodation runs which traditionally were regarded as the main source of wayside freight. Nor was carload freight of any importance initially. The two main line steam railroads already had the advantage of tariffs based on through freight with direct interchange at each of the two principal cities; while the largest customer in Annapolis (the Naval Academy) had long since been captured through a subsidiary of the competing Baltimore and Annapolis Short Line RR.

In 1907 the WB&A's only non-passenger equipment consisted of two heavy (forty-eight-ton) freight motors of high-gear ratio and twenty-five flat cars used mainly for ballasting the new roadbed and subsequent service in maintenance of way. So, by opening day in 1908 there had been no real effort toward freight business, except perhaps to sustain a modest, albeit well established, farmer clientele inherited from its predecessor AW&B (Annapolis Division) Railroad.

In July, 1909 a contract for promoting less-than-carload package freight was concluded with the Electric Express Company, an agency which appears to have been reasonably successful in the New England States. A special tariff was printed listing rates for garden produce (by the basket); and a conductor, riding the gasoline speeder, traveled up and down the line to visit farmers and arrange for shipment of each harvest, and the free return of empty containers.

One condition of the express contract provided that all equipment for that service, including the cars, was to be furnished by the Electric Express Company. Toward that end, the express agency had agreed to purchase the two freight motors (1&2) at a cost of $25,540 which amount would include the expense of re-adapting those AC single-phase cars with new motors to conform to the impending change-over to a direct-current system. However, before that transfer was accomplished the contractor had defaulted on other conditions, and the agreement was cancelled on April 14, 1910; to be replaced by another concession granted to the Adams Express Company. After only two years, that agreement was succeeded in June 1912 by a new freight contract awarded to the American Railway Express Company.

From then on, the volume of less-than-carload and package express increased, partly through promotional efforts mounted by American Express, though largely because it filled a void created by the steam railroads' recent decision to discontinue pick up and delivery service to the smaller merchants in Baltimore and Washington. Thus, the inventiveness and initiative which had characterized early efforts for passenger patronage were, for the first time, extended to a serious bid for new freight customers.

A flourishing business in trolley freight soon prompted an expansion of facilities, including the purchase of four new express cars and the construction of a new freight terminal in Baltimore. Designed by one of the city's leading architects, Otto Simonson, the modern freight station was opened for business on March 12, 1914. It was located on Pratt Street, immediately to the rear of the car barn which until then had also served as the express depot. The two adjoining parcels of land now provided a corridor through the middle of the block. So, although the freight station was listed as 312 West Pratt Street, the cars serving it came through from Lombard Street a block away.

Back in 1909, Congress had prohibited horse

Right: Freight motor number 1 at Annapolis Junction, June, 1908. Author's collection.

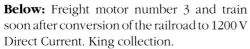

Below: Freight motor number 3 and train soon after conversion of the railroad to 1200 V Direct Current. King collection.

12 and 17 switching at Bladen Street, Annapolis July 1, 1935. 18 is at the right. Note the Maryland State House in the left background. James P. Shuman photograph.

racing within the District of Columbia; and although Benning was no longer the scene of local racing events, the Washington Jockey Club continued to board horses at their stables there. When the new facilities of Prince George's Park (at Bowie) were opened in October 1914, it was not uncommon for many of the racing mounts to be transported regularly from their Benning stables via *horse cars* of the interurban line.

The four new baggage-express cars of 1912 were built by the Niles Car & Manufacturing Company. They were wooden arch roof bodies, fifty-one feet over buffers, mounted on standard Baldwin type 78-25A trucks. Three of these were trailers, each provided with a full complement of controls, enabling them to operate as a leading car in any consist. Because the Baltimore yard tracks then entered Lombard Street eastbound, departing freight runs were required to change ends in the middle of the street before starting out westbound. Apparently, the rather expensive electrical equipment for these cars (averaging some $3250 per set) was justified to obviate an otherwise awkward practice which would have required the motor to run around its train standing on a grade, involving additional dual gauge switches, as well as delays to the street cars that also used the same tracks. In any event the control equipment was removed from the express trailers in 1921 with the completion of a new

terminal which provided a convenient loop. The fourth car of the same 1912 order from Niles was designated as express motor number 7, equipped with GE-205 motors corresponding to the passenger cars.

Late in 1913, another order for two more of this type was placed with Niles. They were delivered in May 1914 and equipped as high speed baggage/express motors numbers 8 & 9. Inasmuch as the WB&A never owned motorized work equipment, number 8 had end train doors (the only one so equipped) apparently to facilitate work assignments with line cars or the caboose.

By 1916, the thriving trade in less-than-carload shipments was averaging nine carloads daily between Baltimore and Washington. With the war and its after-effects, the volume of "Fast Freight" reached its crest; until by 1921, that department alone had reached a gross revenue of $300,000 annually. Over these first thirteen years, the encouraging growth of the WB&A's freight and express traffic is again shown by the increase in this type of equipment operated: from two freight motors and four combination cars in 1908, to fifteen freight motors and thirty-nine combination cars by 1921.

In fact it was so encouraging that an added service of refrigerated express had been inaugurated for meats, seafood, and garden produce,

Above: From 1908 to 1914, the express office and freight station were at 317 West Lombard Street. Tracks entered the street eastbound so that arrivals always backed in while departing trains had to change ends on Lombard Street before departing westbound. Special dual gauge trackwork in the street accommodated the streetcars which also ran on Lombard Street. **Below**: To accommodate the increasing volume of package freight handled in connection the American Express Company, a new freight station was built at 312 W. Pratt Street. Here, the loading docks are seen to the left. At the extreme right the bumper of one track extended from the Lombard Street car barn immediately to the rear. In 1921, the station was demolished to make way for a new terminal yard. Both photos, Author's collection.

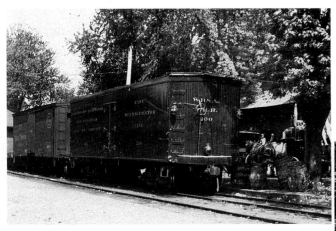

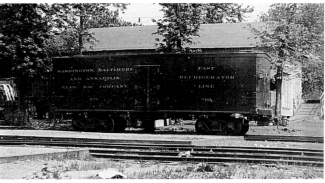

Two different views of reefer car 200 of the WB&A Fast Refrigerator Line. The car was equipped with rounded buffers and jointed drawbars for operation on the sharp curves on the streets of Baltimore. **Above:** Author's collection. **Right:** J. B. Yeabower collection.

handled by the interurban's own reefer cars. The first of these (200) was a small thirty-seven foot refrigerator car (of five ton ice capacity) acquired second-hand in 1914. In the company's shops, it was modified for sharp-radius curves and repainted the standard dark green, trimmed and lettered in gold. Again in 1915 and 1917, two more of this series were purchased from Swift & Company of Chicago, and numbered 201 and 202. But manual servicing of refrigerator cars was costly, and the corrosive effect of salt on older cars not in continuous use led to maintenance disproportionate to revenues. The service was discontinued in 1923, and the 200 class cars were scrapped in November 1926.

But the railroad's contract with the express agency had to be renewed periodically—and in 1923, it wasn't! Quite remote from the local scene, another express company had been organized shortly before as an affiliate of the Southern Railway System. It was incorporated October 6, 1920 under the laws of Alabama as the Southeastern Express; so named for the large region of southeastern states served by the Southern's lines. With main offices in Atlanta, Georgia, this new company soon negotiated additional agreements with a number of other carriers, including: the Mobile and Ohio Railroad, the Tennessee Central Railway, and the Maryland and

Pennsylvania Railroad. Up until this time, the American Railway Express Company had enjoyed a virtual monopoly of most eastern rail carriers. But early in 1921, a dispute with the Southeastern Company had resulted in serious delays where the two agencies exchanged shipments in Washington. Here, the WB&A moved in to bridge the breach by accepting cargo in Baltimore for delivery direct to the wagons of the Southern Railway in Washington. Although first announced as a temporary mediating effort, the interurban continued to handle a combination of express traffic for both agencies until a permanent agreement was reached on March 1, 1923, awarding all business to the Southeastern Express Company. At the same time, their small Baltimore branch office across the street from the WB&A station was moved into the new freight terminal at 135 South Eutaw Street.

American Express, by now deposed from its lucrative satellite status in the Washington-Annapolis territory, founded its own motor trucking service in competition with the interurban. By a reorganization of December 7, 1928 American Railway Express was expanded to handle a nationwide business, redesignated as the Railway Express Agency.

Facilities offered by the Southeastern Express were the same as those rendered to any major steam railroad. The WB&A company furnished

WB&A 74 showing Electric Express emblem. Jacques Kelly collection.

and moved the cars, while the express company adjusted claims, loaded, unloaded, and handled all accounting from the point of origin to destination; using its own delivery trucks to and from the major freight terminals.

As in many another realm of public service, the bureaucracies of administration, public relations, legal work, insurance, etc. expanded in inverse ratio to the basic business of hauling cargo; wherein the returns claimed by the auxiliary agency grew larger than revenues due the railroad. This trend is reflected in the apportionment of gross earnings (accruing on WB&A lines) as prescribed in successive express contracts; namely:

	Express Company	Railroad
1909*	60%	40%
1912	50%	50%
1923	55%	45%
1932	65%	35%

*cars furnished by agency

From an advertising standpoint, the earliest emblem was a gold shield and arrow inscribed with The Electric Express Company which was stenciled on the baggage doors of the combine cars.

Subsequent arrangements with the American Express were never advertised as such; and to the casual observer the railroad's agent was the representative for both passenger and baggage service. During those years, a rather modest marking indicating merely "Fast Freight" was lettered mid-way along the express car body.

The Southeastern Express Company adopted as its trademark a gammadion in gold superimposed on a field of red which embodied the letters "S E C O" in the four angles of the cross. While the emblem was later defamed by a notorious political party, it is intriguing to speculate (had the company survived the war) whether it would have had the conviction to retain its established trade mark.

Apace with continuing efforts to stimulate express business in LCL Fast Freight, there were changes afoot, somewhat belatedly, that were to awaken a new interest in interline traffic of carload shipments which, because of heavier tonnage, more often moved as Slow Freight.

For years the Western Maryland Railway had cast covetous glances toward the possibility of establishing competitive freight rates to Washington and the region of southern Maryland then served by the Chesapeake Beach Railway. The WB&A afforded the crucial link. Invariably, the question arises why

Number 16 at Baltimore in April 1935 showing distinctive Southeastern Express insignia. George Votava photo, King collection.

this important source of carload revenue was not tapped until 1924, nearly seventeen years after the electric line began. Although a survey for a proposed interchange at Westport had been attempted years before, it was generally regarded as not feasible. Here it will be recalled that the route of the original Baltimore Terminal Company had been purposely planned to avoid all grade crossings by passing under or over five different rail intersections. In the case of the Western Maryland crossing, the interurban's viaduct was built forty feet above the steam road, with much of the adjacent quadrants being restricted by Gwynns Falls and marshland on the one hand, and by the street plan of Westport on the other. Thus, it was not until the consolidation with the Annapolis Short Line that the WB&A, through its subsidiary the Terminal Real Estate Company, had acquired an alternate right of way which joined the Western Maryland's tracks at grade. For a brief period, it appeared that this bypass route would be

WB&A first number 1 at a gravel pit in 1928 or 1929. The car was destroyed by fire soon after this photograph. Author's collection.

10 and 13 switching at the gravel pit near Bowie Road, Md. July 12, 1935. James P. Shuman photograph.

abandoned, until October 1924, when the Western Maryland company offered to rehabilitate 1.92 miles (Westport to Rosemont), providing the WB&A company would thereafter maintain the track bonds and overhead work to serve a connection for carload freight. Both sides agreed, and a new interchange near Eyon Street was opened for traffic November 22, 1924.

Early in 1928, the Arundel Sand & Gravel Company acquired excavation rights to a tract of nearly 170 acres near Pasadena on the North Shore Division, from which the railroad carried carload sand and gravel to a siding on the elevated structure near Bush Street in Baltimore. This traffic was handled in eight hopper cars (501-508) and ten older-type gondolas (701-710) which the company had acquired several years before. Beside the main line at Bowie and Bragers (Little Patuxent) there were other gravel pits that had once been mined for track ballast during the construction days. One of these sites was included in a large parcel of land north of Bowie Road, which had been purchased in 1928 by Charles L. Ruffin of Fredericksburg, Virginia, with plans to ship sand and gravel to a distribution yard at 16th and Benning Road, N. E. In order to accommodate the increased business, a notable expansion of rail facilities, both as to rolling stock and terminal yard space, was required. The company purchased a total of fifty rebuilt fifty-ton hopper

cars (comprising two different types, 900-949) which enabled the retirement of eighteen older cars. There are indications that the relatively large increase in their roster of hopper cars at just this time also figured in planning for the Chesapeake and Potomac Railroad.*

To receive the sand and gravel trains, yard tracks of the former White House Station might have been adequate, except for the impending widening of Benning Road, which then threatened a sizeable slice of railroad property. During the spring of 1928, the company leased a strip of land fifty by 1000 feet along the north side of the yard, where the contractor erected five large storage silos which were filled from a tipple conveyer installed beneath one of the tracks. And from the gravel pits at Bowie, unit trains of hopper cars behind electric freight motors now delivered the raw materials for a fleet of transit-mix cement trucks advertised under the name of C. L. Ruffin's Massaponax Corporation.

For thirteen years after the founding of Camp Meade, the Baltimore and Ohio Railroad held a traffic agreement with the WB&A for government freight arriving via Annapolis Junction. While cars destined for Annapolis and intermediate points were interchanged at the Junction, most of the military shipments arrived behind steam locomo-

_____
* see page 97

Freight motor number 8 and one of the 10-17 group at the Eutaw Street freight terminal in 1935. Photograph by William Lichtenstern.

tives running directly to the base over a parallel B&O track on right-of-way owned by the electric line. And with the establishment of the US Army Tank School, and later the mechanized cavalry at Camp Meade, trainloads of heavy ordnance in addition to routine supplies for the Army had generated shipping invoices of enviable revenues. In the first year of the Great Depression, being hard pressed by dwindling returns in other areas, it was only natural the WB&A should now be unwilling to share a division of rates which it might claim exclusively as its own.

On September 29, 1930, the WB&A filed notice to terminate the agreement granting the B&O access to the base, now called Fort Meade.* After

securing approval of new freight tariffs, etc., the B&O Railroad discontinued through service effective February 6, 1931 and subsequently removed 4.12 miles of the northerly track from Annapolis Junction to Admiral. At the same time the WB&A obtained from the War Department a license for a period of five years to electrify and maintain those sidings serving the warehouses and depots which formerly had been reached by the steam railroads. And for intramural switching, it also stipulated that:

"We (the WB&A) will arrange for the same tariff charges that have been in effect with the B&O and Pennsylvania Railroads covering special movement of cars within the camp that have no connection with a road haul."

---

* see page 60

Motorman McCroy and Conductor Bindeman pose before a late afternoon departure for Washington. After arrival from Washington, the articulated car has been positioned over the track four inspection pit for a light inspection and the addition of a headlight. The express car in the rear is for a later Annapolis train. For several reasons, the preferred heading for articulated trains in Washington service was to have the toilet end forward. The hanger for the underground conduit plow used in Washington was placed on the truck on the opposite end of the train from the toilet. With the plow at the back of the train, motormen could attain a higher speed before the mandatory cut off at switches and crossings. Also, since the smoking compartment was always the rear section, non-smokers who wished to use the lavatory didn't have to navigate the smoking compartment. Norman Nelson collection.

11

NOT BY RAIL ALONE

"Change doth unknit the tranquil strength of things"
Matthew Arnold

Toward the mid 1920's, as many county roads were being paved for the first time, fledgling bus companies appeared everywhere. And with that ironic symmetry history abounds in, they grew in a kind of inverse ratio to the decline of the traction lines. The largess of publicly-built tax-supported rights-of-way was an opportunity to be seized by bus and rail operators alike. Or stated another way, there was every reason why the railways, in order to maintain an equal footing, should also compete "Not By Rail Alone". In 1927 the Company purchased three Type -Y six cylinder Yellow Coach busses for a duplicate service from Washington to Annapolis via the newly completed Defense Highway. Quite elegant by the standards of the day, the buses, seating 29 passengers, offered interior appointments of matched mahogany trimmed with velour, plate glass windows draped with sliding curtains and French plate mirrors at every side post, among other luxurious appointments. Bus chauffeurs always wore Sam Brown belts, riding breeches, and puttees.

Meanwhile in 1913, the WB&A Railroad Company had diversified slightly by acquiring the old Annapolis Gas & Electric Light Company of Anne Arundel County which, through successive reorganizations, became a wholly-owned railroad subsidiary called the Annapolis & Chesapeake Bay Power Company. In time the public electric service area was incorporated into the railroad's power transmission system; and the independent power house on St. Johns Street was closed and remodeled to enlarge the gas plant.

Swiftly, in these years, electricity proved itself in new ways. Largely through the vision and shrewd direction of George T. Bishop, the commercial gas and electric services were extended into territories far beyond the bounds of the original franchise. The voracious demands of new uses for electric power were endless— and the Company prospered! On June 16, 1925, Mr. Bishop was promoted from President to the newly-created post of Chairman of the Board. Only weeks before, a spectacular flurry of bidding for WB&A issues on the Baltimore Stock Exchange had resulted in sharp demands for the railroad's stocks and bonds. Despite diplomatic denials by Mr. Bishop, an avalanche of rumors persisted that certain utility interests in Philadelphia and Baltimore were seeking to gain control of the Company; as indeed they were. In the months that followed an ever increasing share of the railroad's outstanding securities were purchased by a new bidder trading as the Baltimore Corporation of Maryland. Finally in June 1927, it was announced that a controlling interest of fifty-four percent of the WB&A's stock had been acquired by the new company which, in turn, was revealed as a holding company of the Consolidated Gas Electric Light & Power Company of Baltimore. And so came to pass a rather ironic turnabout, where the parent railroad management of a satellite power company emerged the other way around.

After twenty-two years, on a day not otherwise remarkable in the running of a railroad, George T. Bishop resigned. And such was the esteem he had earned among his colleagues, that the Board, meeting on July 26, 1927, passed a resolution the eloquence of which is better quoted than rivaled.

Shortly after the Gas & Electric Company assumed control, Herbert A. Wagner the recently elected Chairman of the Board, announced plans for a new branch line of The WB&A that would serve the highly industrialized Curtis Bay area.

BE IT RESOLVED: That it is with the keenest regret that this Board accepts the resignation of Mr. George T. Bishop as a member of the Board and its Chairman, and desires to record among its minutes an appreciation of his services to the company and its predecessor, extending over a period of twenty-two years.

It was in the early part of 1905 that Mr. Bishop first took an interest in the predecessor of this company. At that time the predecessor company was in the hands of receivers appointed by the United States Court, a part only of its proposed single track line between Baltimore and Washington having been constructed. Mr. Bishop, with his associates, formed a syndicate to take the property out of receivership and to complete its construction and equipment. It was his vision that at that time realized that the proposed line of single track road of the ordinary suburban type running from the outskirts of Baltimore at Westport to the District Line would be unsuccessful commercially and insufficient to create the demand and to meet it in the communities and territory which it would serve. He therefore completely revised the plans of construction, made its main line a double track railroad and equipped it with high speed interurban cars. Later, in 1909, it was his courage, fearlessness and resourcefulness which reorganized the property, extended its service into the heart of Washington and acquired new terminals in both Baltimore and Washington. Subsequently, under his leadership, the company acquired what was known as the old Short Line, and what is now known as the North Shore Division. In 1912, due to his farsightedness, the company acquired the gas and electric plant of the Annapolis Gas & Electric Company, which had then less than four hundred subscribers; rebuilt its plant and extended its lines into new territories, and increased the number of its patrons to about seven thousand.

These are but the high points of the services he rendered the company. His kindliness and many other fine personal qualities made all of his associates on this property his true and loyal friends and admirers.

RESOLVED FURTHER: That a copy of these Resolutions be sent to Mr. Bishop.

Thomas P. Littlepage
Secretary

July 26, 1927

One of WB&A's three Type Y Yellow Coaches at Naval Academy Junction. Photograph by William Lichtenstern, King collection.

Commencing in November 1927, a right-of-way of 4.38 miles was purchased for the proposed route which extended from Woodlawn Heights on the North Shore Division, following roughly beside the north bank of Cabin Creek, via Harris Heights, then crossing above Pennington Avenue onto a curving descent to the streetcar tracks along Curtis Avenue, leading to Fairfield in East Brooklyn.* The idea was certainly not new; for as far back as June 1906, the Baltimore & Annapolis Short Line Railroad had drafted plans for a nearly identical route that would have tapped the then expanding shipyard and factory district of Curtis Bay. Now, twenty-one years later the project was being revived under a new Company to be known as the Chesapeake and Potomac Railroad, a subsidiary of the WB&A.**

Only this time, more elaborate plans would envision heavier construction, easier grades, and flatter curvatures. Since much of the line within

---

* The port activity of Fairfield was served by a large loop of streetcar and railroad tracks.
** The Railroad Record, Md Sec of State, Vol. 4 Page 227

Brooklyn (Baltimore City) would be shared with the United Railways & Electric Company, their tracks would have to be relaid with greater center clearances and a third rail to provide for the difference in track gauges. However, in view of numerous points of interchange with other railroads in the port area, practical considerations would dictate use of gasoline or steam locomotives for that portion.

Press releases and other public reports had scrupulously avoided any reference to the purpose of such an undertaking, the capital stock of which (authorized at $1,000,000) was being subscribed by a relatively small coterie of the WB&A's new directorate. Be it noted that the region in question was already served by a direct streetcar line for passengers, and a long established division of the Baltimore & Ohio Railroad for freight. What then, was the rationale for yet another line?

Without positive proof, justification for this scheme was ascribed to a more economical shipment of industrial coal, which was then the

W. B. & A.
Washington-Annapolis
MOTOR COACH SCHEDULE
Effective Oct. 7, 1930
EAST BOUND

EASTERN STANDARD TIME		
Leave	A.M.	P.M.
WASHINGTON		
TERMINAL	10.00	5.00
(12th St. & N. Y. Ave.)		

Coaches will stop to receive passengers at the following hotels: Annapolis, Sterling, Harrington, Washington, Willard, Occidental, Oxford, Houston, Capital Park, Grace Dodge, Continental, Hamilton.

	A.M.	P.M.
Bladensburg	10.33	5.33
Ardwick Road	10.40	5.40
Lanham	10.44	5.44
Vista	10.48	5.48
No. 2 Glendale Road	10.50	5.50
Springfield Road	10.54	5.54
Road to		
Bowie Race Track	11.00	6.00
Priests' Bridge	11.05	6.05
Head of South River	11.17	6.17
Three Mile Oak	11.24	6.24
Arrive ANNAPOLIS	11.40	6.40
(Carvel Hall Hotel,		
opp. U. S. Naval Academy)		

FARE
(One Way $1.22, Round Trip $2.32)
Intermediate Fares—One Way

Bladensburg	.25	Road to Bowie Race Track	.75
Vista	.50	Head of South River	$1.00

(M-115)—D-147—19900—10-30

W. B. & A.
Annapolis-Washington
MOTOR COACH SCHEDULE
Effective Oct. 7, 1930
WEST BOUND

EASTERN STANDARD TIME		
Leave	A.M.	P.M.
ANNAPOLIS	8.00	3.00
(Carvel Hall Hotel,		
opp. U. S. Naval Academy)		

Coaches will stop to receive passengers at Bladen Street Station, West Street Station and Crandell's Lunch Room, O'Neil's, West St.

	A.M.	P.M.
Three Mile Oak	8.16	3.16
Head of South River	8.23	3.23
Priests' Bridge	8.35	3.35
Road to		
Bowie Race Track	8.40	3.40
Springfield Road	8.46	3.46
No. 2 Glendale Road	8.50	3.50
Vista	8.52	3.52
Lanham	8.56	3.56
Ardwick Road	9.00	4.00
Bladensburg	9.08	4.08
Arrive WASHINGTON		
TERMINAL	9.40	4.40
(12th St. & N. Y. Ave.)		

FARE
(One Way $1.22, Round Trip $2.32)
Intermediate Fares—One Way

Head of South River	.25	Vista	.75
Road to Bowie Race Track	.50	Bladensburg	$1.00

Frank Tosh collection

most highly regulated of all railroad freight. Various categories of anthracite and bituminous coal, lignite, and coke were further classified according to their intended use (as that for generating steam, metallurgical purposes, or export), and still further grouped according to mode of transport and handling, wherein that destined for a port was generally moved cheaper than to other domestic points. *

From earliest times, agreements between competing railroads had been complicated by an archaic interpretation of government regulations, stratified over many years, that had produced rates without rhyme or reason. So, seeking to circumvent these restrictive tariffs, two of the largest purchasers of industrial coal had discovered a cheaper way to supply their needs. The "Chesapeake" utility which now owned its own railroad, and the "Potomac" utility that generated power for it were about to declare independence from shipping rates decreed by others. And their railroad had just purchased fifty reconditioned hopper cars to prove it. Despite prolonged delays in starting the trackwork, another development nearly three years later would indicate that the branch line to Curtis Bay was still being actively considered.

Dating from the merger of 1921, the junction at Linthicum involved a crossover located south of Maple Avenue, where southbound trains crossed to the northbound track before taking a single switch leading off to the North Shore Division. Although adequately protected by signals, this two-way operation through a single track constituted a bottleneck that augured even greater delays if Linthicum Junction were to handle increased traffic from the proposed Curtis Bay line. On June 30, 1930, work was started on a revised track layout at the junction that provided

---

* Terminal facilities required holding yards for unit trains, ways to thaw frozen cars in winter, a mechanical dumper, and even means to mix different grades for a specific use.

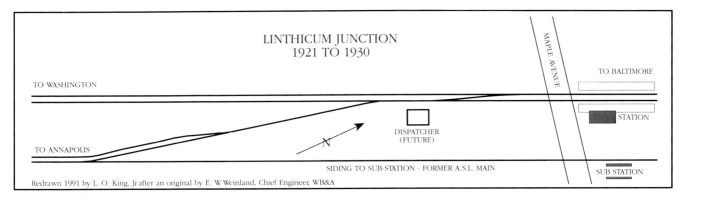

LINTHICUM JUNCTION
1921 TO 1930

TO WASHINGTON

TO ANNAPOLIS

N

DISPATCHER
(FUTURE)

MAPLE AVENUE

TO BALTIMORE

STATION

SIDING TO SUB-STATION - FORMER A.S.L. MAIN

SUB STATION

Redrawn 1991 by L. O. King, Jr after an original by E. W Weinland, Chief Engineer, WB&A

Right: Front view of Linthicum interlocking tower, based on architects drawing with details added from the picture below. Drawn by L..O. King, Jr .
Below: Linthicum Junction looking north. Tracks of the Annapolis North Shore line in the foreground join the Washington Division shown at left. Revised trackwork with a new interlocking plant completed in 1930 had eliminated the delays previously occasioned by a single switch turnout as shown in the drawing above. The articulated car at the junction was photographed August 17, 1935. James P. Shuman photograph.

At the height of controversy over the revised traffic pattern at Church Circle, a car bound for the wharves is negotiating the turn against oncoming auto traffic. Note the conductor who is carrying a red flag. Jacques Kelly collection.

a double-track turnout, complete with the latest interlocking plant that was installed by the Union Switch & Signal Company. With the completion of this project in October 1930, the grade crossing at Maple Avenue had automatic blinker lights, and even the old dispatcher's booth was replaced by a more pretentious interlocking tower. But ominous portents of the Great Depression had by then overruled any chances for finishing the branch line to Curtis Bay.

By means of its railroad, the Baltimore Gas & Electric Company had secured new resources over and above the business of transportation. Through franchises of the Annapolis & Chesapeake Bay Power Co., it had acquired a greatly expanded service territory, encompassing the larger part of Anne Arundel County, and

stretching through Prince Georges County all the way to the District Line on the south, and well beyond Laurel to the west. It now owned substation-stations and power lines over well-established rights-of-way, and controlled easements (along the tracks) for pipe lines.

In October 1928 a high-pressure gas main was constructed from Linthicum to Annapolis. An attractive addition to the Linthicum substation was built to house a booster station which fed the six-inch to four-inch all-welded pipe line that conveniently crossed the rivers and highways, being attached to the railroad's bridges. Thus, the utility company had gained not only a vastly enlarged field of electric service, but the gas customers of the Annapolis area—and all points between. And again, its assets were measured "Not By Rail Alone".

Today, in the lengthening perspective of time, and the musing of a record closed and done, there is small doubt that several events which then befell the railroad did much to hasten the decline. Briefly stated, these unhappy events involved a tangled web of franchise, labor, and taxes.

The town of Annapolis had always been hostile toward the railroad's use of its streets and the congestion caused by the big cars on sharp curves in very close quarters. At various times it was claimed that sewer pipes had been damaged, and that some of the old colonial houses had developed serious cracks brought on by the vibration of heavy trains rumbling through the narrow lanes. According to a local doggerel of the day:

"Tracks laid upon our streets so fine
   Would ruin all their arches,
   But everything must get in line
   When progress forward marches.
   And all the balance of your days
   You will repent your folly
   Repeating as you go your ways,
   Too bad we 'llowed the Trolley"

A twenty-five year franchise which the city fathers had granted back in 1907 was now nearing its end. President Doyle had fostered an amicable relationship with the mayor and aldermen; and when, in 1928, they wanted to repave Main Street, the railroad had obligingly relinquished about one half of its local street trackage. The compromise was not without certain advantages. First, it had demonstrated the Company's willingness to accede to public opinion. Second, since the town itself had initiated the paving project, the Company would be required to defray only half the expense of restoring the street after the rails were removed. And third, abandonment of the railroad's overhead would allow the Annapolis & Chesapeake Bay Power Company to reconstruct its transmission lines along Main Street, using the existing steel trolley poles instead of a more costly underground conduit system, as first proposed by the town authorities.

For its part, the railroad was to construct a short connection between the Bladen Street yards and the existing track on College Avenue, after which all service of both the North Shore and South Shore Divisions would use the station on Bladen Street. However, until those plans could be worked out, arrivals via the South Shore line would continue to operate over West Street to Church Circle, and there take the reverse direction on College Avenue and King George Street to the ferry wharf. So the town's repaving work started, and service via Main Street and Market Space was discontinued as of October 10, 1928. This meant that the former one-way operation around a town circuit was now aggravated by an awkward left turn at the Circle and a congested two-directional movement of trains (over only-half the original route) against a menacing mass of automobiles.

Seldom have differences between the letter and spirit of an agreement deteriorated more sharply than during the months that followed. In January 1929, a stalwart friend was lost with the untimely death of the WB&A's President and long-time General Manager, James J. Doyle. He was succeeded as President by Herbert A. Wagner of the Gas & Electric Company. The post of Vice President and General Manager was filled by Harry T. Connolly, whose long career with the railroad dated from the building of the line in 1907; first as a substation operator, then as Superintendent of Power, and more recently as Manager of Utilities for the Annapolis & Chesapeake Bay Power Company. Then six months later, the municipal-elections of July 1929 found the amiable mayor replaced by a new one.

Thus, the business of rerouting the local traffic, at this point only partially implemented, fell to a new cast of principals whose mutual antagonism went from bad to worse. Mr. Connolly argued

81 & 42 arrive at Naval Academy Junction from Washington May 30, 1934. George Votava photograph.

that the new trackwork, estimated to cost up to $14,000, was not justified unless the town would guarantee an extension of the expiring franchise. The town council countered with a set of ten conditions* so vindictive as to be totally unacceptable. The new mayor, perhaps a bit overzealous as defender of the public interest, saw the railroad's case as a good political issue; and vowed to solve the traffic problem by banishing the trains altogether. Now when it is recalled that virtually the whole Eastern Shore of Maryland came to town via the bay ferries and The Electric Line, it will be seen that the Interurban's necessity of serving the ferry wharf was its main reason for being in Annapolis.

On October 14, 1929, the town council passed a traffic ordinance declaring the left turn at Church Circle illegal, and served the Company with notice to cease and desist. The railroad people insisted that they still held a valid franchise. Moreover, that the left turn was necessitated by their removal of the right turn in order to accommodate the town. For the next thirty days, local news provided grist for the political mill with glaring headlines, such as: "New Plan in Trolley Snarl", "Town Acts Against WB&A" or

* See page 149

"Railway to Fight Traffic Rule Enforcement". Finally, affairs had reached the level of comic opera when, on the thirty-first day, the crew of the 9:30 train turning left as always, were arrested. It was a grand show attended by his honor the mayor, his Chief of Police, and the press, complete with jeers and guffaws from the sidewalk audience.

As always, the train crew that morning were Harry and John (Wes) Basil, brothers, who had devoted a lifetime to railroading; specifically together; and more specifically to this particular run of the Annapolis Division. Like sands through the hour glass, so passed each day with Harry and Wes on eastbound 205 making that turn. In serving the summons officialdom was attempting a flourish of political grandstand for the sake of news. In accepting the ticket, the conductor evinced only a flush of disdain for the whole charade for the sake of his duty. Stuffing the paper into his pocket as he waived the highball, the only reply was: "Alright Harry, let's get the train through".

At a hearing next day, the case was dismissed on grounds that a local traffic ordinance was contravened by the town's prior legal obligations under its franchise; that the council had failed to

Long before there was a bay bridge, trains and busses made direct connection with the ferries from the Eastern Shore. The end of King George Street, seen here, has since become part of the Naval Academy grounds. Author's collection

approve an alternate plan for rerouting the trains via Bladen Street; and that harassment of the Company's employees amounted to an obstruction of public service within the purview of affairs governed by the Interstate Commerce Commission and State Public Service Commission. Temporarily embarrassed, the town decided, for the moment, to drop the whole thing. After all, this irksome franchise had less than three years to go.

Despite its feuding with the city fathers, the railroad bent every effort to promote travel to and through Annapolis, which was warmly endorsed by the business community. To encourage shopping in Annapolis, there were one dollar excursions from Baltimore, and from intermediate points, a round trip ticket was offered for the normal one-way fare. During the late summer of 1929, the Company announced an expenditure of a quarter million dollars toward improvement of passenger service along the North Shore suburbs. With complete renovation of seventeen of the existing motor cars (new seats, tight-lock couplers, etc.), there were nine modern all steel trailer cars added to the North Shore schedules. It was an impressive commitment made only weeks before the October stock market crash was to spread shock waves felt around the world.

On January 27, 1931, the railroad was placed in receivership for the third time. George Weems Williams, the receiver, lost no time in getting to

Hazleton car 86 crossing College Creek as it enters Bladen Street yard. Author's collection.

the State House where he had a bill introduced before the State Senate which would absolve the Company from taxes levied against its real estate by each of the five Maryland jurisdictions. In years to come, massive and direct public subsidies for various cures to rescue or promote mass transit would become so widespread as to make this limited tax relief appear modest indeed, but the idea then was so arrant as to raise violent objections. At issue was a yearly tax bill of some $80,000. in Maryland assessments (not to mention another $10,280. claimed by District of Columbia and the federal government).

After much debate, an amended measure was passed* to grant a remission of state taxes for two years from June 1, 1931. This benefit was immediately challenged by the city councils of Annapolis and Baltimore, to win a favorable verdict in the Fourth Circuit Court of Appeals.

The decision was quite a blow to the railroad, and it could not have come at a worse time. The Annapolis franchise, governing the line's access to the ferry wharf, would expire on June 30, 1932 and the town was not about to renew it. Just a week before, the Company had filed a petition in the US District Court which challenged the town's

* Chapter 497, Md Acts of 1931

authority to terminate their rail service."Railroad to Battle City Government" the headlines declared; and again the struggle was revived in full fury. Across the bay, the *Easton Star Democrat* joined the chorus with denunciations such as:"Demands on WB&A Are a Direct Slap at All of the Traveling Public" or "Annapolis Trying to Throttle Shore Traffic". It was the stuff of real melodrama as the waning hours of June approached ere a last-minute injunction was issued allowing the WB&A to continue for another sixty days. Next morning the railroad announced that only six trains daily would make connections with the boats, instead of the 23 trains which had theretofore operated through town.*

Were one to review the deliberations of the town council, it will be found that there were individual members who questioned the fairness of the town's official attitude toward the WB&A. But the voices of reason were overruled and the mayor's intransigence prevailed. If he could not foresee the consequences, they were all too apparent to most of the merchants and civic leaders. The Chamber of Commerce, the Rotarians, the American Legion, and various

* During the winter months, street operations were further reduced to four trains daily, except for certain charter trips serving the Naval Academy

In 1929, the five St. Louis cars were completely renovated for service with the new trailers which arrived that summer. King collection.

other civic groups called upon both sides in attempts to reach a settlement; but each side remained adamant. And the running charade, however amusing to the spectators, mounted daily as a legal contest to be continually worried about and wrangled over.

Back in 1872, the Annapolis & Elk Ridge Rail Road, a direct corporate antecedent of the WB&A, had been authorized by the General Assembly:

> "to extend its tracks to the harbor of Annapolis, or to any wharf or pier adjacent to said harbor; and for the purpose of such extension, to use any street, lane, or alley to reach the waterfront."

Unless a compromise could be reached, the Company was now ready to invoke this long-standing right of condemnation of the streets for service in the public interest. Obstinate to the bitter end, the mayor and council retained a private law firm to continue the fight. And encouraged by their successful appeal in defeating the railroad's tax exemption, they would oppose this too. But there was to be one more skirmish.

George Weems Williams, the Company's trustee, meanwhile had taken the railroad's tax case to the US Supreme Court. On March 13, 1933 the high court reversed the ruling of the Appeals Court, and thereby upheld the validity of tax relief for the WB&A. With this decision, the railroad had won all of its legal battles except the one, still pending, to permit condemnation of the streets in Annapolis. Most of the town council were crestfallen, and to save more legal expense and bother, decided to drop any further protests.

Following the inauguration of March 1933, a bank moratorium declared by President Roosevelt had postponed all large corporate transactions, but as soon as it was lifted the Annapolis & Chesapeake Bay Power Company on March 15, 1933 was officially merged with the Consolidated Gas Electric Light & Power Company of Baltimore. When divorced from the combined balance sheet of railroad and power revenues, the rail statistics, alone, were made to appear even worse; and the uncertain future of the Company's financial affairs was to provide convincing argument for the State Legislature to renew the tax exempt status in 1933, and again in 1934.

During the brief period that the 200 series operated to Washington, an inbound train is seen here at Fifth and Massachusetts Avenue, N. W. The newly rebuilt cars were painted tuscan red instead of the then prevalent green. John B. Yeabower photograph.

A small part of the contention in winning these motions was a plea by the trainmen and other employees that their railroad was not only essential as a public service, but it was as well a source of employment for their own livelihood. It was a plausible argument during those depression years when all jobs were at a premium. But in September 1934, the Brotherhoods * voted to strike against this still rather precarious source of employment, with demands which would have further increased operating costs and deepened the deficit. At issue was a guaranteed work day of 160 train miles, regardless of the

_____

* The strike of September 21, 1934 involved three union agencies: the Order of Railway Conductors, the Brotherhood of Railway Trainmen, and the Brotherhood of Locomotive Engineers

time required in making scheduled runs, with overtime rates for all time exceeding an eight-hour day. The court ruled against it. And although the strike was soon ended, it had served mainly to arouse public sentiment and official resentment against the strikers, whose very livelihood had been prolonged through the special tax dispensation.

So there were intense feelings at the State House, both pro and con, as the 1935 Legislature met to consider the railroad's tax exemption for another year. "All citizens were being asked to support this service for the benefit of a relative few" some said. "Why shouldn't public transportation be self-sustaining?" others asked. A rather amusing question in the light of years to come. Strongest opposition had been led by the

This scene near Bragers typifies the miles of straight track on minimum grades which enabled the high speeds attained.
James P. Shuman photograph

Anne Arundel delegation, including the by-now familiar protagonists from Annapolis. Though their efforts notwithstanding, the railroad tax bill on March 19, passed the Senate by a healthy margin of 19 to 8. Within the week, it was late one night when many members of the House of Delegates had already gone home that Senate Bill 192 was unexpectedly brought to the floor— a grubby tactic not unknown to those who call it *political science*. The railroad's tax measure lost by a single vote! Even that crucial count of one was a last-minute switch as Theodore Berman, R-(Balt), changed his vote, thus defeating the bill. Next day there was a spirited attempt to call back the measure on a question of rules, but the motion failed. Almost at once, the railroad's bondholders' committee filed foreclosure proceedings,and a petition to abandon all service. As reporters, seeking some official statement, crowded around Mr. Williams, they

all had the same question. "As there is no purchaser in sight", he explained, "it means simply that the property will be sold for junk". And as a state senator was heard to say: "I took no part in the fight, but I'm afraid this has gone a little too far".

Just two months before, on January 20, the Company had issued its latest Timetable No 28, listing twelve trains that ran terminal to terminal in 65 minutes—the fastest time ever! It had been achieved at a cost of some $151,000 spent in refurbishing the main line tracks; and by the assignment of nine of their newest cars geared for experiments in speed approaching 90 miles per hour. This involved a somewhat paradoxical truth that the elapsed time between cities was actually shorter than that required within the cities. All equipment and physical property had been maintained in excellent condition; and unlike many another interurban whose final days were overtaken by weeds and rust, the service here was still first-rate, and the high-speed cars still as spruce and efficient as they had always been.

These were not the symptoms of a management that had lost faith, or had intended to quit! Rather, they were evidence of a resolve to ride out the operating losses of a temporary depression until business conditions might improve (which of course they did). Then where, in the chain of very recent events, had this opposite choice been reached? One can only conclude that a certain ill will of state and local government, inflamed by the incessant quarreling among contending factions over a period of six years, had left the owners morally and financially exhausted.

On the positive side, the Secretary of War interceded in the interest of continued service to Fort Meade. The Secretary of the Navy entered an eloquent plea on behalf of the Naval Academy. Commissioners of the District of Columbia protested that abandonment would nullify their plans for a $2,000,000 sanitarium, whose location at Glendale (Hillmeade Station), had been decided because of the railroad; and little committees from practically every stop along the line were demanding to be heard.

From the first of May, the dominoes fell in rapid succession. After only two days of public hearings, the Public Service Commission on May 4 approved abandonment. On May 8, a decree of the U S Court for the District of Maryland authorized the sale of the entire system, which was promptly advertised by Sam W. Pattison & Company, the auctioneers presiding; and on June 14, 1935, a public auction was held at the Court House in Annapolis. Though heralded in a way by other signs at other events this was, nonetheless, a moment of foreclosure which arrived brutally swift. But, as the Company went on the block, something more than real estate, track and inventories fell to the singsong of an auctioneer's patter. In human terms, the livelihood of 442 employees was at stake. In the course of America's worst economic disaster, when unemployment was averaging twenty-

three percent, the so-called social safety net of jobless compensation or public welfare hadn't been invented yet. Among the spectators that Friday afternoon were many of the railroad's own people who numbered among the Company roster that classified:

General Administration:
  General Officers   2
  General Office Clerks   54
Maintenance of Way & Structures:
  Superintendent   1
  Other Employees   110
Maintenance of Equipment:
  Superintendent   1
  Other Employees   119
Power:
  Superintendent   1
  Other Employees   17
Transportation:
  Superintendent   1
  Trainmen   136

On its financial statement then, the railroad carried assets valued at $15,674,966. Among those bidding at the sale, the Bondholders' Committee reacquired most of the real estate and city terminal properties, which were transferred to the WB&A Realty Corporation for liquidation, a process that was to last until March 1946. Included in various long-range obligations guaranteed by the WB&A Railroad, was a forty year mortgage of one million dollars dating from the Annapolis Short Line's original electrification project started in 1906. When the end seemed inevitable, a Bondholders' Protective Committee had been organized in a gallant effort to salvage the investment represented by this mortgage. With the aid of numerous engineering studies previously made by the Baltimore & Ohio Railroad, they would again separate the Short Line as an independent operation. For a very nominal bid, though subject to all liens ($1,990,741) then outstanding, the Annapolis North Shore Division, comprising two parcels of right-of-way (totaling 22.9 miles of

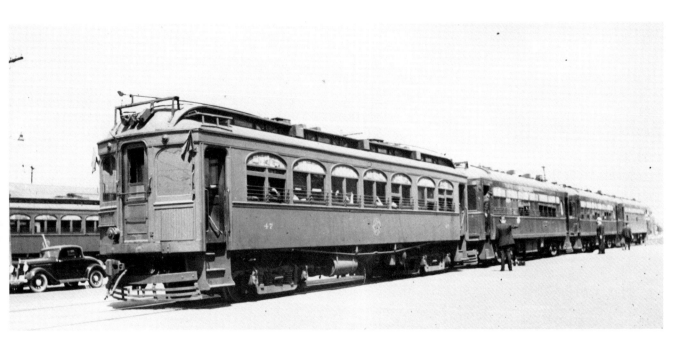

The maximum allowable train length in Washington streets was two cars and here two two-car trains are at the beginning of private right of way at 16th and Benning Road. A possible explanation of this scene is that the first three cars have been made up as a Bowie Race Track Special while the rear car is a Baltimore local. The date is 1934. John B. Yeabower photograph.

95, inbound from Annapolis, descends from the elevated structure to enter the streets of Baltimore at Scott Street on August 17, 1935. James P. Shuman photograph.

line), with its fifteen original cars, were purchased on behalf of the Committee, who then formed the Baltimore & Annapolis Railroad Company. That Company later purchased 6.90 miles of the South Shore Division (from the West Street yards to Crownsville) which it operated as a freight only service for another year, until August 25, 1936.

A belated offer by the Pennsylvania Railroad to buy and operate for at least three years the entire South Shore Division was rejected, notwithstanding their tender which had amounted to some $15,000. more than the scrap values bid at the auction.

Under an agreement negotiated with the junk dealer, a section of 5.8 miles from Odenton to Annapolis Junction (less overhead trolley, transmission wires, and substation apparatus) was later purchased by the Baltimore & Ohio Railroad*.

The ten articulated trains, in use barely eight years, reverted to the J.G. Brill Company through default on the equipment notes still outstanding. They were offered for sale by the United Iron & Metal Company of Baltimore, as agents for the

---

* ICC (FD) 10916,Vol. 207 Page 727

builder, but were never sold. Everything else including rails, bridges, overhead, signal equipment, substation machinery, car house and shop apparatus, cars, busses, and the existing stock of spare parts went to another iron dealer for the scrap price of $252,150. Twenty of the cars were eventually resold and continued in service on other lines.

Although the District Court had set a deadline of mid-September, the Receiver decided on an earlier date. Without fanfare, the service ended

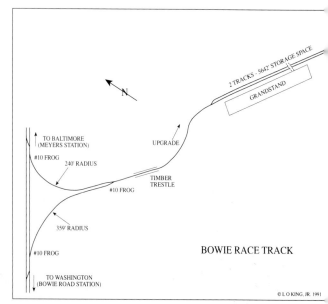

© L.O KING, JR. 1991

91 arriving from Baltimore at the Bladen Street yard in Annapolis, on July 13, 1935. James P. Shuman photograph.

on August 20, 1935. People long afterward would recall that night as one of uncanny disbelief. For all the disturbing news of recent weeks, everyone, the commuters as well as employees, said that surely a way would be found to save the line. Next morning, more from force of habit, a few of the old timers gathered at the station on West Street. But the waiting room was padlocked and the yard was empty There was no place else to go. And there, in the glare of the August sun it seemed, of a sudden, that enforced idleness could be every bit as ruthless as this recent turn of events which had robbed them of their self-

assurance, a job, and a paycheck.

To allow time for the new Baltimore & Annapolis Railroad to arrange for the transition, the junk dealer was requested to postpone possession of his purchase. Even so, the Master Mechanic would later recall that certain shop equipment would have to be forfeited for lack of space at the smaller building in Annapolis.

Meanwhile, the traditional racing season had been announced for November 15-30, 1935 at Bowie. Apparently the racetrack management were slow to realize what impact the recent abandonment would have on this event, for it was almost six

Posed before the last run to Washington August 20, 1935 from left to right are Walter Merkel, brakeman, Charles Mattingly, conductor, Albert E. Braun, motorman and Bruno Lorenz, last passenger. Jacques Kelly collection.

Despite the recent abandonment, the fall of 1935 would witness heavy traffic through Baltimore Highlands, as seen in this scene of one of the Naval Academy Specials bound for the football games only days after the racetrack specials bound for Bowie. In addition, there were regular trains bound for Annapolis. Thomas H. Arnold photograph.

weeks after the August 20th shut-down before the Southern Maryland Agricultural Association applied for some train service to Bowie.

The B&A Railroad still maintained schedules as far as Linthicum; and with cars and rosters of recent employees still intact, service might have been reinstated via the electric operations of proven suitability for the line; except for a few critical elements of the electrical plant, now missing. The alternative would be a more costly modification of the line for operations via standard railroad equipment.

An urgent estimate prepared by the Baltimore & Ohio Railroad outlined the reinforcement of certain bridges and removal of all trolley fixtures at six overhead bridges to obtain a minimum clearance of 16-feet 6-inches. Through the tunnels at Westport, the roadbed would be excavated for a single track that would increase lateral as well as vertical clearance for the steam locomotives.

Under a four party agreement, the Southern Maryland Agricultural Association would advance $6000 toward renovation of the line; the B&A Railroad would manage the operation using B&O equipment; the WB&A Bondholders' Protective Committee would grant the use of the right-of-way; while the Boston Iron & Metal Company would permit the use of track and railroad structures.

The schedule provided freight trains for the horses, and four daily departures from Camden

Station, with extra runs on Thanksgiving Day. It lasted only two weeks.

Then winter came once more—and for the first time in twenty-eight years an unbroken mantle of snow lay cold and deep across Arundel's woods and fields, where only a swath of silent white marked the path where once The Big Cars ran.

With the demise of the Electric line, there was no real successor. In fact, as the suburban peripheries expanded and the so-called blight of urban centers contracted, the need for commuters' channels grew ever more acute. For a time there was even some mention of a rapid transit plan. Though, through sheer default, the impacted commuters soon resorted to rubber tires in a scheme of things which became increasingly sensitive to congestion, collision, excessive delays, bad weather, parking, even air pollution; and a workable answer to these problems remained unsolved. But ours is a Dynamic Age of great change, where each attempt shall have its day— and pass away. The Interurban era was gone! And thus was ushered from the scene, one of man's noblest efforts to answer a question which, to this day, is still very much unsolved.

ΩΩΩ

Washington Baltimore-Annapolis Time Table

Fast electric trains between Washington, Baltimore, Annapolis, Fort George G. Meade and intermediate points

EFFECTIVE APRIL 12, 1931

(Subject to change without notice)

Time shown is Eastern Standard time. Time from 12.01 A. M. to 12 o'clock noon, inclusive, is indicated by light face type; from 12.01 P. M. to 12 o'clock midnight, by bold face type.

Washington, Baltimore & Annapolis Electric Railroad Company

Baltimore Terminals: Howard and Lombard Streets
Washington Terminal: 12th St. & New York Ave., N.W.

HARRY T. CONNOLLY
Vice-President and General Manager

Washington Baltimore-Annapolis Time Table

Fast electric trains between Washington, Baltimore, Annapolis, Fort George G. Meade and intermediate points

EFFECTIVE APRIL 12, 1931

(Subject to change without notice)

Time shown is Eastern Standard time. Time from 12.01 A. M. to 12 o'clock noon, inclusive, is indicated by light face type; from 12.01 P. M. to 12 o'clock midnight, by bold face type.

Washington, Baltimore & Annapolis Electric Railroad Company

Baltimore Terminals: Howard and Lombard Streets
Washington Terminal: 120th St. & New York Ave., N.W.

HARRY T. CONNOLLY
Vice-President and General Manager

(B-3030—27272—3-31)

A Visit to Washington

❧ Hardly an American approaches his first visit to Washington without emotion. And even those to whom it is a familiar experience are not wholly unmoved. For almost at every turn are buildings and memorials rich in patriotic and historic interest. Among the places you will want to visit are:

The White House and President's Park.
The Treasury and the State, War and Navy Buildings.
The Lincoln Memorial and Washington Monument.
The Corcoran, Freer and National Art Galleries.
The Pan-American, Red Cross, Continental Memorial Buildings and Octagon House.
The Bureau of Printing and Engraving.
The National Museum and Smithsonian Institution.
The Capitol, Botanical Gardens, Library of Congress, House and Senate Office Buildings.
The Cathedral of Sts. Peter and Paul, containing the tomb of Woodrow Wilson.
Embassies and other diplomatic buildings.
The Scottish Rite Temple.
The U. S. Marine Band, which plays every evening at Potomac Park.
Griffith Park—World's Championship Baseball Teams play here.
Arlington National Cemetery, containing Amphitheatre, Tomb of the Unknown Soldier, home of General Robert E. Lee.
Fort Meyer, adjoining Arlington—polo contests, drills, by crack cavalry.
Mt. Vernon—home of George Washington.
Alexandria, containing Christ Church, where Washington worshipped, Carlyle Mansion and Masonic Memorial to Washington.

❧ A complete illustrated guide book describing these and other places of interest in Washington may be obtained upon request at any of the W. B. & A. terminal stations, or by mail from the Passenger Traffic Manager, Howard and Lombard Streets, Baltimore, Md.

ELECTRIC TRAINS · BALTIMORE TO WASHINGTON AND FORT GEORGE G. MEADE

Time Shown is Eastern Standard Time

(Change at Naval Academy Junction for Fort George G. Meade)

[Detailed timetable with stations from Baltimore (terminal), Bush St., Westport, English Consul, Rosemont, Baltimore Highlands, Dodge Park, Pumphrey, No. Linthicum, Linthicum, Ripley, Dorsey, Waltham, Kelley, McPherson, Crystal Springs, Elkhurst, Dolment, Clarke, Conway, Maryfield, Naval Academy Jct., through Waugh Chapel, Priest, Primrose, Conway, Myers, Boon Road, Lloyd, High Bridge, Hillsmeade, Dodge Park, Bell, Lincoln, Clarke, Vista, Cherry Grove, McCarthy, Johnson, Glenncastle, Dodge Park, Hyattsville, District Line, Arr. Washington (terminal), New York Ave. & 12th St., N.W.]

f Daily except Sunday.
f Stops as prints North of Linthicum to receive passengers, only, for points South of Linthicum.
a Makes connections at Naval Academy Junction for Annapolis.
θ Makes connections at Naval Academy Junction for Fort George G. Meade, Sundays only.
6 Makes connection at McPherson, Elmhurst, Dolment, Clarke, Severn Run, Maryfield, Sundays only.
○ Trains stop at McPherson, Elmhurst, Dolment, Clarke, Severn Run, Maryfield, Sundays only.

ELECTRIC TRAINS · WASHINGTON TO BALTIMORE, FORT GEORGE G. MEADE AND ANNAPOLIS

Time Shown is Eastern Standard Time

(Change at Naval Academy Junction for Fort George G. Meade and Annapolis)

[Detailed timetable with stations from Washington (terminal), District Line, Gregory, Hyattsville, K. Columbia Park, Dodge Park, Glenncastle, Ardmore, McCarthy, Cherry Grove, Vista, Lincoln, Bell, Hillsmeade, High Bridge, Boon Road, Lloyd, Myers, Crystal Springs, Francis, Wough Chapel, Naval Academy Jct., through Maryfield, Severn Run, Clarke, Dolment, Elmhurst, McPherson, Francis, Kelley, Waltham, Dorsey, Ripley, Linthicum, No. Linthicum, Baltimore Highlands, Rosemont, Westport, Bush Street, Arr. Fort George G. Meade, Arr. Annapolis (West St. Sta.), Arr. Annapolis (terminal), Bladen & Lathrob Sts.]

f Makes connection at Naval Academy Junction for Annapolis. Daily except Sunday.
- Daily (except Sunday).
a Train stops at Mayfield, Severn Run, Clarke, Dolment, Elmhurst, McPherson, Shipley, Linthicum, Sundays only.
x Makes connection at Naval Academy Junction for Annapolis.
4 Saturdays only.
□ Discharge passengers from points South of Linthicum.
□ Operates between Naval Academy Junction and Baltimore, Sunday only.
θ Daily except Saturday and Sunday.

NORTH SHORE — BALTIMORE TO ANNAPOLIS
Time Shown is Eastern Standard Time

Stations (Leave): Baltimore (terminal), Bush Street, Westport, English Consul, Rosemont, Baltimore Highlands, Pumphrey, No. Linthicum, Linthicum, Shipley, Woodlawn Heights, Gorhard, Marley, Glenburnie, Benson's Range, Oakland, Elvaton, Howell, Jones, Winchester, Bervale, Westover, West Annapolis (Bladen St. Sta.), Arr. Annapolis (Bladen St. Sta.)

* Daily except Sunday. F Stops between Baltimore and Linthicum daily, except Sunday, to receive passengers only; makes all stops Baltimore to Linthicum on Sunday. S Saturday only.

NORTH SHORE — ANNAPOLIS TO BALTIMORE
Time Shown is Eastern Standard Time

Stations (Leave): Annapolis (Bladen St. term.), West Annapolis, Bervale, Winchester, Jones, Howell, Elvaton, Oakland, Benson's Range, Glenburnie, Marley, Gorhard, Woodlawn Heights, Shipley, Linthicum, No. Linthicum, Pumphrey, Baltimore Highlands, Rosemont, English Consul, Westport, Bush Street (terminal), Arr. Howard & Lombard Sts.

* Daily except Sunday. S Saturday only.

SOUTH SHORE — BALTIMORE TO ANNAPOLIS
Time Shown is Eastern Standard Time

Stations (Leave): Baltimore (terminal), Bush Street, Westport, English Consul, Rosemont, Baltimore Highlands, Pumphrey, No. Linthicum, Linthicum, Shipley, Dorsey, Ferndale, Glenburnie, Nippersville, Elbaburst, Ordnance, Shipman, Severn Run, Naval Academy Jct., Depplatt, Davidville, Holladay, Arnold, Salsbury, Gut, Crownsville, Millersville, Arth., Andover (Bilwood Forest), Waytorn, Hockley, Camp Parole, Cedar Park, Arr. Annapolis (West St. Sta.), Arr. (U. S. Naval Academy)

* Daily except Sunday. ¶ Sunday only. ▲ Change at Naval Academy Junction for Annapolis. ★ Makes all stops between Naval Academy Jct. and Annapolis, Sunday only; except Sundays, stops to discharge passengers east of Naval Academy Jct. All South Shore trains from Baltimore connect at Naval Academy Junction with train or bus for Fort George G. Meade.

SOUTH SHORE — ANNAPOLIS TO BALTIMORE AND WASHINGTON
Change at Naval Academy Junction for Washington

Stations (Leave): Annapolis (U. S. Nav. Acad.), Annapolis (West St. Sta.), Cedar Park, Camp Parole, Hockley, Best Gate, Waytorn, Andover (Bilwood Forest), Arth., Belvoir, Crownsville, Gut, Waterbury, Salsbury, Millersville, Arnold, Holladay, Davidville, Depplatt, Naval Academy Junction, Severn Run, Shipman, Ordnance, Elbaburst, Nippersville, Glenburnie, Ferndale, Dorsey, Shipley, Linthicum, No. Linthicum, Pumphrey, Baltimore Highlands, Rosemont, English Consul, Westport, Bush Street (terminal), Arr. Howard & Lombard Sts., Arr. Washington (terminal) New York Ave. & 13th St. N.W.

* Daily except Sunday. ¶ Sunday only. § Change at Naval Academy Junction for Baltimore. All South Shore trains from Baltimore connect at Naval Academy Junction with train or bus for Fort George G. Meade.

NAVAL ACADEMY JUNCTION TO FORT GEORGE G. MEADE
EXCEPT AS INDICATED, THIS SCHEDULE WILL BE OPERATED WITH MOTOR COACHES
TIME SHOWN IS EASTERN STANDARD TIME

Leave Naval Academy Jct. / Arr. Fort George G. Meade

T Train service to Loop Station. o Daily except Sundays and Holidays.

FORT GEORGE G. MEADE TO NAVAL ACADEMY JUNCTION
EXCEPT AS INDICATED, THIS SCHEDULE WILL BE OPERATED WITH MOTOR COACHES
TIME SHOWN IS EASTERN STANDARD TIME

Leave Fort George G. Meade / Arr. Naval Academy Jct.

T Train service to Loop Station. o Daily except Sundays and Holidays.

QUICK
COMFORTABLE
CLEAN
DEPENDABLE

Colonial Annapolis
and the
U. S. Naval Academy

¶ Few places in America or elsewhere repay so well the interest of visitors as the mellowed, unspoilt old town of Annapolis.

Most visitors, of course, are attracted by the United States Naval Academy. And a visit to the Academy is, indeed, worth even the longest journey. It would be impossible here to enumerate even a few of the things to be seen there. Most of the buildings remain open to visitors during all seasons. Among these are:

The magnificent Chapel, where lie the remains of John Paul Jones, first Admiral of the American Navy.

Dahlgren Hall, the Armory of the Academy, containing specimens of almost every kind of ordnance used in all the wars of mankind.

Bancroft Hall, one of the world's largest buildings said to occupy more ground space than any other.

"La Reina Mercedes" (in the Santee Basin), a famous prize of the Spanish War.

"The Cumberland", antique ships-o'-war, famous in American naval history.

¶ Much of the historic interest of Annapolis, however, lies without the Naval Academy reservation, in the shady, sleepy streets, still called by the titles of archaic royalties. They contain such buildings as:

The Old State House where Washington resigned his command of the Continental forces, and where the commissioners of five states gathered, at the call of Madison, to prepare the way for a Federal Constitution.

Home of Charles Carroll of Carrollton, Samuel Chase, William Paca and Thomas Stone, famous Maryland signers of the Declaration of Independence.

Home of Anthony Stewart, owner of the brig "Peggy Stewart", and the spot where the brig was burned.

St. John's College, founded in 1696, and the "Liberty Tree", on its campus, which is said to be more than 600 years old.

Carvel Hall, old Colonial home, a romantic and colorful spot during June Week.

State House, established by Act of the English Parliament in 1692.

Mansion of the Governor of Maryland.

Old State Treasury Building (Council House), which was erected in 1694.

Richard Carvel House, subject of Winston Churchill's novel of that name.

The Harwood House and its famous Colonial doorway, praised for its artistic purity.

¶ A complete illustrated guide book describing Annapolis and its places of interest may be obtained upon request at any of the W. B. & A. terminal stations, or by mail from the Passenger Traffic Manager, Howard and Lombard Streets, Baltimore, Md.

George Krambles collection.

This scene, at 15th & New York Avenue N. W., looks west toward 15th Street in 1920 and shows the Washington end of line for the WB&A. Out of the picture at the left is the US Treasury. Note the staggered double trolley poles on the roofs of the WB&A cars, the Capital Traction Company cars in the background without trolley poles and the electric automobile behind the truck. King collection.

12

THE TERMINALS

THE WASHINGTON OFFICES

Washington's introduction to the new interurban line was a large electric sign erected atop the Oxford Hotel which stood at the northwest corner of 14th and New York Avenue N.W. This sign, composed of myriad light bulbs, dominated the roof tops with its modern message of: "Palace Electric Cars to Baltimore-Annapolis". The cars themselves, however, came only as far as a new terminal known as White House Station, that had been built at 16th and Benning's Bridge Road N.E. opposite the Columbia Line car house.

Land for this station had been acquired back in 1901 as part of the plans which then envisioned a depot to be used jointly with the Chesapeake Beach Railway When that company was unable to fulfill the terms of its traffic agreement, which had called for an electrified terminal operation, a later contract was signed on December 9, 1907, wherein the Washington Railway & Electric Company undertook construction of the buildings and track layout for the White House Station to be occupied by the WB&A alone. Facilities there included the passenger station with five stub-end tracks for the interurban cars on the east side, and a conduit loop track for the streetcars arriving on the opposite side. In time, the terminal yard was enlarged to add a sixth track which served a long freight shed. The seventh track along the south side of the yard was, in fact, a siding owned by the streetcar company.

But the plans for interurban trains to enter Washington had been laid years before, in June 1902, when promoters of the original Washington & Annapolis Railway had negotiated trackage rights over the new suburban extension of the city's Columbia Line. That agreement was amended in more specific terms by another contract signed on April 15, 1907, which provided for compensation at a fixed rental for track and overhead; plus a rather

complicated formula based upon mileage, revenues, and surcharges combined with similar payments then being made by the WB&A owners on behalf of their Washington Berwyn & Laurel Electric Railroad. In broad outline, the formula is set forth on the following page.

Benning's Bridge Road was part of the distant suburbs, and the location of a passenger terminal that far out had been deferred against the possibility that a way might still be found for the big cars to run all the way into town. But requirements of the yet unproven single-phase electrification had steadily added to the equipment, in both weight and complexity, to a point where street operations via the underground conduit system were no longer feasible. So the White House Passenger Station was started in December 1907, and by late the following month, Smethurst & Allen, in charge of overhead construction, were making the final adjustments to strain insulators, span wires, and guy anchors through the yard. According to the specifications: "The ends of the lead wires into Benning Road to be anchored and left of sufficient length to enable later double frog connections with the car company's two-wire trolley system".*

In days to come, residents and employees along the Columbia Line were to marvel at the first appearance of these big "Electric Pullmans" making their initial runs into streetcar territory. As one of the older inhabitants remembered it: "It snowed that day as the test car came through about dusk. It was

---

* At a switch to be used by cars of appreciable differences in length, the trolley frog was often located, temporarily, until a working compromise between smooth running and excessive wear could be determined -- a decision somewhat compounded by the double-wire system. For years, six such junctions along the Columbia Line continued without trolley frogs, requiring the conductor to manually transfer both poles of a car branching from the main line.

Some details of the operating agreement between WB&A and Washington Railway & Electric Company.

- Rental of $ 300. per annum for each mile of single track, there being 4.16 miles of r-of-w, or 8.32 miles of track between the District Line and White House Station.
- A fare of .0425 for each revenue passenger carried.
- A surcharge of .0075 for each revenue passenger carried.
- An accounting for all cash, tickets, identification checks, etc. by means of fare registers installed at expense of the Washington Railway & Electric Company; plus payments under contract to the City & Suburban Railway for:-
    Car miles operated between Berwyn and Laurel @ .025 per mile.
    Electric current used between Berwyn and Laurel @ .03 per car mile.
    An apportionment of reasonable wages for crewmen.

And when totals computed as above should reach $ 50,000. annually, the surcharge was to be cancelled; or, if exceeding $ 70,000. per annum, then WRy&ECo was to return excess over the rate of .04 per total number of passengers carried including passes..

a great sight! Much like a big day coach, even to the point of sounding a railroad whistle, this handsome new electric car with all its lights turned on and a brilliant headlight shining out through the snow, presented quite a spectacle to everyone who stopped and stared."

The Washington Jockey Club was part of the high rollers horsey set, and while it lasted, their race track at Benning generated a seasonal ebb and flow of race fans between Pimlico, Upper Marlboro, and later, Bowie. With this in mind, the WB&A Company had contracted for W Ry & E Company to build a long side-track west of the right-of-way (later Kenilworth Avenue), where interurban trains would deliver horses as well as humans.

Immediately east of Kenilworth Junction, the B&O and Pennsylvania Railroads crossed Deane Avenue on parallel bridges which spanned the trolley tracks, the road, and a placid little stream called Watts Creek—placid, that is, except at the most inopportune times when heavy rains caused it to flood the low point of the underpass. While a matter of some dismay to the W Ry & E Company, this flooding was of far greater concern to officials of the WB&A. Whenever cars were stranded, the

heartier among local streetcar passengers could make it home on foot, while interurban travelers spent the night aboard the trains—the longer the delay, the shorter the tempers.

With conversion of the first single-phase electrification to a 1200 volt DC system, the WB&A Company sought to eliminate the inconvenience of transferring passengers at White House Station with renewed plans to operate trains into the center of town. To this end, Senator Raynor and Congressman Taylor of Ohio had introduced bills in January 1909 seeking Congressional approval for the interurban to build its own line through the city. In support of these measures, the Company proposed an investment of some $3,000,000 for new line construction. The project outlined their intended route westward along Florida Avenue and K Street to Sixth Street N.W., south to H Street, thence westward along H Street to Thirteenth Street N.W., with a loop around 13th; E Street; 11th Street; and back to H Street N.W. Though, as with any plan of this magnitude, the press and public debate lent far more emphasis to the idea than an accurately proportioned chronicle of the facts should allow; for just as the public hearings reached a crescendo,

WRY&ECo number 4 stranded near the Benning Race Track as a result of a flash flood April 28, 1923 illustrates the problem occasionally faced by both roads. Library of Congress.

it was announced on February 6th that a compromise had been concluded whereby the interurban service would operate over the full length of the Columbia Line to the Treasury building at Fifteenth and New York Avenue N.W.

In preparation for the much heavier interurban cars, the city tracks would have to be rebuilt. These tracks, remnants of earlier cable car operations, had been laid on cast iron yokes, placed five feet apart on tangents. At 40 tons, the big cars represented more than twice the weight of anything previously operated on this line; and because of the tapered (narrow base) form of the lighter weight cable conduit yokes, the effect of increased stress on the rails would be to depress them, widen the slot, and eventually crack the yoke. After several methods of bracing were tried, it was decided to support each rail on a beam of reinforced concrete eight inches wide by sixteen-and-a-half inches deep, running as a continuous longitudinal stringer (1800 cubic yards of concrete per mile). Shortly after the concrete was poured, iron bearing plates, 11,480 in all, were placed at intervals between the yokes, and allowed

to set in the concrete. Later a small wedge was driven between the top of the plate and base of the rail to secure a rigid and uniform bearing surface along the stringer.

Another part of the project involved nine intersections with other car lines, where the specialwork at crossings had to be re-grooved through extensive grinding of case-hardened steel to accommodate the deeper $15/16$ inch flanges of the interurban cars. At the new mid-town terminal, they also built two cross-overs and an additional stub track of 110-feet - a scant space for two cars to lay over in the middle of a very busy street. By November of 1909, this reinforcement and modification of 5.64 miles of street trackage had cost a total of 175,676.33 uninflated dollars.

The upkeep of underground current collectors (plows) was always an expensive item, requiring frequent inspections, leading to early replacement of the friction wear plates, new contactor shoes, waterproofing, and other steps to preclude dangerous flash-overs or short circuits. All this was provided by the streetcar company which was reim-

Above: Except for five of the largest bridges, which were of open girder construction, most of the crossings over highways or streams were of reinforced concrete having a solid floor filled in with stone ballast. Examples of these at Horsepen and Cat Tail Branch have survived, intact, for over eighty years. Others however fell early victims to the erosion of high water, as in the case of the accompanying view of the one at Cabin Branch which in April 1923 was rebuilt as a deck-girder trestle. **Left:** Temporary bypass at Cabin Branch during repairs following the flood damage of 1923. Author's collection.

bursed through a monthly billing known as "plow trips". Thus, while the average MU train was charged as two plow trips, the articulated cars of later years were to achieve the same result at half the cost. The new schedules which touted "Mid City Terminals" began on March 1, 1910. And by virtue of this close working arrangement with the streetcar company, incoming passengers via the interurban were issued free transfers valid on all lines of the Washington Railway & Electric Company.

Meanwhile, the city ticket office had been moved in July, 1909 from the Oxford Hotel, across the street to the Evans Building at 1424 New York

Avenue. Three years later, November 1912, it was again moved to a much larger corner location in the Bond Building at 1400 New York Avenue.

By 1918 the bustle and traffic congestion of wartime Washington was nowhere more evident than at the so-called "World Corner" at 15th & New York Avenue. This was the site of the great triumphal arch erected to welcome the returning troops; this was the avenue of four car tracks abreast; and it was the destination (or point of turn-around) for three different car lines, including the interurban. The time required for loading and unloading was aggravated by the big cars whose narrow door-

The downtown station was originally located in the Oxford Hotel. From there the ticket holders were entitled to ride streetcars of the Columbia Line that carried special signs announcing connections to the interurban. In July, 1909, the city ticket office was moved across the street to the Evans Building; the second of four locations over the years. After that came the location at 1400 New York Avenue and, finally the terminal at 12th and New York Avenue. Station photo, Author's collection. WRy&ECo 256 at their P Street yard. Photograph by LeRoy O. King, Sr.

Three views of the original White House Station copied from an early company brochure. King collection

White House Station. The car is a Columbia line shuttle which has just arrived from the District Line. Library of Congress.

The new terminal in Washington was opened January 31, 1921. It occupied one half of the block bounded by New York Avenue, 12th, H and 11th Streets, N. W. Trains entered from the west on 12th Street and left through a double curve into 11th Street and New York Avenue. Facilities included three parallel tracks which accommodated fifteen cars. Author's collection.

ways, steep steps, and passengers with baggage tended to delay the other cars.

To relieve this, there were various solutions proposed* which, though widely debated, never came to pass. In one of these, a franchise was requested for a track southbound on Twelfth Street and westward on H Street N.W., with curbside loading from a waiting room adjoining the south entrance of the Masonic Temple at Thirteenth and New York Avenue. Another plan involved negotiations with builders of the Annapolis Hotel then being planned for 1111 H Street N.W. Under this joint venture, the interurban trains were to run through the proposed building, serving a lower level concourse with an upstairs waiting room in the hotel proper.

As an alternative to that project, the railroad company had reserved an option on part of the land which included the site fronting on New York Avenue between Eleventh and Twelfth Streets N.W. In January 1919 application was made through the WRy&ECo. which would negotiate under its

---

* U.S. Congress. Senate. Beeler Report. 65th Cong., S. Doc. 197

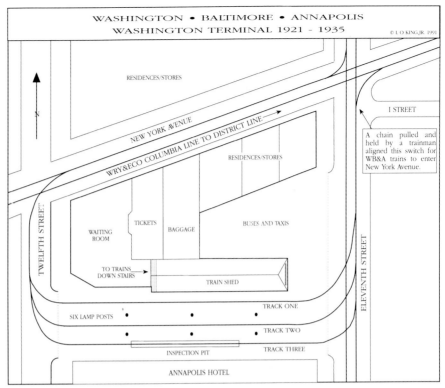

franchise for the city's approval of a station. Although a hearing was convened on February 6, 1919, actual construction was beset with delays that would last another two years. In the matter of real estate, there were seventeen cases of ejectment proceedings against tenants which had to be resolved in court. Next was the uncertainty of plans for the hotel, whose role would greatly influence the design of the terminal; and third, was a debate concerning different track layouts then under consideration. In the first track plan, which the com-

Washington Terminal, looking northwest from 11th Street in 1935. William Lichtenstern photograph, King collection.

Washington terminal from the 11th Street side in the early thirties. Note the two-car train of orange and cream cars at the left. Author's collection.

Note, on the rack at the right, the portable headlights and jumper wires for moving cars off dead spots in the underground conduit. The view looks toward 11th Street from the passenger platform. King collection.

pany favored, trains would enter from Eleventh Street, arrive westbound through the station, and leave via Twelfth Street and New York Avenue. From an operating viewpoint, this entailed one left-turn and three right-turns which could complete a loop with less chance of traffic mishap, fewer crossings of other tracks, and a correspond-

ing saving of some $7,500 in cost of original construction. Its objectionable feature, however, required a diagonal ladder track on Eleventh Street, whose curvature (after allowance for property lines, minimum radii, etc) had placed the conduit switch points squarely in the sidewalk. Under the alternate layout, which was finally adopted, trains entered from Twelfth Street, arriving eastbound on three parallel yard tracks (of an aggregate 0.339 mile) and departed via Eleventh Street and New York Avenue.

After numerous minor revisions, the order was placed on February 2, 1920 for all specialwork to be fabricated by the Lorain Steel Company of Johnstown, Pennsylvania. An obscure feature of the blueprints for that contract is a tentative sketch of "Probable Future Tracks" drawn as two leads from the yard tracks Nos 2 and 3 turning south into Eleventh Street. It lends credence, however slight, to financial news of that day that the Bishop-Sherwin syndicate might acquire a controlling interest in the

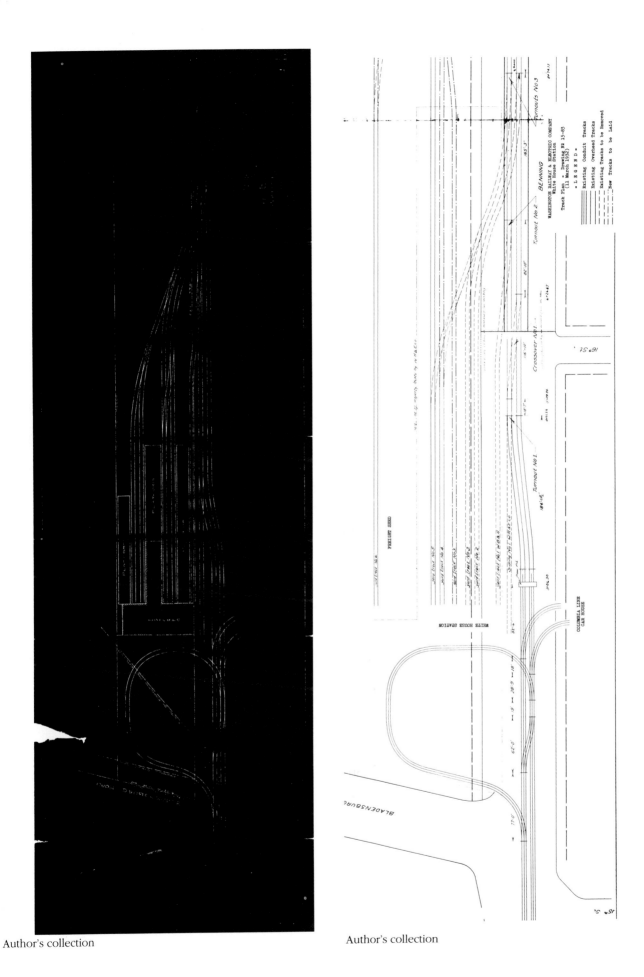

Author's collection

Author's collection

Washington-Virginia Railway, whose terminal was just down the street.

Among the buildings that remained intact was an existing store on the corner of Twelfth & New York Avenue, which was remodeled into an attractive waiting room and baggage office. The principal costs of the new station were expenditures for roadway, tracks, and structures which, exclusive of real estate, brought the completed project to $179,920.

And amid congratulations and floral tributes from the Washington business community, the new terminal was opened on January 31, 1921. The novelty of opening day was slightly marred by a minor mishap when one of the first cars was derailed at the new switch on Twelfth Street, requiring several of the morning trains to continue on to the former terminal at Fifteenth Street.

After fourteen years as an interurban terminal, the station loop was again used in 1936 for street-cars of the Columbia Line to turn back during major reconstruction of the city tracks at Fourteenth and New York Avenue.

Inasmuch as the freight motors were never permitted to operate on conduit track, the old White House Station continued to serve as the Freight Depot, and as a storage yard for cars. In 1928, five large silos were erected along the north side of the property and a tipple conveyor was installed beneath one yard track to handle sand and gravel for the Massaponax Corporation. Hopper cars were spotted on an incline stub at the east end of the yard, to be released one at a time for unloading at the conveyor. With the widening of Benning Road in 1932, the yard layout was completely altered to eliminate three of the original terminal tracks, and by moving the yard entrance some 600 feet to the east, thus increasing the capacity of the remaining yard.

THE BALTIMORE STATIONS

By the summer of 1901, surveyors and real estate agents for the Washington & Annapolis Electric Railway had established the line's northernmost point at Westport. It was then widely conceded that the interurban would enter Baltimore under trackage rights to be leased from the United Railways & Electric Company; but dissension would soon prevail sufficient to defeat such a plan.

Six years before, the Columbia & Maryland Railway had started another interurban line to Washington that was in fact acquired and essentially built, before bankruptcy ensued in 1897. As the result of a foreclosure sale on March 25, 1898, that interurban was severed to become two suburban properties, extending from Washington via Berwyn to Laurel; and from Baltimore via Catonsville to Ellicott City. Despite this adversity, the unfinished project still represented large investments whose backers (together) remained serious contenders for the interurban franchise between Baltimore and Washington. So to protect that possibility the bond-holders, organized as the Baltimore Security & Trading Company, had obtained an agreement on April 20, 1901 from purchasers of the Ellicott City line that whoever might complete the original project, and thereby form part of a through route from Washington to Baltimore, would be granted preferential rights to the tracks which they (the original builders) had laid via Edmondson Ave., Catonsville, and Ellicott City. Such preference afforded the incentive for further investment in their interurban line; and at the same time prevented the URys&ECo from granting trackage rights to any other company which might interfere or compete with inter-city travel. By that arrangement, the Washington & Annapolis Railway was denied a street car route into Baltimore. A short time later the W&A Railway (now WB&A) itself fell upon hard times; and with the cessation of all construction in July 1903, the question of access to Baltimore became a moot issue of no particular urgency.

The WB&A was revived by new owners under George T. Bishop who, in 1905, introduced some of his own ideas, representing a change from the first plans. According to him, the advantages gained through high-speed interurban schedules ought not be dissipated by having those schedules subordinated to the stop and go operations of city street cars. To that end, he organized the Baltimore

The Terminal Building at 108 North Liberty Street as it appeared shortly after the line opened in 1908. To commemorate the event, souvenir buttons were distributed bearing the company's green and white emblem similar to the official monogram stenciled in gold over the ticket window. Author's collection. For a view of the Park Avenue side of this station see page 24, See also map on page 12.

Terminal Company June 5, 1905 and its contracting agency, the Traction Construction Company October 27, 1905 which would oversee all aspects of building an independent approach within Baltimore City and County. The resulting access over city streets, avoiding the more direct avenues already occupied by the city company, was a rather circuitous route through narrow secondary side streets (Scott, McHenry, Portland, Greene to German Street) which involved tortuous curves, made even more so by projected dimensions of the big Niles "Electric Pullman" cars then on the drawing boards. Considering the width of certain intersections, a sixty-three foot car mounted on thirty-seven foot five inch truck centers, when negotiating a sharp curve, would overhang the sidewalk by as much as five feet. This was solved by cutting back the curb line; and by the use of so-called "spiral"

curves—a wide sweep of more than 90 degrees to accomplish a right-angle turn.

In 1905, German Street (later Redwood) was the only east-west street of the downtown district without trolley tracks. Although the URys&ECo had plans for a route along German Street to relieve the congestion of too many lines concentrated on Baltimore Street, the Baltimore Terminal Company had also applied for a city ordinance to authorize their tracks on German Street as the only alternative for interurban trains to reach a mid-city terminal. On April 27, 1906, a compromise was reached wherein the streetcar company would acquire the German Street privilege in return for an agreement to allow dual-gauge tracks for the Terminal Company to share a route on Lombard, Liberty Streets, and Park Avenue. After months of negotiations, a trackage lease was finally signed on December 28,

On Liberty Street, the inbound track continued past the station to a stub end at Lexington Street. This spur could accommodate up to three cars, but trains standing continually on the street soon brought serious complaints from the city. The large doorway at left is the entrance to the building at 108 N Liberty Street which included the General Offices and a Passenger Terminal. Author's collection.

1906 which set forth conditions for reconstructing and adapting the existing streetcar tracks, the rights of joint users of the outside rail over streets in question, and the modification of overhead work other than trolley wires. It will be recalled that the AC single-phase electrification, then being planned for the interurban, was unacceptable over city streets, necessitating a different character of current locally which had not yet been determined. Nor was dual-gauge track quite as simple as laying a third rail. In that construction, the inner rail was secured by an elaborate series of wedges and tie rods, and even the outer rail was replaced in order to accommodate the wider tread wheels on the common side.

The interurban terminal would be located on the site of premises to be razed from 108, 110, 112, 114 North Liberty Street and from 107, 109, 111, 113 Park Avenue. The new station was designed by the architects Simonson & Pietsch and erected by J. Henry Miller under contract for $51,000 which specified that all work involving the basement and first story, including the sidewalks, would be completed and ready for use by WB&A trains within 105 working days from date of the contract, May 18, 1907; and that the entire building be finished within 150 working days. As the press announcements had indicated, they were planning to start operations that fall.

A single track loop passed through the station which provided a ground floor waiting room with entrances from both the Liberty Street and Park Avenue sides. Beside the ticket window, a concession for cigars, confections and fancy fruit was run by Petrohilos and Pappas. There was a large freight elevator which served the basement baggage room.

On the second floor, a Directors' meeting room and offices provided headquarters for the Baltimore Terminal Company and the Washington Berwyn & Laurel Electric Railroad, whose officials for a time served in joint capacities as executives of all three companies. As a technicality, the Baltimore Terminal Company owned the station and tracks from Clifford, as well as all passenger equipment, which it leased to the Railway Company.

It was shortly before midnight on March 19, 1908 that the very first test run was made through downtown streets. Despite the hour, hundreds of people had been attracted by the novelty of the big car which created a rather awesome spectacle of arcing and smoke caused by sand and construction dirt still on the rails. For the next ten days the public was invited to inspect one of the new Niles cars on daily exhibit at the Terminal, Regular service was inaugurated on April 3, 1908.

In keeping with its high standards for safety and upkeep of equipment, the WB&A Company required that cars be inspected and cleaned upon completion of each round trip. This routine included some window washing, sweeping, servicing the toilets and water coolers, checking brake rigging and journals, and constant inspection of the AC motors which, originally, had caused considerable difficulty with over-heating. In fact, the manufacturer had specified a lay-over of 20 minutes at each end of the main line limited runs, or a minimum 40 minute cooling off interval between each round trip.

Inasmuch as the Baltimore Terminal on Liberty Street provided only one track through the station, servicing was regularly performed in the yards of White House Station in Washington. But in February 1910, the line in Washington was extended some thirty blocks beyond the original station to terminate in the middle of a busy street at 15th and New York Avenue N.W., which also precluded facilities for the inspection and cleaning of cars. And deadheading the sixty blocks to and from White House Station yards was manifestly impractical. Accordingly, it was decided to establish a yard at the Baltimore end. In January 1910, the International Harvester property at 317 West Lombard Street* was acquired for use as a car barn and express depot, which was completed the following June. The storage tracks, with all overhead work, as well as the three-rail specialwork in the street, were installed and thereafter maintained by the United Railways & Electric Company. The Lombard Street Station comprised four stub-end tracks which entered the street eastbound; so that arrivals always backed in, while departing freight runs had to change ends in the middle of the street before starting out westbound. To overcome this somewhat awkward maneuver, the later Express Trailers 4, 5, and 6 were equipped with controls, which enabled them to operate as the lead car in any freight consist. Lombard Street also afforded a storage point for about ten cars, from which trains could be dispatched in proper sequence to the Liberty Street Terminal.

During these years, an increasing business in package freight being handled in connection with the American Express Company had indicated a need for more space. In the fall of 1913 a small, though very attractive, brick freight station was built at 312 West Pratt Street; at which time one of the tracks entering from Lombard Street was extended through the middle of the block to a bumper adjoining (and at right angles to) the sidewalk on Pratt Street.**

The nation's entry into the first World War unleashed a deluge of travel via The WB&A, which grew from two million passengers carried in 1916 to over 5.9 million in 1918. The frequency and length of trains, and the crowds involved, had far exceeded the capacity of the downtown station. In February 1918 a track connection was installed at Pratt and Greene Streets that enabled certain trains to use the single-track on Pratt Street under rights leased from the Baltimore & Ohio Railroad.*** While the base schedules continued to operate from Liberty Street, extra runs of five and six-car

---

* see photograph page 88, top.
** see photograph page 88, bottom
*** see Baltimore City Ordinance 322, page 53.

President Wilson's Inauguration, March 4, 1913

TREMENDOUS CRUSH AT ELECTRIC LINE
Police Reserves Had To Be Called To The WB&A Station
RUSH TO GET ABOARD CARS AT TERMINAL
Thousand Persons Sent Each Hour,
But Great Throng Packed Streets

A mad rush which swept the police off their feet, rendered them helpless for a time, and brought about great crushing in which women were caught, occurred at the station of the Washington Baltimore and Annapolis Railroad. Men fought to get into the cars as the trains were on their way to the station. Many of the passengers went as far south as Lombard Street, only to be refused admittance to the cars.

Then they hurried back to the station, where they renewed their fighting to get on. Many men jumped up between the cars and clung to the bumpers. The train crews had to battle in some instances to get them off; and several times the police had to run down the street beside the cars, pulling the men from the steps.

Cars were run at anywhere from 5 to 14 minutes apart, and it is estimated that the people were leaving at the rate of 1000 or more per hour. The cars seat 54 persons, but the travelers did not confine themselves to the seats. They sat all over the arms of the seats and the aisles were packed. Some of the cars carried as high as 120 passengers.

The Company has 40 cars and every one of them was pressed into use. Six more cars were added. These were secured from the Chesapeake Beach Line and were pulled by the W B & A motors.

Inasmuch as coaches of the Chesapeake Beach Railway could not clear the tunnels at Westport, nor negotiate the sharp curves in Baltimore, that equipment was assigned to the Annapolis Division to release regular cars for service on the main line.
Dispatching was further complicated in attempts to maintain some local schedules interspersed in the close headway between high-speed trains.

Views on Washington, Baltimore & Annapolis Lines, March 4, 1913

A Big Day for Washington, Baltimore & Annapolis Electric Road— 1200 Volt D. C. System

The heavy traffic of inauguration week necessitated the operation by this road of two-car trains in and out of Washington on a ten-minute schedule. Every passenger car owned by the Company and every substation unit was in practically continuous service for three days. The average daily mileage per car on March 4th was 447, and several cars were operated over 600 miles.

With heavy traffic, frequent stops, the consequent pushing of the equipments for speed, and extreme load on the entire transmission and distributing systems, there were no detentions—not a single failure of any portion of the electrical equipment.

These cars equipped with G-E 600/1200-volt motors and type M control have now run about 175,000 miles each, and none of the original brushes, armature bearings or contactor arc shutes have been replaced for wear.

It pays to buy equipment which can be depended upon absolutely when extraordinary traffic demands must be met.

General Electric Company

Opening date for the new Baltimore Terminal was still six weeks away when this picture was taken in September, 1921. Note temporary overhead for the ramp track and wooden poles used during construction of the yard. The newly remodeled Short Line car has only one doorway for both passengers and baggage on the side visible here. Jacques Kelly collection.

trains for the military traffic originated in the middle of Pratt Street at Eutaw. *The Official Railway Guide* of July 1918 lists thirty-three daily departures for Camp Meade alone. In addition, there were five trains daily (six on weekends) which soon became known as "Bootlegger Specials" with another five to six special runs added for the Bowie Races - in season. In order to accommodate this influx, the Freight Station at 312 West Pratt Street was enlarged to serve as an auxiliary ticket office.

Even as the war ended, the ever-increasing schedules of regular passenger trains had long since outgrown the terminal on Liberty Street. Then, with acquisition of the Annapolis Short Line in

February, 1921, the North Shore trains which theretofore had used Camden Station, were also re-routed via WB&A tracks to the interurban terminal; and the need for an adequate Baltimore station became urgent. It will be noted that the single-track loop there handled no less than 105 daily departures. And compounding normal congestion, the specials added for events like Navy football games or the presidential inaugurations created crowds bordering on turmoil.

Up until 1921, the railroad's real estate adjoining the Lombard Street yard comprised only a narrow north-south corridor through the middle of the 300-block of West Lombard/Pratt Streets. For over

The new Terminal Building facing Howard Street. Lombard Street is to the right. Author's collection.

three years the Company had negotiated for acqui- sition of additional property next to the car barn; but efforts each time were thwarted by tenants still under lease. The largest owner was Schoenewolf's Wholesale Grocery Company which stood at 100- 102 South Howard Street. Finally, in early 1921, this building was vacated; and on its site a handsome new four-story limestone edifice took form which, with the new freight depot and train yards,eventually reach a cost of $1 million. Because the big terminal was to occupy the exact site of the old WB&A car barn,inspection facilities had to be moved temporarily out to Baltimore Highlands, where they dug a pit and erected a make-shift shed for work on the cars.

The new station building, now facing Howard Street, was planned by the architects Dreher-Churchman-Paul & Ford of Philadel- phia, and built by the George A. Fuller Construc- tion Company. Work started in April, and six months later the new terminal was dedicated on October 30, 1921. It was, beyond a doubt, one of the finest facilities of its kind. The main building provided for the General Offices, a commodious waiting room, baggage room, trainmen's room, lunch counter, barber, and other concessionaires. In the main hall with its big sky-lightthat dominated a high ceiling banded in interlacings of ormolu, the south wall displayed a large topographic mural painting outlining the geography served by the

WB&A System. And it was this canvas depicting the aerial view from Baltimore which, when reproduced in company literature, accounted for their rather uncustomary map oriented with north at the bottom.

The improved freight station (40 x 260 feet) was fully inclosed and included a long loading dock for delivery vehicles on the Eutaw Street side which paralleled an incline ramp track on the station yard side. So critical had been the need for some means of handling freight that a portion of the station was opened in July, some three months ahead of time, using temporary overhead and tracks still under construction.

October 30, 1921 was an auspicious day in Baltimore, for it marked the dedication of the Electric Line's new Terminal at Howard and Lombard Streets. Gathered for the occasion are a group of company officials shown here from left to right: William M. Garrett, Treasurer, E. W. Weinland, Engineer of Maintenance, Mrs. J. J. Doyle, A. S. Osbelt, Master Mechanic, George T. Bishop, President, Mrs. Bishop, James J. Doyle, Vice President and General Manager and Harry T. Connolly, General Superintendent. Author's collection.

Entering from Pratt Street, there were two ladder tracks that afforded access to any terminal track from either the eastbound or westbound main line. The yard offered storage space for approximately 48 cars on five parallel tracks (four with inspection pits), surrounded by a seventy-two foot radius loop track which, as a technicality, added 0.160 mile of new construction to the main line mileage. And perhaps not as readily apparent were the collateral costs of work involved in rerouting the street approaches just to reach the new station location. Under terms of a city ordinance*, the interurban company was required to move the B&O Railroad's existing single track along Pratt Street in order to accommodate double tracks, with the necessary reconstruction of four industrial sidings** and two street car crossings.

* S.B.No 339, May 1921
** The commercial sidings were: Sonneborn & Company, Schauman Company, Pittsburgh Plate Glass Company and Armour & Company, on S. Eutaw Street

Special trackwork in the street, with the entrance to the terminal yard, accounted for $106,248 of specialwork ordered from the Lorain Steel Company. And to that were to be added the costs of removing the third rail and repaving within street car tracks no longer used on Lombard and Liberty Sts and Park Avenue. For the statistically-minded, it may be of casual interest that the use of 0.899 mile of gauntlet (dual-gauge) city track, over a period of thirteen years (1908 - 1921), had amassed a record of 572,323 car miles operated by The WB&A Company. The new routing via Pratt Street had eliminated joint trackage with the city cars which for the first time, enabled the interurban to use its own overhead without power purchased through the local system. The maintenance of way over city streets, however, continued under contract to the United Railways & Electric Company.

Time is often perverse in the way it sorts and rearranges the values we assigned to achieve-

The freight terminal loading dock on Eutaw Street. Note section insulators where the high-voltage overhead crosses the streetcar wires on Eutaw Street. Author's collection.

ments of great effort, expense, and seeming importance. Completion of the new Baltimore Terminal Station—the Company's pride—this paragon of its day, was to arrive as an anti-climax; for the fortunes of the Interurban, generally, and this one in particular, had already entered the vale of years.

When the railroad was sold on June 14, 1935, the Baltimore Terminal was acquired by the Bondholders' Protective Committee who, in turn, organized the Baltimore & Annapolis Railroad Company While the tracks into Camden Station were being electrified for the new service, regular passenger trains of the B & A Railroad continued to use the Howard Street Terminal until September 28, 1935. Soon thereafter it was

bought by Harry G. Pappas, the concessionaire of long standing. And lest memories might fade in the alien days to come, he kept the name, WB&A Restaurant, and that big canvas railroad map hanging on the south wall. For the next twenty-five years the place served, in varying degrees, as a rather dilapidated bus depot, until:

"that which Man altered not for the better;
Time altered for the worse"

and in April 1963, all remnants of the once-splendorous Interurban Station were demolished to make way for a new hotel which opened the following year.

New Baltimore terminal yard as viewed from Pratt Street. Author's collection.

An articulated train is about to enter the Baltimore terminal from Pratt Street. Author's collection.

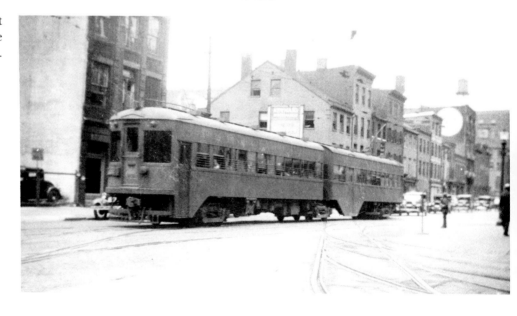

Soon after 1908, one of the original cars is about to leave from King George and Randall Streets in Annapolis. The buildings in the background were Navy quarters known as Porter Row. Maryland State Archives (MSA SC 2140-249).

operations by April 1, 1908.

• That the railway provide a city-type streetcar to give local service from 7 AM to 7 PM daily at a frequency of not less than every 15 minutes.

• That the fare for this local service should be not more than 5 cents per adult or 3 cents for each child passenger, from which the town would receive 4.5 mills and 2.7 mills respec tively as its gross receipts tax against all fares collected.

Construction of street trackwork was started on October 28, 1907. From the old station, the main track was extended to a point where it converged with West Street at the corner of Calvert Street. In the sharp angle thus formed, the Company erected a small triangular-shaped brick building to house a waiting room and sub-station. This original sub-station, somewhat smaller than the electrical plant of later years, supplied only 1.33 mile of street trackage which was then operated as a 550 volt double trolley (overhead return) system. Until this station was finished some two months after the line opened, the first interurban cars terminated at the old Elk Ridge Depot opposite Second Street (Lafayette Street).

In the strictest sense, West Street Station was not a terminal because most of the trains continued onto the street and around a town circuit that included West Street to Church Circle, Main Street to Market Space, Randall Street to King George Street, to the ferry landing; returning via King George Street to College Avenue to Church Circle. At the foot of King George Street, trains terminated on double tracks (812 feet in length) which ended at the very water's edge. During peak periods, the trains for Baltimore and Washington (on parallel tracks) loaded simultaneously, which enabled them to run as first and second sections on the same clearance for single-track operations over the South Shore Division.

For the local service, the Company purchased two Baltimore streetcars which were regauged in the Carroll Park Shops for standard width track. They were brought to Annapolis on April 1, 1908 and placed in service that evening. At a nickel a ride, the new electric cars (one of them an open car) soon proved to be the most popular diversion in town.

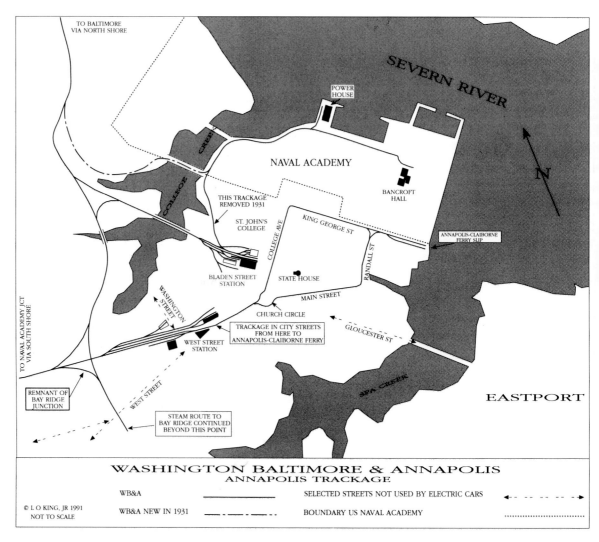

TO BALTIMORE
VIA NORTH SHORE

SEVERN RIVER

POWER HOUSE

NAVAL ACADEMY

BANCROFT HALL

THIS TRACKAGE REMOVED 1931

ST. JOHN'S COLLEGE

KING GEORGE ST

COLLEGE AVE

RANDALL ST

ANNAPOLIS-CLAIBORNE FERRY SLIP

BLADEN STREET STATION

STATE HOUSE

WASHINGTON STREET

MAIN STREET

CHURCH CIRCLE

TO NAVAL ACADEMY JCT VIA SOUTH SHORE

TRACKAGE IN CITY STREETS FROM HERE TO ANNAPOLIS-CLAIBORNE FERRY

GLOUCESTER ST

WEST STREET STATION

SPA CREEK

EASTPORT

REMNANT OF BAY RIDGE JUNCTION

WEST STREET

STEAM ROUTE TO BAY RIDGE CONTINUED BEYOND THIS POINT

WASHINGTON BALTIMORE & ANNAPOLIS
ANNAPOLIS TRACKAGE

WB&A	————	SELECTED STREETS NOT USED BY ELECTRIC CARS	◄ - -- -- -- ►
© L O KING, JR 1991 NOT TO SCALE	WB&A NEW IN 1931 —— · —— · —— · ·	BOUNDARY US NAVAL ACADEMY	··············

Except for minor modifications, the little cars used standard streetcar equipment until 1910, when only one of them (number 10) was refitted with rheostat controllers to run on 1200 volts. With conversion of the entire system to a direct-current operation, the local schedules were extended as far west as Camp Parole. But the little car* was soon victim of several serious accidents in collisions with the heavier freight or faster interurban trains (12/27/12 and 7/21/13), and on June 8, 1914 the railroad was allowed to discontinue streetcar service upon regular payments of a special (extra) franchise tax in lieu of the gross receipts levy theretofore collected by the municipal authorities.

On July 12, 1913, an additional station was opened

---

* Number 10 was replaced by number 19 in 1912.

next to the Baptist Church at the southwest corner of College Avenue and St. John Street. A remodeled store was appropriately painted in The Electric Line's colors of green and white, with a large shingle proclaiming the "State House Station."

Here the trains stopped in the middle of the street in front of a small parkway bordered by ornamental lamp posts and rows of well-kept flowers and hedges which formed the pedestrian entrance to the other company's Bladen Street Station. The depot on Bladen Street was an older building dating from the Annapolis & Baltimore Short Line Railroad's first operations in 1887. Facilities there included the traditional waiting room furnished with a coal stove and rows of oak benches. Outside, there were tracks on either side of a long covered passenger platform, a big freight shed, and five yard

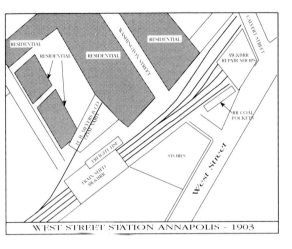

WEST STREET STATION ANNAPOLIS - 1903

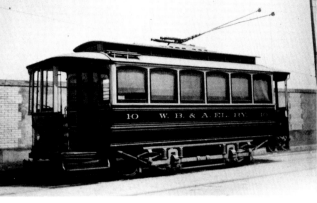

Above: WB&A 10 on King George Street July 23, 1908. Photograph by LeRoy O. King, Sr. **Below:** Baltimore open car of the same series as WB&A 11 which was acquired for local service in Annapolis. King collection.

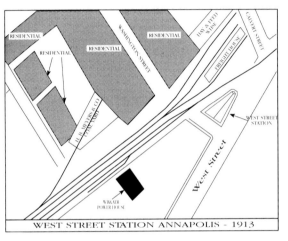

WEST STREET STATION ANNAPOLIS - 1913

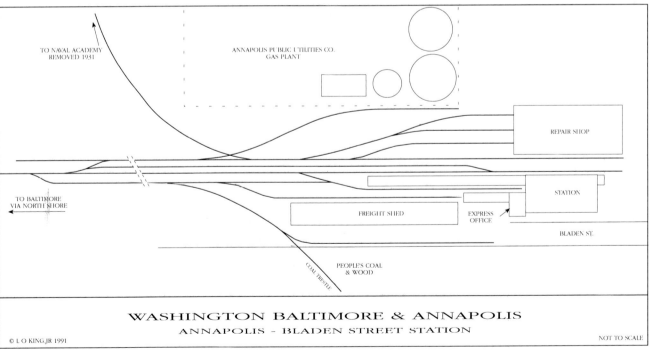

WASHINGTON BALTIMORE & ANNAPOLIS
ANNAPOLIS - BLADEN STREET STATION

© L O KING JR 1991

NOT TO SCALE

Until 1908, steam trains via the South Shore terminated at the old Annapolis & Elk Ridge Railroad depot. When the railroad line was electrified, local service through the town was provided by big interurban trains as well as the city car seen here at the new WB&A station on West Street. Note the double overhead wires which were required by town ordinance at the time. From a postcard. Author's collection.

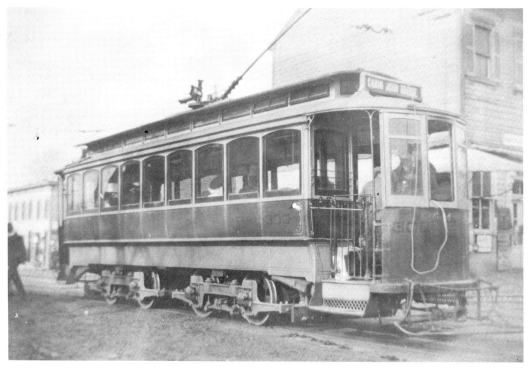

Washington Railway & Electric 300 was one of two Laconia-built cars on the system. The other, 301, was sold to the WB&A in 1912 and became their number 19. See note bottom of page 140. Photograph by LeRoy O. King, Sr.

Car 64 arrives at West Street about 1930. Note the WB&A bus on Washington Street and the "penny" scale near the station door; a fixture typical of the era. King collection.

tracks which led into three bays of a concrete shop building. A large vacant spot in the center of the yard indicated the site of the engine turn-table from earlier days. At the outer end of the yard, all lines converged into a single track crossing the trestle over College Creek. And beyond the trestle, two arms of a sweeping "wye" arrangement joined the line to Bay Ridge. Following this track (southbound) across another trestle over Hutchin's Creek (or Peter's Cove) led to Bay Ridge Junction where the excursion trains, operated by the B & A Short Line, once crossed the AW&B Line. From the very beginning of this intersection in 1886, a connecting curve from west to south had enabled special trains from Baltimore and Washington to run directly to Bay

Ridge Park, some four miles beyond. With the coming of The Electric Line in 1908, the bay resort had ceased to be of any importance as a railroad destination, although the junction continued for many years as an interchange between the two interurban lines entering Annapolis. As a point on the public timetables, it was perhaps better known as Cedar Park. In 1921 this connection assumed added importance when the consolidated operations used it increasingly for freight routed via Odenton. At that time a second connecting arm from west to north was built to facilitate the milk runs and other shipments to and from the Naval Academy. In those days, a regatta event on the Severn always involved one of more baggage cars carrying the racing shells of visiting varsity teams.

The U. S. Naval Academy is an impressive place. It is made so, in large measure, by the stately halls of French Renaissance architecture that were erected in 1899. At first, the granite and other materials for this massive construction were delivered by barge to the Severn waterfront. But on April 25, 1895, an enterprising group of five members from the Short Line's Board of Directors incorporated as the Annapolis & Chesapeake Railroad. They built one mile of track from the Bladen Street yards, across the back campus of St. Johns College, to and within the Naval Academy grounds. It was said to be a temporary construction track, and indeed the beautiful campus grounds, bordering College Creek, had been leased on that basis. But the main power house, with its permanent demands for coal, was to prove otherwise. Several years later, the line within the Academy yard was extended to serve the Brigade Commissary at Bancroft Hall, until the freight business gradually grew to more than 1200 carloads per year.

On January 1, 1921, the Annapolis & Chesapeake Railroad was renamed the Annapolis Short Line Railroad; and, by deed from the Maryland Electric Railways, acquired 18.4 miles of line, being that portion of the North Shore route from Shipley to Bladen Street (Annapolis), subject to various debts (construction mortgage, car trust leases, operating losses, etc.), which, in turn, were guaranteed by the WB&A Electric Railroad Company. By this alliance the WB&A had secured the original Annapolis & Chesapeake track along the edge of Dorsey Creek (College Creek) that, for another ten years, would supply freight to the Naval Academy. Until then, coal and other cargo consigned to the Navy entered Bladen Street Station where the trains changed ends, to be shunted through gate 5 and along the seawall to the shops and power house then located on the Severn waterfront. But in 1929 the Governors of St. John's College had refused to renew the easement for the right-of-way which they regarded as a blemish across their grounds.

During 1930-31, the Navy built an entirely different approach. Leaving the North Shore track in the

In this 1935 view, the car in the distance at the right is beside the West Street terminal building. At the right foreground is the WB&A's sub-station. William Lichtenstern photograph, King collection.

vicinity of Tucker Street (West Annapolis), it wound around the Superintendent's Garden (later the site of a new heating plant) to cross King George Street onto a new drawbridge over Dorsey Creek, there, joining the original line near Gate 5. As part of this project, there were other realignments within the yard, including a new paved track beside the tennis courts along Sands Road leading to Bancroft Hall. A modern day visitor would be hard pressed to place most of these landmarks which have long since yielded to gleaming new buildings and picturesque landscaping of the waterfront.

One of the sharpest thorns in the unfolding

Bladen Street Station in steam days. Note State House in background. Maryland State Archives/Forbes collection MSA SC 182-799.

Bladen Street Station as seen from the former State House Station. The name on the sign is Annapolis and Chesapeake Bay Power Company. Author's collection.

Bladen Street Station looking northwest January 22, 1950. Leonard Rice photograph, King collection.

Above: The original Annapolis & Chesapeake track crossing King Street at Gate 5. Piling has been delivered for the new railroad bridge which will curve to the right (NW) along the near side of the highway bridge. The Annapolis Short Line trestle is shown in the background. **Below:** The same scene in September, 1931. Looking west, the turn-off to the right crosses the new bridge over Dorsey Creek, while the old track through Gate 5 leads to Bladen Street Station.

Above: New tracks into the Naval Academy yard leave the bridge parallel to King George Street (right) as they curve to join the old line seen here between the sheds. **Below:** In 1931, the new track along Sands Road between the Dewey Basin (left) and the tennis courts (right) leads to Bancroft Hall in the background. Four photographs, National Archives.

This accident at College Avenue and King George Street, Annapolis happened during the early hours of November 30, 1929. It was attributed to an iron object in the flangeway of the curve. Author's collection.

dilemma of increasing traffic in very narrow streets had been the Interurban's right to use the ancient streets of Annapolis. In 1928, the railroad had obligingly relinquished almost half of the Annapolis franchise in order to accommodate the repaving of Main Street. It was a compromise made in good faith to ease the traffic congestion; and not entirely without self-interest to gain a measure of concurrence from the town authorities for renewal of the franchise, due to expire four years hence. But this decision did not then presage events that were soon to become a crucial issue. Before the revised traffic plan (which involved some new track construction) was fully implemented, the chief negotiator in these arrangements was lost through the death of the railroad's dynamic President and longtime General Manager, James J. Doyle; and a few months later the town elections of 1929 were to choose a new mayor and council. So what had previously been a reasonable understanding among consenting parties now became bitter dissension among rival interests, and the plan fell apart in midstream. As the matter stood toward the close of 1929, that portion of track recently abandoned now precluded the former one-way flow of traffic around the town circuit, thus compounding the problems caused by two-directional rail operations against an ever increasing mass of automobiles. This inspired a concerted move by the new mayor to force the abandonment of all street trackage.

Local politics played upon confusions which they might have helped correct; and for six years a seemingly endless chain of charges, countercharges, costly litigation, and other disputes finally succeeded in devitalizing all efforts toward a solution. Central to these arguments was the railroad's offer to extend one of the North Shore terminal tracks along the curb of Bladen Street to join the existing track on College Avenue. Under this plan, the West Street Station would be closed, with all passenger service of the South Shore Division routed over the Cedar Park cut-off, and around the Bladen Street Station onto College Avenue and King George Street to the ferry wharf; thereby avoiding the most critical congestion on West Street and at the Circle. Such an investment was, of course, contingent upon renewal of the Annapolis franchise. Ere that came to pass, however, the railroad itself had vanished!

WB&A REPLIES TO TEN CITY DEMANDS

The answer of George Weems Williams, Receiver for the Company, to the ten requirements laid down by the town of Annapolis for granting a franchise to operate from Bladen Street Station to the ferry are as follows:

1. That the railroad complete the Bladen St. spur within 60 working days from time the franchise becomes effective, provided the franchise be accepted or approved not later than Sept. 15th.
Agree to complete within time specified; but franchise details cannot be worked out by Sept. 15th.

2. That town permit the railroad to make ferry connections by bus from West St. until other plans are completed.
As the receiver is continuing operations under court order, there is no necessity for running busses.

3. That the railroad pay $ 384.58, which is one half amount of attorney fees, etc. caused by the railroad's action in contesting legality of the franchise.
Inclination is to acquiesce if everything else is resolved.

4. That the railroad pay the town quarterly rental equal to 4 1/2 mills (each adult) and 2 1/2 mills (each child) passenger carried through streets, provided revenue shall be not less than $ 500. annually; and with the understanding that legislative action or any court orders to the contrary shall not affect this contract.
Railroad is willing to accept tax specified under those conditions.

5. That the railroad pay the town full amount of franchise tax due from 1 Jan 1931 to 30 June 1932.
Cannot recommend that receiver pay tax requested.

6. That the company remove tracks and equipment from West St., Church Circle, and Randall St. and restore streets to original condition within six months from acceptance of franchise.
Cannot agree to remove tracks and easements as requested. Willing that granting of a new franchise shall be without prejudice to town to make claim in the receivership case. Receiver shall, at expense of the receivership, remove the tracks and let court decide the question.

7. That the railroad shall continue the operation of West Street Station for all South Shore trains, except ferry trains.
One reason for making substantial expenditures in order to have a union station (at Bladen St.), the company figured on a saving by discontinuing operation of a separate station at West Street. Railroad regrets cannot recommend continuation of station as requested.

8. That the company grant easements and rights-of-way through its property for the purpose of completing and carrying out plans of the Metropolitan Sewage Commission.
Would be willing to recommend that such r-of-w be granted, provided it does not interfere with operation of railroad; but as all r-of-w are mortgaged to secure various bondholders, neither court nor the receiver could, without consent of bondholders, give Sewage Commission a valid title to such easement.

9. That the railroad agree to abide by all existing and future laws and ordinances of the town.
Will recommend that railroad abide by all valid laws now in effect, or which may be passed from time to time.

10. That the proposed franchise shall be agreed to by officials of the railroad, the receiver, and be subject to approval of the US Court before becoming effective.
Will recommend that proposed franchise be approved as requested.

Naval Academy Junction looking south. The center track curves to the westbound line to Annapolis Junction while the north wye seen at the extreme left connects with the South Shore Division. Author's collection.

13

THE JUNCTION

It would be hard for a curious wayfarer to even locate the spot today, for the cartographer's lexicon acknowledged it only thirty years, which is a mere wink in the boundless years that have gone before and since. But it did exist! The operational hub of The Electric Line was a place just east of Odenton Station where the north-south main line crossed the east-west track of the old Annapolis & Elk Ridge road. As a principal transfer point, this station might have been more fittingly named Annapolis Junction; but that entry had long appeared in B&O timetables to designate a similar point on their line. And so came into use the somewhat vicarious name: Naval Academy Junction.

The track arrangement there involved a right-angle crossing with connecting "wyes" on three sides. On the northeast corner, the dispatcher's tower housed the signal control boards and a bank of manually-operated levers on the upper floor, governing the principal switches, and on the ground floor, the superintendent's office, trainmen's quarters, and a battery room for the signal operations. Across the track there was a small waiting room adjoining a long covered platform provided with rows of wooden benches. In each quadrant, bounded by the intersecting tracks and sweeping curves, the large triangles thus formed were attractively landscaped in beautiful lawns dotted with evergreens, a low hedge, and circular flower beds of red and yellow cannas in season. Andy Hood, the station janitor, and his pride in the junction's grounds, are a part of the legend.

Amid this sparsely-settled locale of pine groves and one dirt road, the dominant landmark was George M. Murray's canning factory. With the coming of The Electric Line, Murray had the foresight to anticipate the surveyors and all that followed. There would be out-of-town contractors, scores of construction workers, a whole array of technicians and artisans employed at the main shops, and eventually, passengers changing trains were the two lines crossed. In 1905 he built a large frame hotel which was run by George M. Murray and Sons. Facing Telegraph Road, immediately beside the main line tracks, the big building housed a tavern and dining room on the first floor, a large ballroom upstairs, and guest rooms on the third floor. One room was always reserved for WB&A crewmen assigned to the first morning run from the junction. And for those on the extra board to while away idle hours, Murray's basement provided billiard tables and a bowling alley.

In the heyday of Murrays' Hotel, the place held promise of even greater things to come. In addition to a couple of ambitious, albeit ill-fated, real estate developments (Bonaventure and Admiral Heights), prospects were heightened with the announcement in May 1908 that the New Era Amusement Company had secured over 100 acres for a summer excursion resort. Designed by the architect Oliver Mitchell, this "Electric Park", as they were then called, had envisioned a large lagoon with an island cafe, broad promenades, and dozens of concessions, rides, and exhibits. The main entrance, facing the interurban line, was conceived as an impressive dome sixty feet in diameter, surmounted by a high tower to serve as a wireless transmitter. Ultimately, the grounds were to include additional enclosed areas, bordering the Pennsylvania Railroad tracks, for a race track and fair grounds. But such grandiose schemes had failed to win adequate financial backing, and the project died aborning.

It thus remained for the hotel at the junction, which would gradually develop as the community center of Odenton. With the coming of the railroad, Murrays' Hotel had added a General Store which, as the only place of its kind, prospered from patronage by the trainmen, shop personnel, and passengers

One of the early landmarks at the junction was Murray's Hotel. This scene, looking east, shows the Dispatchers' Tower at left. Author's collection.

Just north of the Junction, the yard and shops included sixteen parallel tracks which were joined by ladder tracks at each end. Author's collection.

Annapolis Local rounding the North Wye at Naval Academy Junction. One of the original combination cars still equipped with locomotive type pilot and double trolleys places this scene about 1912. Karel Liebenauer collection.

waiting between trains. Although the railroad had connecting curves (or wyes) on three sides of the junction, Murrays' property, abutting squarely into the south-west corner of the intersection, had precluded sufficient radius for a curved track from east to south (i e: from the Camp Meade line into the Washington line). In 1918, heavy traffic from the Army base made such a connection almost imperative; but the railroad's offer to buy a very small corner of Murrays' land was effectively thwarted by their asking price of $2500 for 1/25 of an acre. A short time later, however, the Murray brothers agreed as a patriotic (wartime) gesture to donate the small corner on condition that the railroad management

would forever disallow use of its station for the sale of tobacco, refreshments, or any items in competition with the lucrative business then enjoyed by the Murrays' General Store. The necessary deed was executed on November 20, 1918, and a double-track curve, thereafter known as "Murrays' Wye", was installed and attractively landscaped. Three years later (March 1921), as part of an economy move to eliminate the expense of a ticket agent, the management leased a station concession to George Pappas of Baltimore who already ran the magazine-lunch counter business at each of the principal terminals, and who further agreed to staff the ticket office as part of his contract. The Murray Brothers

Above: In addition to trains scheduled direct from Baltimore, service along the fourteen mile Sou[t]
Shore Division was also provided by a city type car operating between Naval Academy Junction a[nd]
Annapolis. This car, number 19, ex-Washington Railway & Electric 301 was originally from th[e]
Washington and Great Falls Electric Railway Company. Author's collection. **Below:** Double tracks [at]
Murrays' wye curve north to west from the main line to the Fort Meade branch. Here two freight moto[r]
switch cars on May 19, 1935. James P. Shuman photograph.

Left: An articulated car from Annapolis discharges passengers at Naval Academy Junction on May 19, 1935. Compare this scene with one at the top of the opposite page. **Below:** Two articulated trains pass just north of the Naval Academy Junction station which can be seen in the background. The train on the right is a Baltimore-Annapolis South Shore through train and the train on the left is a Washington-Baltimore Limited. Note that, in the left foreground, there is a derail which is set on the lead track to the yards to protect the main line. Both photographs by James P. Shuman.

Above: Freight motor number 10 about to enter the branch to Fort George G. Meade on May 19, 1935. The view looks toward Baltimore. Naval Academy Junction yards and shops are in the right background. **Below:** An articulated car leaving the Junction for Annapolis May 19. 1935. Both photographs by James P. Shuman.

Above: Baltimore-bound 24 at Naval Academy Junction, May 30, 1934. George Votava photograph. **Below:** From the opposite direction, looking toward Washington, another Baltimore bound train has just arrived. The date is May 19, 1935. Note the WB&A bus connection to Fort Meade at the far right. James P. Shuman photograph.

The modern shops included such innovations as arc lighting, heated pits and the latest design of overhead sprinkler systems. In one bay, the gantry crane (of forty-two foot span) enables a car body to be hoisted for an exchange of trucks, completed in a matter of minutes. Author's collection.

charged this to be in violation of their earlier agreement, but were overruled in court. During the active construction period at Camp Meade and throughout the tumultuous war years, Murrays' Hotel was a scene of bustling activity for all who came, or went, or waited on the railroad. In October 1923, the big wooden structure was destroyed by fire, and was never rebuilt.

Just north of the junction there was a small lake surrounded by marshland. For that reason, the general shops had been built about ¼ mile farther up the line at a place first known as Voltage, later called Mayfield. Branching off to the right of the northbound main, the yard track led into a series of sixteen parallel tracks which were joined by ladder tracks at both ends. Five of these tracks ran into or through the main shop building. Of reinforced concrete and brick, the shop (257-feet x 84-feet) included two bays for inspection and repairs; and was equipped with such innovations of the day as heated pits, arc lights, and the latest type of fire-fighting devices. The center track of the Machine Shop crossed a short transfer table. While a car body was hoisted by the large overhead crane, the car truck could be moved sideways and a replacement installed in a matter of minutes. With the war,

Above: The dispatcher's building at Naval Academy Junction. Herbert H. Harwood collection. **Below:** A Washington-bound articulated train approaches the Junction August 18, 1935. E. Alfred Seibel photograph.

Car 52 leaves the Junction for Annapolis on August 18, 1935. E. Alfred Seibel photograph.

the number of cars was greatly increased; and in 1918 another building was added to afford two additional tracks, which thereafter became the "new" Paint and Carpenter Shops.

Turning east from the yard, a short spur served a separate building which housed the substation, where the 33,000 volt feeders were relayed to Baltimore and Annapolis; in addition to the panels for two pairs of (300 kw) rotary converters that fed the adjacent main line, the South Shore Division, and the yards. The trolley wire was broken by section insulators at the entrance to the yard which operated on 600 volts.

The Washington Railway & Electric Company had two small electric locomotives (052 and 053) which were permanently assigned to their Potomac Electric Power Company Plant at Benning. Being equipped for the standard railroad (coal) interchange, these locomotives had wheels and flanges which prevented taking them over city streetcar tracks in order to reach the company's shops in Georgetown. The simplest alternative was to haul them out to Naval Academy Junction, to shops equally capable of all types of railroad maintenance. The standard billing for moving a locomotive from Benning to the junction and return was $20.

Over the years, the WB&A Shops held to a strict schedule of faithful maintenance. They turned out numerous cars remodelled from other lines, and even rebuilt one car in its entirety. Whatever the job to be done, the facilities of Naval Academy Junction, and the craftsmen who worked there, proved always equal to the task. Here was the car barn, redolent of fresh paint and ozone. Here, the glistening copper of newly-turned armatures, or wet cars right off the wash track, and that staccato bark of their line switches as they coupled up in trains. On the platform, a row of battered drum-type headlights and lanterns awaited the evening runs. And beyond were the dwarf semaphores (red and white—yellow and black) responding on command from the tower. Or the Westbound Local impatiently "whistling for the block". Of such was the daily scene at the Junction. Of such was the "stuff" of real railroading—ever since railroads began!

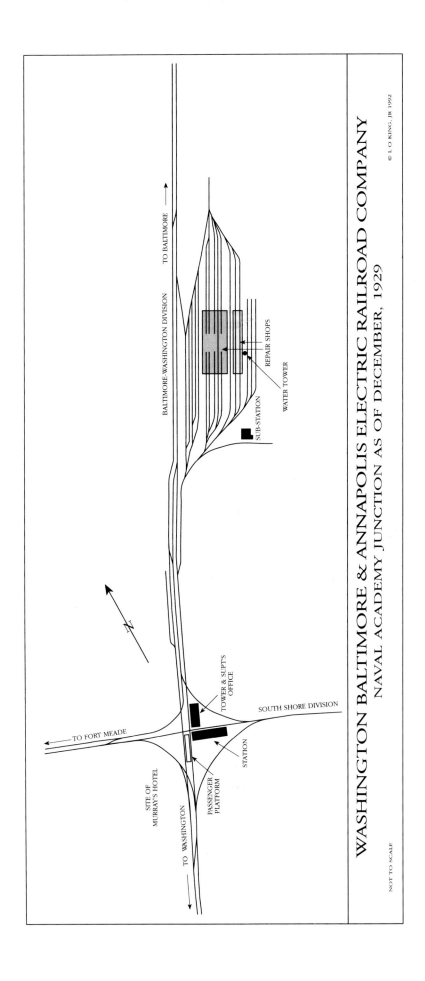

NOT TO SCALE

WASHINGTON BALTIMORE & ANNAPOLIS ELECTRIC RAILROAD COMPANY
NAVAL ACADEMY JUNCTION AS OF DECEMBER, 1929

© L O KING, JR 1992

Semaphore mechanism and signal relays installed on the Annapolis Division June 1912. Author's collection.

14

THE SIGNALS

Considering the speed and frequency of their limited trains interspersed with locals and carload freight, the Electric Line amassed an enviable score of safe operations; and whether by fate or otherwise, the fortunately few collisions to be ascribed of major consequence were in each case antecedent to the Signal Systems described here.

In 1907, a contract for manually operated signals to be installed over the single-track Annapolis Division was awarded to the Blake Signal & Manufacturing Company of Boston. C. Chandler Blake, the inventor, had previously applied his system in conjunction with direct current railways, but in this case was faced with certain changes necessitated by the single-phase AC operation. Because of possible interference with track circuits caused by induction from the high-voltage alternating current, there were numerous technical problems to be resolved. For this reason, an operating signal system did not become effective until June 25, 1908, some four and a half months after the road was opened. The first Blake signals functioned more as an auxiliary to the working timetable. By pressing a button, the Dispatcher could release a semaphore arm from its position in the upper quadrant, and thus summon a train crew to the telephone box. Upon reporting in, standing procedure could be amended by verbal orders that had to be written and acknowledged by both the Conductor and Motorman; after which the signal blade was reset by means of a rope.

Four years later the dispatching procedures were greatly improved with the installation of a fully automatic block signal system between Annapolis and Naval Academy Junction. All equipment for the new plant was furnished and installed by the Union Switch & Signal Company of Swissvale, Pennsylvania in the remarkably brief period of thirty days. The new system became operational on

June 24, 1912, just in time for the increased traffic attending the Democratic National Convention which was held in Baltimore that summer.

In 1914, automatic signaling was extended to include the double-track main line from the Junction to Scott Street in Baltimore. Inasmuch as the South Shore schedules traditionally provided most of the local service all the way in to Baltimore, the increased frequency of all classifications over the northern half of the main line had accorded it a higher priority for new signals. It remained for the stimulus of heavy wartime traffic, some four years later, to warrant these improvements over the southern half of the main line which was

One of the first electric cars waits at the Waterbury siding. Note the Blake semaphore that was reset by means of a rope. Author's collection.

All track circuits are of the double-rail type which provide a two-rail return for the propulsion current. At the impedance bonds, located on either side of insulated track joints, the propulsion current divides so that each half passes around the iron core of the bond in opposite directions (an equal + and -); its magnetizing action upon the core being zero. On the other hand, the bonds afford full impedance to the signal current by preventing the passage from rail to rail of the higher frequency AC used in signal circuits. Author's collection.

similarly equipped in the fall of 1918.

Unlike the principal signals of the Annapolis Division, which were semaphores, the main line, and later the North Shore Division, employed a three-lens colored light indicator (US&S Company's Type "N") that was adapted from a design first used by the United Railways & Electric Company.

The total project included 66.56 miles of protected main line track, divided into 39 standard blocks; and 33 signals comprising eight standard blocks which governed 13.6 miles of single track on the Annapolis Division. Each signal block averaged 1.66 miles in length. Signals were numbered to correspond with mileage from Annapolis, designated to the nearest even tenth of a mile for westbound movements; and to the closest odd tenth for those governing eastbound trains. On the main line, all signals were numbered from Baltimore in the same manner with odd numbers to control the southbound and even numbers to regulate the northbound operations. For ready identification, this numbering conformed to the time-

Signal 47 holds an eastbound movement at Iglehart while the other semaphore, number 46, is cleared for the block westward to Crownsville. Annapolis South Shore Division. Author's collection.

= Annapolis South Shore Division =

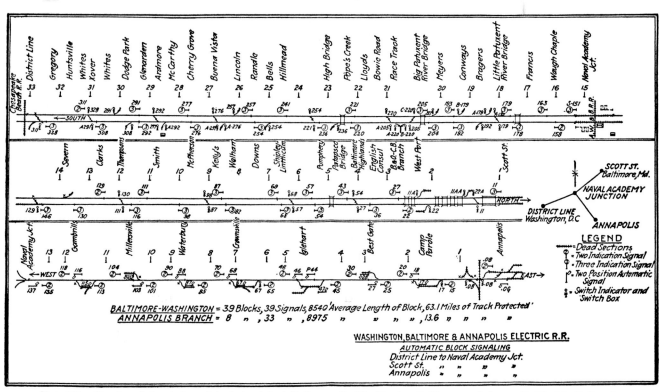

FIG. 271.—Track and signal plan of single track installation on the Washington, Baltimore and Annapolis Electric Railroad.

Above: The 1200 volt trolley contact is aligned parallel with the north-south wires, cleared for Pennsylvania Railroad trains. **Below:** The 1200 volt contact arm is rotated ninety degrees where it bridges the interurban overhead and is cleared for WB&A trains. In both views, Naval Academy Junction is to the right. Author's collection.

tables, wherein north and westward runs were assigned even numbers, while south and eastbound trains were odd numbered. Switch indicators were unlighted dwarf semaphores which generally controlled clearances from the siding into the main line; and at the same time afforded a distinct proceed indication for trains approaching at high speed.

Along single track of the Annapolis Division, each block extended from one passing siding to the next with a light signal of red and green indications placed about 1000 feet in advance of the semaphore which was located at the fouling point instead of at the switch point in order to minimize delay to opposing trains approaching the siding.

Following the merger of 1921, automatic signals were installed along the newly-acquired North Shore line from Linthicum to Bladen Street, Annapolis; and a second Dispatcher's office was established at Linthicum Junction to direct the operations of that Division. At the same time, a series of seven additional color light signals were interspersed between Baltimore Highlands and Scott Street to coordinate extremely close headways occasioned by the Short Line cars operated jointly with the regular WB&A schedules. Moreover, throughout the spring and summer of 1921 the density of traffic over this portion was further aggravated by numerous trains being deadheaded to and from the storage sidings at Baltimore Highlands during the construction of new terminal tracks in downtown Baltimore.

In time, the protection of automatic signals was extended to all operations of the WB&A, except for that portion west of Naval Academy Junction which covered 6.25 miles to the B&O interchange at Annapolis Junction. Even this Division was a double-track line as far as Fort Meade Station, which had precluded the urgency of elaborate signals within the Army base. Interline freight and special moves to the western end of track continued to be governed via written train orders or wayside telephones. Yet despite the absence of modern signal devices, this Division was eventually to feature an innovation of electrical engineering rather novel in the technology of that day.

According to local idiom, the "trolley gate" soon became a term to mean the Catenary Bridge of Odenton Junction. When the Pennsylvania Railroad was electrified in 1934, their grade crossing with the WB&A at Odenton involved two distinct electrical systems. Since each railroad employed overhead wires, the decussation of power lines so totally incompatible was resolved by means of an interlocking catenary bridge which stood astride the tracks. North-south trains operated on double tracks from an 11000 volt 25 cycle single-phase system supplied in each direction through parallel catenary wires suspended 22 feet above the rail. The Pennsylvania's overhead was continuous (unbroken) except for insulators. The single-track interurban line, crossing at right angles, employed a 1200 volt direct current overhead wire that was interrupted for width of the actual intersection. It was suspended at a height of nineteen feet above the rail.

Spanning the intersecting tracks, the steel superstructure provided a vertical spindle on which was mounted a horizontal rotating arm sufficient in length to bridge the break in the 1200 volt cross wire. This independent segment could be aligned for the interurban trains using the lower level east-west wire, or it could be rotated ninety degrees where it then stood parallel with the north-south wires. Although three feet lower than the Pennsylvania's overhead, it was centered directly above the interval between these double tracks so as to permit unobstructed pantograph running of the Pennsylvania locomotives. Radial movement of this independent section of the interurban's overhead contact was controlled from the adjoining signal tower; and further interlocked to protect the high-tension characteristics of each system, as well as the approach signals from all four sides.

The Catenary Bridge was officially listed as the Pennsylvania Railroad's way structure No E 324-A, designed by Gibbs and Hill, Consulting Engineers of New York City. Although constructed in 1934, the first Pennsylvania trains via electrification were not inaugurated until January 28, 1935. Hence, this elaborate installation was used less than seven

Articulated car 22 at Millersville, on the Annapolis South Shore line enroute to Naval Academy Junction July 14, 1935. John J. Bowman, Jr. photograph.

months before the WB&A road was abandoned.

The folklore of railroading, more often than not, is drawn from the rota of quaint personalities, the spectacular, the tragic, or incidents unusual amid the plainsong of daily routine that sometimes stretched uneventful from winter to summer and back again. But the unsung safety record, more often than not, was a journal of that which did not happen. In the recurring drama of a high-speed limited barreling past the slow freight, or the dilemma of schedules thoroughly deranged by the extras running late, or the special work train cleared with rights over all others, it was this marvel of what did not happen that bears eloquent tribute to the discipline of rules, the lonely dispatcher, and the distant red light. It was this symphony of signals that made it work!

AUTOMATIC BLOCK SIGNALING

Protecting High Speed Traffic
on the WASHINGTON BALTIMORE and ANNAPOLIS ELECTRIC R.R.

UNION

Style "N" Color Light

SIGNALS
controlled by continuous

A. C. TRACK CIRCUITS
make

MAXIMUM OPERATING SPEED
possible on the W. B. & A. with

ABSOLUTE SAFETY
to the important interurban freight and passenger traffic now moving in and out of Baltimore and Washington from naval training stations, cantonments, etc.

"Union" Standard Uniform Equipment Throughout

SOLID LINE ———
Block Signaling in service.
BROKEN LINE – – – – –
Signaling now being installed.

Union Switch & Signal Co.

SWISSVALE, PA.

Potomac Electric Power Company's Benning power plant about 1914. King collection.

15

THE ELECTRICAL SYSTEM

For years rumors persisted that the WB&A System would be a third-rail operation. As late as September 1906, the supervising engineers were accepting bids for a standard 600 volt direct-current electrical plant, with 25 sets of car equipment which specified third rail shoes. But later that month, it was the contract awarded to the General Electric Company that reaffirmed a much earlier decision to adopt an entirely new system of electric traction which, of necessity, would employ a high-tension overhead trolley. That decision to undertake one of the first alternating current (AC) single-phase electrifications, an unproven departure from the more fundamental types of direct current (DC) railway apparatus then in use, represented a choice that was bold in its concept, albeit a fateful one in its later implications.

Time and the frailty of man's records have obscured many of the considerations which led to that conclusion; though in light of its consequences, a few of the more obvious reasons should be noted:

- In 1902, Benjamin G. Lamme, the distinguished inventor and Chief Engineer of the Westinghouse Electric and Manufacturing Company, had perfected a series-commutator type of motor having characteristics suitable for railway use, which he described along with a new plan of power distribution, in a famous paper read before the American Institute of Electrical Engineers on September 26, 1902.
- His eloquence, and the results of his tests conducted in Pittsburgh, had for the first time outlined a practical means of adapting single-phase alternating current to an interurban line such as was then being built by the original WB&A

Electric Railway Company. Almost immediately, this plan was endorsed by the Cleveland Construction Company, as consulting engineers, and approved by the WB&A Company.

- Years later, the original plans inherited by the successor WB&A Company (of 1905) were still predicated on a company-owned generating station, which had been partially completed in accordance with Westinghouse designs. Thus, to some extent, the subsequent owners were influenced by large investments already committed by their predecessors.
- Also important were the initial costs which are reflected in a comparison of the two systems then being considered:*

  A 600 volt DC electrical plant comprising eleven substations and equipment for twenty-five cars at an estimated cost of $446,340.

  A 6600 volt AC single-phase system comprising only two substations and equipment for twenty-five cars at an estimated cost of $341,445.

Dating from the first survey of operating requirements which had been commissioned in May 1902, the consulting engineers had recommended this AC system, which would operate from a power house to be built in East Hyattsville. Its three 1500 kw Westinghouse generators were specified of more than average capacity to accommodate, in addition to the proposed interurban route, a 600 volt suburban trolley line (the Washington Berwyn

---

* From proposal submitted by General Electric Co. September 24, 1906.

& Laurel Electric Railroad then nearing completion) which the WB&A owners had acquired the year before (May 6, 1901). At the same time plans were already underway for a partial electrification of the Chesapeake Beach Railway whose requirements would also be supplied, at least in part, from the WB&A power house.

As President of the Cleveland Construction Company, Will Christy and his staff were just then enjoying a measure of fame for their work in having completed another high-speed interurban (The Great Third Rail) which opened on August 25, 1902. In many respects, there is a remarkable similarity between features of the power house designed for Hyattsville and the one built by the same Cleveland Construction Company at Batavia, Illinois for the new Aurora Elgin & Chicago Railway.

On August 22, 1902, land for the Hyattsville plant comprising 4.0134 acres, was purchased from J.H.Rogers and Philip Clarke.* On March 3, 1903 a contract was awarded to D.W. and G.H.Thomas for the power house building, specified to be of brick and stone construction 122 feet x 130 feet x 40 feet high; having a sheet metal smoke stack of ten feet inside diameter x 220 feet high. J.H.Conner was the engineer in charge. At a contract cost of $44,750, the building was essentially finished before work was halted on July 12, 1903. In addition to the building itself, work on related contracts had already begun for a railroad siding, coal trestle, and certain foundation work involving tie rods, base plates, and settings for the pumps and condenser by Henry R. Worthington; boilers by the Stirling Company; the steam machinery by Hooven Owens Rentschler; and other steelwork by Mayer & Englund Company. Completion of the project was announced for October 1, 1903 at a cost of $350,000. But with the WB&A bankruptcy of July 1903, the contracts were cancelled. Under subsequent railroad ownership the building was demolished in 1910, and the land was sold on December 21, 1912 to the

---

* Land Records PGC, Libre 9 Folio 355; and WB&A Prop Plat 89-C

Hyattsville Gas & Electric Co. Foundations and footings were never removed, and in the grassy area where they stood may be found a partial outline of the outer walls, within which are various geometric patterns in masonry that still define the bases for boilers, the smoke stack, etc. Being in the flood plain of the river, whose course has been altered by dikes and levees, the land became public parkland, and was thereby protected from the encroachment of surrounding commercial development.

The Westinghouse system of 1902 had specified a single-phase trolley operating on 1000 volts at a frequency of $16\frac{2}{3}$ cycles. On the cars there were to be four motors of 100 HP each, wound as plain series types having field circuits laminated throughout to eliminate, or reduce, arcing at the commutators. From all sides, doubts persisted about the ability of an AC machine to develop an adequate range of torque/speed with variable control for traction work, while at the same time overcoming its inherent defect of inductive sparking. Despite skepticism expressed by his colleagues, Lamme insisted that such a motor would work. Indeed he maintained that the future for interurbans of any length lay in the economical transmission of power which could only be attained by the use of high-voltage AC. In this belief he was sufficiently persuasive that Westinghouse was now committed, to the tune of $359,000, to demonstrate a very practical application of the single-phase theory. Throughout the scientific community at home and abroad, Lamme's work was attracting considerable interest, so that progress was eagerly watched for the results to be achieved on this new WB&A project.

In place of the familiar series/parallel controller with its objectionable features of make-and-break contacts and wasteful losses in resistance, these plans adopted an induction regulator. This was, in effect, a transformer whose primary and secondary windings mounted on separate cores could raise or lower the motor voltage by rotating the angular position of the secondary field in relation to the primary. The idea had many advantages, but by his own admission Lamme conceded that AC equipments could not be conveniently operated on DC lines, because complications of the dual control were sufficient to prevent its use, at least for some time to come.

An interesting contradiction here is an earlier agreement signed by the WB&A Company (April 1902) for joint use of a Washington terminal at White House Station, which could only be reached via a 500 volt direct current streetcar line. But as mentioned, these technical considerations were preempted by the realities of finance, and all work stopped.

The brief period from 1902 through 1904 was to witness remarkable advances in development of the AC traction motor. Shortly after Mr. Lamme had unveiled his single-phase motor at Westinghouse, a similar railway motor was introduced at General Electric. It was the work of a young Swedish inventor, Ernst F. W. Alexanderson who was later to achieve world fame for his high-frequency alternator which enabled trans-Atlantic radio communication and wireless telephony. But in 1904, Alexanderson called his new motor a "compensated" repulsion design; compensated, because of the distribution of additional field windings which neutralized, or compensated, for the armature reaction. Under this system, both motors and control could be adapted to operate on either AC or the standard 600 volt DC trolley, a capability that opened up enormous possibilities for interurban lines to secure the benefits of running over existing streetcar tracks, in cities, without sacrificing the advantages of long distance sections equipped with AC trolley. Although the refinements developed at General Electric may, to some extent, have overlapped certain inventions previously attributed to Westinghouse, it is to the credit of both companies that the manufacture of components which embodied experimental knowledge about transmission, motors, and control apparatus would become available to either under license from a Board of Patent Control, a sort of truce reached between Westinghouse and General Electric back in 1896, which had worked to the decided advantage of all concerned.

By 1905, responsibility for overall design of the WB&A had passed from the Cleveland Construction Company of Akron to the Roberts & Abbot Company of Cleveland. Upon their advice, the new contract for an AC single-phase electrical installation to operate 96.33 track miles (exclusive of the District of Columbia) was awarded on September 24, 1906 to the General Electric Company. So here was General Electric, whose predecessors had long been advocates of Edison's steadfast contention of direct current for railway use, now about to undertake a major project under the opposing theory theretofore expounded by their competitors. Actually, they had offered a choice of either system, wherein cost was a persuasive argument in favor of alternating current. But General Electric may have still retained some doubts, for their contract guaranteed that expense for maintenance of the total AC plant would not exceed that of a corresponding DC system; and, in the event it should not prove satisfactory, it would be replaced by a complete DC installation (distribution system, substations, and car equipments) upon payment of the difference in cost between the two systems.

In place of the original plan for a company-owned power house at Hyattsville, a contract was signed on January 18, 1907 for power to be purchased from the Potomac Electric Power Company of Washington.

Within the District of Columbia, an agreement with the streetcar company (April 15, 1907) provided for joint use of the Columbia line. Under that arrangement, costs would include a fixed rental for track and overhead; plus a formula for current that was limited by maximum revenues combined with similar payments then being made on behalf of the Washington Berwyn & Laurel Electric Railroad.* All responsibility for a 500 volt two-wire trolley system within the District of Columbia was thus assumed by the Washington Railway & Electric Company. The size and weight of the proposed interurban

---

* For details see page 118.

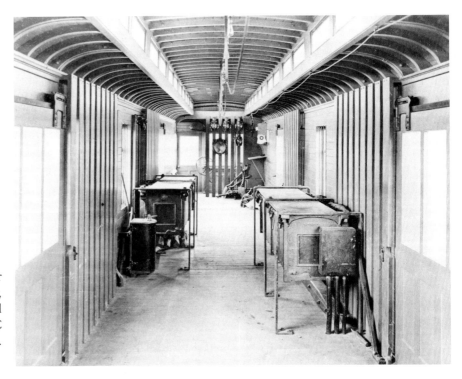

This interior view of freight motor number one, equipped as an AC car, shows the space taken up by electrical equipment not needed in the DC electrification which followed. Author's collection.

trains to operate over modest grades, in conjunction with streetcar traffic, created power demands far exceeding anything experienced up until then. And to insure that the system would carry the full load, the contract stipulated:

"At no place on its line shall the voltage between the two trolley wires drop below 350 volts for a period of longer than ten seconds, and, after the expiration of such period of ten seconds, the line voltage shall rise to at least 400 volts; provided, however, that the Washington Company shall not be liable for temporary total cessation of power".

Nineteen Cars, described as the high-speed Limiteds , were each equipped with four motors (weighing 5800 pounds apiece, or some 12 tons per set) which, together with car body, trucks, and brake accessories, amounted to a total weight of 59 tons per car (light).

Four of the Local cars were each provided with two motors and one main transformer which, with the other equipment, specified a complete car of about 35 tons (light).

Two freight motors carried the standard four-motor equipments, having a somewhat higher gear reduction intended for slower service in work trains, or for hauling carload freight.

The road was officially opened on February 7, 1908. On open track the cars proved to be very fast at speed; but in starting, their excessive weight, and the heavy line surges thus induced made for poor acceleration, blown circuit breakers, and even occasional damage at the substation. Unusual wear in the brushes caused an accumulation of carbon dust within the motor housing, resulting in short circuits or flashovers. And vibration in the motor mounts soon caused excessive wear in gears and pinions. Another problem was the tendency of the motors to overheat. Although the time tables were planned to allow a minimum layover period between trips, excessive heat generated under normal service conditions often required that the cars be set out to cool off. This problem was further aggravated by the high torque demands of frequent stops within city limits.

Running on direct-current with motor fields in series, the cars were capable of a free running speed of about 60 percent of their balancing speed on alternating-current with fields in parallel. But this change-over entailed other problems attending operations over the streetcar tracks in each city, having the rather diverse characteristics of a single grounded DC trolley, or a 600 volt DC double overhead with varying potential. And where these conditions, with the basic 6600 volt AC, were placed in combination on the same car, the intricacy of wiring, working parts, and control were such as to practically condemn the apparatus from the start.

First plans had envisioned city operations as far as the US Treasury building in downtown Washington, but complexity and weight of the AC cars, as ultimately developed, had far exceeded the forty ton restriction imposed over conduit tracks of the Washington Railway & Electric Company, necessitating transfer of all passengers to streetcars for the city portion of the trip. Within a year it was painfully apparent that the AC single-phase system was unable to meet all requirements, and in March 1909 the General Electric Company was requested to replace it under terms of the guarantee.

Meanwhile, in 1907, the first high-potential DC equipment was developed. Charles E. Eveleth, one of G.E.'s leading proponents of this plan, noted that the running current of a train is about one third that of the starting current and (especially on long interurban stretches) there are considerable periods during coasting and stops when the train is taking no current; so that a substation unit required to commutate up to its overload guarantee was seldom fully utilized. His system, designed as a combination 600/1200 volt DC operation was intended to save costs by reducing the number of substations needed by increasing the track mileage fed by each, and thereby increase its efficiency by improving the load factor. Moreover, this use of high voltage could exploit existing capacity of layouts which the AC system had created.

It was thus decided to convert to the new 600/1200 volt direct current electrification. To supervise engineering aspects of the changeover, the management again retained the original Cleveland Construction Company, while General Electric, within the short span of eight months, built all apparatus and car equipment required for the conversion. Inasmuch as the contracts specified that transition was to be made without interruption to regular service, it was required that the massive transformers, control panels, and other heavy equipment at each substation be transferred by stages to a nearby temporary shelter before the new machinery could be installed in the existing buildings. This demanded a coordinated plan of heavy moving each night, so that before morning, the assembly being shifted on rollers might be reconnected in multiple with that part still in place to assure continued service until the following night. During September 1909, an additional substation was built at Ardmore to reinforce line voltage for the first 11 miles north of the District Line.

The substation at West Street, Annapolis at first had two 300 kw motor generator sets (for the 600 volt town circuit) which were changed to two 300 kw converters, connected permanently in series, inasmuch as the 1200 volt system, after 1910, extended through the streets of Annapolis. To accommodate this change, the local streetcar had to be rewired from the series/parallel control to a straight (R-200-A) rheostat controller. In later years, two more 300 kw Westinghouse rotaries (acquired from the Short Line) were added to the West Street station to carry the Annapolis North Shore line as well as the South Shore Division.

In Baltimore the current for that short portion of the overhead operated jointly with the city cars had been purchased under contract dated November 28, 1907 with the United Railways & Electric Company at 2 $\frac{1}{8}$ cents per kw hour. As the conversion project began, the substation at Scott Street was shut down completely, during which period (August 13, 1909 to February 15, 1910) a supplemental contract provided for the URys&ECo to furnish all current used on city streets in Baltimore (Terminal to Viaduct). It will be recalled that the Scott Street station had theretofore fed only the 600 volt city circuits; but that after the complete change over, it also assumed a section of seven miles of the 1200 volt line from Scott Street (Viaduct) to Shipley.

After weeks of moving and testing equipment,

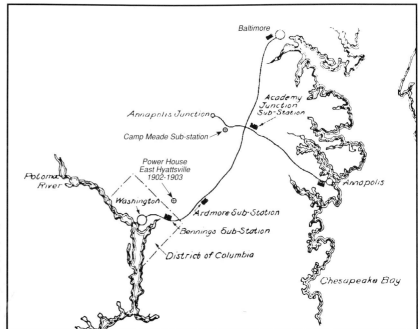

For the new 1200 volt DC electrification, energy was purchased from the Potomac Electric Power Company at 6600 volts three-phase . At the primary substation located at Benning, it was converted to a potential of 33000 volts for transmission at three-phase 25 cycle to each of five substations. Author's collection

inspecting line work instructing the station operators, wiring the new cars, and retraining the crews, a test run was made during the late hours of January 24, 1910 using one of the new type cars. It is fascinating to imagine the midnight precautions that preceded that tryout, but having worked successfully, the main event had at last arrived. In the early hours of February 15th, the last AC car made its final trip, and at 5:20 that morning the first DC car was started. Throughout that first day of operation, the new cars ran over 4500 car miles without missing a single trip of the regular schedule. Two weeks later, on March 1st, the company announced direct service from downtown Baltimore all the way through to the Treasury building in Washington. Thereafter, the conduit plows used on city trackage were leased on a mileage basis from the Washington Railway & Electric Company.

Five of the original cars were re-equipped with new motors; while all of the heavy high-speed Limiteds were replaced by twenty-seven new cars, whose smaller dimensions reflected a corresponding reduction in weight, size of the motors, and complexity of control apparatus. However, notwithstanding this adoption of the more conventional DC equipment, WB&A Cars, by virtue of such varied operating characteristics; demanding 600/

1200 volt circuits; single or double trolleys; conduit plow collectors; multiple-unit Sprague Type-M controls; and later Westinghouse Type HL controls; were always to remain among the most complicated of any interurban equipment. During 1200 volt operation, a dynamotor furnished 600 volt current for the lighting circuits which, during city running were fed directly from the trolley. Car heaters which originally were wired directly to the 1200 volt side, functioned at only half capacity within city limits. This resulted in inadequate heat, especially throughout the layovers at each terminal. Incredible as it may seem, the solution to that problem was a brief conversion to Peter Smith-type coal stoves installed at a cost of $175 per car.* But improved technology would soon prevail, and in later years all cars were effectively heated by electricity.

In preparation for the change over of 1910, a new freight motor was added, bringing to 33 the total number of DC motor cars. There were no passenger trailers. Though unlike the original Limited cars which had usually operated as single units, the smaller Niles cars were now required in two-car trains to maintain the main line service. It was soon apparent that 30 passenger cars were

* Md. PSC Cases 861 (1914); 914 (1914); and 1249 (1915).

The substation at Naval Academy Junction is, at this writing, still in use as part of a larger grid served by the Baltimore Gas & Electric Company. Author's collection

insufficient to handle the volume of traffic. Accordingly, ten additional cars were ordered in September 1910, and were delivered the following April.

Under terms of the original contract, General Electric Company had built and installed the new system at a cost of $92,508 with allowances for much of the single-phase apparatus returned. To that were added construction costs of the supervising engineers, construction of additional transmission lines, and the purchase of 38 new cars fully equipped; all of which amounted to slightly more than $880,000 as the total price of the conversion.

The trolley overhead was constructed as a nine-point catenary suspension between poles placed 150 feet apart on tangent track. This design served its purpose well, both as to flexibility of the trolley at high speed, and for economy of upkeep by reducing the wire stress and wear inherent in any type of direct suspension. At first the overhead had employed a system of side brackets mounted on each pole, which in 1925 was changed to a triangular rigging of span wires, replacing the metal cross arms.* The standard height of the trolley wire was nineteen feet six inches on open track; although this varied considerably at freight sidings where it was as high as twenty-three feet; or where, under

---

* ERyJ Vol 65 No 14 April 1925, Page552

bridges and through tunnels, it ranged to a minimum of sixteen feet.

From the beginning, a lightweight trolley wheel of bronze alloy had been the standard. Unless maintained in perfect balance, both as to rotation and vertical tension, the slightest skip at high speed would cause rapid arcing, and gradually, a blistering effect with resultant wear against both the wheel and wire.

Years later, a carbon shoe contact would, in time, give the wire a lubricity which reduced wear. However, since it was uneconomical to operate different trolley contacts over the same wires, conversion of the interurban cars would be delayed until 1934 in order to coordinate joint operations with the city cars.

The duties of a substation operator were not unlike those of a fire fighter whose long hours, though often quiescent, could never allow for any lapse of dozing or inattention. As the guardian of high-tension electricity, he was constantly faced with circumstances that could erupt with explosive force. Emergencies such as a flash-over, a broken trolley wire, or a sudden overload required immediate response to avoid damage to equipment or even loss of life.

Another event that was sure to register at the

substation was an offense, fortunately rather rare, known as a "HI-POT". As each run left the city in Baltimore, or the District Line in Washington, it passed from the lower voltage streetcar circuit into the high-tension interurban overhead by drifting through an insulated break in the trolley wire. At that point, the motorman threw a double-pole knife switch that transferred the train's wiring from 600 to 1200 volts. A failure to change over in time meant that the train had run into High-Potential while still connected for Low Potential circuits, causing a massive overload of equipment, resulting in blown fuses, burned out lights, or other damage; and a summons to visit the General Superintendent next morning. Thus, to "HI-POT" was to blow the works, literally as well as figuratively.

On March 19, 1913 the railway acquired the franchise and all property of the Gas & Electric Light Company of Anne Arundel County, which they renamed the Annapolis Public Utilities Company. Realizing that the long-term power contract with Potomac Electric Power Company offered a significant cost advantage over existing arrangements for independent electric service in the Annapolis area, the Board of Directors authorized a much larger substation to be built on West Street with additional equipment to incorporate all power facilities for the railroad as well as for the street lights and local commercial service. At the same time they approved a duplicate 33,000 volt three-phase transmission line to be built from Naval Academy Junction to Annapolis. Design and supervision was carried out by the Cleveland Construction Company under a project that eventually reached a cost of $80,000. ($79,260.27 plus the necessary transformers at Benning). The decision was a wise one, for the ample capacity thus created would in time enable the company to absorb a number of smaller utility franchises extending over five counties.

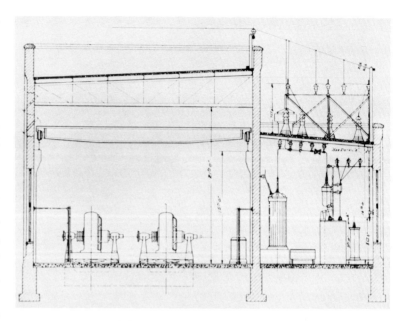

Transverse section (above) and plan of the Ardmore substation which was built for the 1910 DC electrification and is typical. From a General Electric Company Bulletin. King collection.

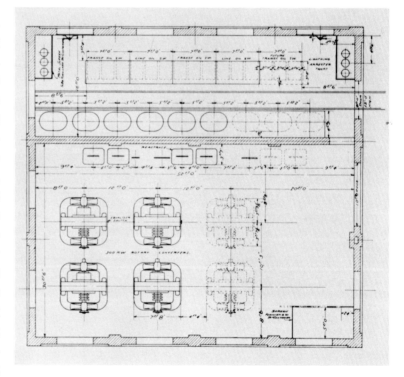

In 1918, the opening of a new substation at Admiral was charged to railroad improvements, but the entire output was soon diverted to meet the ever-increasing demands of Camp Meade. After the war, that station was maintained on behalf of the US Government, although by then the light traffic over that branch no longer justified it as a railroad requirement.

With acquisition of the Annapolis Short Line in 1921, the WB&A Company had gained two more substations; namely, a set of Westinghouse equipment which had been established just two years before at Linthicum; and a similar though larger (900 kw) Station Number 2 near Jones Road. That station was built in 1913 as part of the Short Line's conversion to a 1200 volt DC system; and is designated Jones Number 2 to distinguish it from another Jones substation just 500 feet to the south.

From 1914 to 1921, Jones Substation Number 2 was supplied from the Westport power house owned by the Consolidated Gas Electric Light & Power Company of Baltimore. The plan of power distribution was such that during off-peak hours, it could carry the entire load, unmanned; automation rather innovative at the time. By 1919 traffic had increased to justify another station established at Linthicum,

After 1921, as the Short Line's network became integrated into the WB&A power system, the station at Jones number 2 was dismantled, the line being fed from both ends rather than the middle. But upon abandonment of the WB&A in 1935, the new Baltimore & Annapolis Railroad, then deprived of its power source from the Annapolis end, was compelled to reactivate the Jones number 2 station, which, by now was little more than a vacant building. Moreover, even the building, 45 feet x 30 feet x 8 feet, had to be enlarged to receive a complete set of GE equipment salvaged from the station discontinued at Ardmore. To this day, the cement block annex is readily distinguished from the original brick structure.

When the new Baltimore terminal opened in October 1921, rerouting via the new trackage on Pratt Street had, for the first time, eliminated a joint trolley operation with United Railways & Electric Company. This had the advantage of allowing interurban trains to reach the city destination on their 1200 volt overhead.

By 1927, the Consolidated Gas Electric Light & Power Company of Baltimore had gained a controlling interest in the WB&A, but it was not until the existing power contract with Potomac Electric Power Company expired on July 31, 1933, that the primary source of all electrical energy consumed by the railroad and the territory of its commercial users was transferred from long-standing ties with Benning, on the south, to the power house at Westport on the north. At the same time, the entire electric utility systems of Baltimore and Washington were interconnected to afford a reciprocal grid network which was to insure continuous service throughout periods of peak loads, disaster, and mechanical failures.

When the railroad was discontinued in 1935, the substation at Scott Street was retained to supply a section of B&O track then being electrified for the Baltimore & Annapolis Railroad's rerouting into Camden Station. It will be recalled that Scott Street, although by this time somewhat isolated from the rest of the railroad, was nevertheless required for its 1200 volt output; because the established power system for the B&O tunnel locomotives through Camden Station operated on a different (675) voltage. An agreement between the B&O and B&A Companies dated September 29, 1935 describes the interurban's responsibility for its own power transmitted from Scott Street over lines to be placed on poles owned by the B&O Railroad.

So remnants of the former network at Scott Street, Linthicum, and the plant reactivated at Jones Road would survive another fifteen years, until 1950, when the B&A Railroad abandoned all electrified operations. In the years since then, the facilities at Naval Academy Junction and Fort Meade have been enlarged as part of the commercial network served by the Baltimore Gas and Electric Company. All others have been abandoned — though at each location the four walls they once occupied still stand as forlorn derelicts from another age.

Freight motor number 1 in front of the shops at Naval Academy Junction on July 23, 1908. LeRoy O. King, Sr. photograph.

16

CARS

THE FREIGHT MOTORS

Until the war of 1917, motive power for freight consisted of six cars built by Niles. As already mentioned, the first two which had been readapted from the original AC electrification, and a third (number 3) acquired at time of the change-over, each carried four 140 HP motors. According to *Electric Traction Weekly* of September 2, 1911, these motors were capable of hauling as many as twenty loaded freight cars. They were geared for slower speeds than the later three (numbers 7, 8 & 9) which, operationally, were similar to the passenger equipment. While all freight motors routinely negotiated the tortuous curves leading into downtown Baltimore, they never entered the city tracks of Washington.

A misfortune all too common was a short-circuit of high-voltage that sometimes occurred along private right-of-way at some point inaccessible to immediate help. That was the case on June 6, 1929 when freight motor number 1 was destroyed by fire near Westport. She was carrying a cargo of near-beer* at the time, and although the spirituous effects of that beverage are only mildly intoxicating, there was an ample supply that night to insure that it was. The motors and controls were promptly repaired, and a new all-steel body delivered by the J.G.Brill Company in November 1929 completed the restoration of freight motor number 1. Through subsequent owners, with a new identity (number 7) and various alterations, it continues to this day as an operable museum exhibit.**

The eight freight motors (10-17), or locomotives as they were usually reported, had their beginning as AC passenger cars of The Annapolis Short Line. There were originally nine of this series, which comprised five straight passenger types and four of the combination passenger/baggage design. They had been ordered in 1907 from the Southern Car Company at an average cost of $16,588 per car. When the Short Line was converted in 1914 to a 1200-volt DC system, the original cars were stripped of their electrical equipment for use as trailers. In October, 1914, one of the combination cars (number 31) was rebuilt as a baggage trailer numbered 211.

In December, 1916, the WB&A Company acquired two of the combination cars which were rebuilt into package express trailers, equipped with controls. Within a matter of weeks, the remaining six were also purchased for use as passenger trailers numbered 12 through 17. This arrangement, however, was only short-lived.

Four months later, the country was at war! And within a year, the number of revenue passengers had climbed to 5,946,697. In order to cope with this sudden influx, all eight of the former Short Line cars were rebuilt as locomotives. During the summer of 1917, the Carpenter Shop at Naval Academy Junction closed in the side windows and train doors; while the Mechanical Department installed the latest type train brakes; type 15-D-9 controllers: and Westinghouse type 557-W-8 motors of 140 HP

---

* The popular term "near beer" was derived from the legal limit of alcoholic content allowed during prohibition.

** With exception of the ten articulated units, all of the steel body cars were eventually acquired by other lines. Freight motor number 1 became Central California Traction Company's number 7 where, with various modifications, it ran between Sacramento and Stockton until 1946; and continued for a brief period in Sacramento until all electric operations ceased in October 1947. For the next twenty years, it was stored in a junk yard in Stockton. In 1967, number 7 was donated to the Bay Area Electric Railroad Association. Through dedicated effort and expense of their members, it was moved to the Western Railway Museum at Rio Vista Junction, California. As of 1992, it still runs as the sole survivor from the WB&A roster.

Above: Number 2 in Baltimore about 1935. Note differences in the pilot and the front window arrangement when compared to number 1 on page 180. King collection. **Below:** Second number 1 at Baltimore September 6, 1934. M. D. McCarter collection.

Above: Second number 1 at 16th & Benning Road, Washington, about 1933. John B. Yeabower collection. **Below:** Central California Traction Company number 7, ex-WB&A number 1, at Stockton, California, in 1937. King collection.

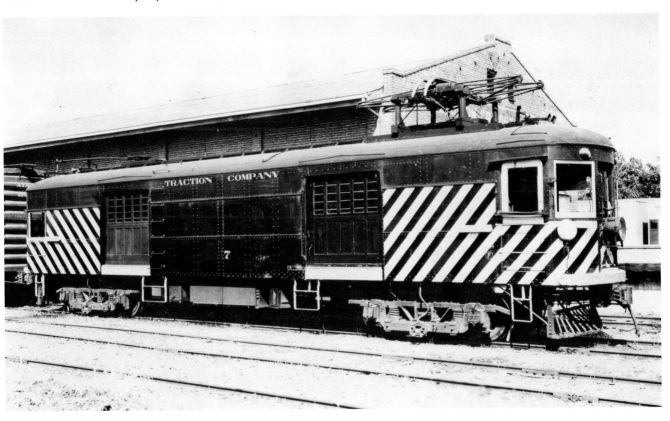

Number 3, as built at the time of the changeover to DC. King collection.

Number 3 in Baltimore in its final form with an arch roof. M. D. McCarter collection.

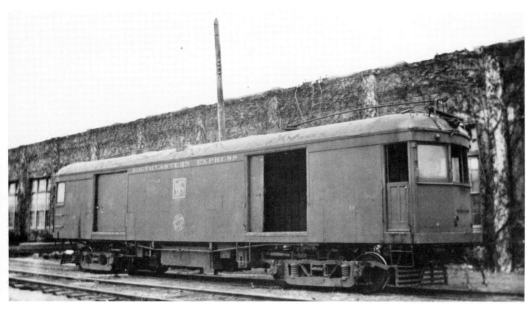

Number 9 at Naval Academy Junction, April, 1935. See page 93 for a picture of number 8, which is different. George E. Votava photograph.

rating, at an average expenditure of $13,881 per car. So acute was the need for additional motive power at this time, that several of the rebuilt cars were wired to run temporarily on two motors, until the rest of the equipment was received from Westinghouse. Throughout the war, these locomotives hauled long trains of the Long Island Railroad trailers in passenger service, in addition to a record traffic in heavy freight attending the construction and opening of Camp Meade.

In the spring of 1921, one of the cars acquired by merger with the Maryland Electric Railways was the baggage trailer number 211, which became WB&A number 20, later 601. Apparently the freight motors sustained some weakening effect of the car frame caused by draw-bar stress; for in 1924 an additional side-sill of heavy steel was installed on all four corners of each locomotive. The renovation work, however, omitted one car. On August 30, 1922, freight motor number 15 was badly damaged in a fire, and was later stripped of its equipment and redesignated baggage trailer number 602. While its origins, in common with number 601, now gave the two cars an overall sameness, a closer comparison is not without interest. Number 601 (rebuilt 1914 in the Short Line shops) had extra wide cargo doors, rounded at the top, whereas number 602

(rebuilt in WB&A shops) had standard-width freight doors, similar to the others. Moreover, placement of the two personnel doors at diagonally opposite corners, in the case of number 601, was the reverse of all others.

In the post-war years, the 10-17 class motors furnished the mainstay of equipment for the Southeastern Express Company as well as a refrigerator car dispatch which operated until 1923. The timetable for that year, for instance, lists twelve daily freight runs. In still later years, these cars were the motive power for trains of hopper cars that hauled sand and gravel from the pits at Bowie and Bragers.

When the line was discontinued in 1935, the two trailers (601 and 602) with a freight motor number 18, went to the newly-formed Baltimore & Annapolis Railroad. The other wooden freight motors were scrapped; except numbers 16 and 17, which survived on the Benning coal interchange run by the Capital Transit Company. As the Washington company gradually acquired other second-hand locomotives, number 17 was sold in February, 1944, to the Potomac Edison Company, where it again performed wartime service on the Hagerstown & Frederick Railway.

Gone is the path where once the Big Cars ran. Though it takes but small imagination to visualize a

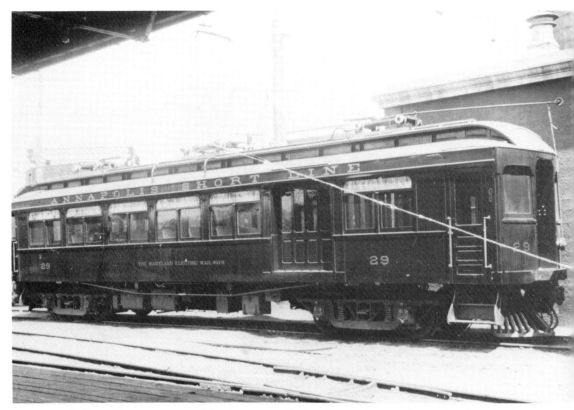

Annapolis Short Line motor combination car at Bladen Street, Annapolis. Author's collection.

For a short time in 1917, number 17, among others, served as a WB&A passenger trailer before being rebuilt as a freight motor. Mr. A. S. Osbelt, Master Mechanic, is in the foreground. Author's collection.

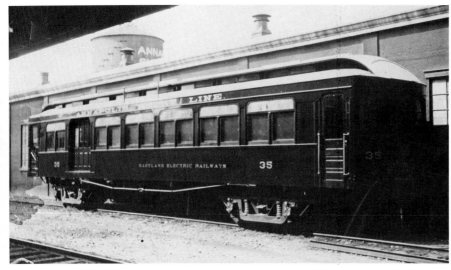

Annapolis Short Line 35 as a trailer at Bladen Street, Annapolis, July 23, 1908. LeRoy O. King, Sr. photograph.

601, above, which was rebuilt in the Short Line shops from number 31 in 1914, had extra wide cargo doors, rounded at the top. Number 602, below, which was rebuilt from number 15 in the WB&A Shops in 1917, has standard width freight doors similar to all of the freight motors in the 10-17 series. 601, George Votava photograph; 602, Author's collection.

Number 17, typical of the class, at the yard at 16th and Benning Road, N. E. M. D. McCarter collection.

Number 12, the only one of the 10-17 group to have an arch roof, at Baltimore, September 6, 1934. King collection.

train of open platform trailers behind number 12 thundering down Scott Street, with white flags fluttering, as she made a run for the incline. Or, of a summer's evening, the plaintive notes of an air whistle, a great amber headlamp, and the smell of smoking brakes as "The Night Merchandise" entered the yards at White House Station. To be sure—'twas a generation fortunate beyond its comprehension!

In addition to the freight motors already mentioned, the last one acquired was number 18, in point of gross tonnage and maximum tractive rating, the largest. It was originally one of three fifty-six foot passenger/baggage types built by the Jewett Car Company for the first electrification of the Annapolis Short Line. Electrical equipment was supplied by Westinghouse and the trucks by the American Locomotive Company. As delivered in 1909, each car had a pantograph and two trolleys (which were never used). In this configuration the three Jewett cars operated less than five years, when they were replaced by twelve new steel cars that had been ordered for the conversion to a 1200 volt DC system which was inaugurated on January 4, 1914. Until that time, all freight schedules had been hauled by steam

Number 18 at Annapolis, September 26, 1941. It was essentially unchanged after its transfer to the Baltimore & Annapolis. George Krambles collection.

locomotives, two of which were kept as standby engines for another six years.

In March 1914, Jewett car number 37 was rebuilt as the Short Line's first and only electric locomotive, number 300. Initially, its performance was rather sporadic as a result of the motors overheating. Upon recommendation of engineers called in from Westinghouse, there were horizontal ducts installed at floor level with a blower (a full-size traction motor) which directed forced draft into four Type 562 motors of 145 HP rating that were geared at a rather high ratio of 3.53:1. A secondary floor covered a spread of steel rails within the car to increase weight for better traction. At the scales it weighed in at 119,000 pounds, or 59 ½ tons. Although number 300 was capable of handling standard railroad passenger trains for special

events at the Naval Academy, there were times when these assignments were assisted by the company's steam engines.

With the merger of 1921, number 300 from the Short Line became number 18 of the WB&A. The pantograph was replaced by two trolleys, and solid steel sheathing was installed over the pilots to serve as snow plows on each end.

Upon the abandonment of the WB&A in 1935, number 18 was the only freight motor retained by the newly-formed Baltimore & Annapolis Railroad, where it continued until the end of electric operations on February 5, 1950. Through forty odd years of service, mostly as a utilitarian work motor, the clerestory transoms and beautifully arched end windows would remain as reminders of its more elegant features when new.

This photograph, taken July, 23, 1908, is the best one extant of the original Limited cars. To some, they were the handsomest interurbans of all. LeRoy O. King, Sr. photograph.

THE NILES CARS

Much has been written about the *classic interurban*. Depending upon the locality, travel to the big city was at times the high-speed mainliner, serving meals enroute; or it might have been that meandering local that collected milk cans and mail. The car itself was often a case of the old coach builder's craft done in ornate woodwork, cast iron, and heavy brass; or it might have been that streamlined version of the welder's work fashioned of lightweight aluminum. Why, even the exact definition of an "interurban" is ofttimes apt of argument.

But whether such diverse views stem from one's memories of certain operating practices; from one's notion of stylish paint or appearance; or merely from separate vantage points on the scale of years, the common heritage whence they came has produced a reasonable prototype not unlike the accepted standard of a Mississippi stern-wheeler, the covered wagon, or the steam locomotive.

Whether its nameplate was Niles, Jewett, Cincinnati, St. Louis, or Brill, this interurban car offered a commodious interior of high-back seats covered in leather or plush, which all seemed the more elegant under prismatic colors refracted from the fancy clerestory transoms, or the Gothic arched window sash of stained glass. Sometimes there was a baggage compartment at one end, and the big headlight and pointed

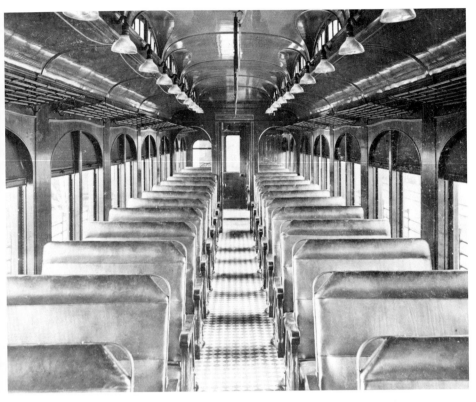

The first cars had an attractive interior of inlaid mahogany and leather seats. There were clerestory transoms of stained glass on either side of the full Empire ceiling as well as stained glass in the upper curved portion of the side windows. They afforded an atmosphere of elegance unequaled at the time. Herbert H. Harwood collection.

pilots on both ends were reminders of its recent forerunner: the steam engine.

The first cars for The WB&A were built by the Niles Car & Manufacturing Company. And because plans had then envisioned fast through service in competition with the other railroads, the new cars were to be comparable to standard coaches of the mainline steam roads. Thus, the concept of smaller cars in trains was overruled in favor of a single large car. A single car would obviate the problem of radial couplers for the twists and turns through city streets; the longer wheelbase of bigger trucks would afford a smoother ride at high speed; and the larger car body provided room for the additional equipment required by the AC system. The finished car was indeed large: measuring sixty-two feet overall, mounted on heavy-duty Baldwin trucks which, with four 125 HP traction motors (weighing 5800 pounds each), brought the total car to more than fifty-nine tons.

From the viewpoint of passenger comfort, the seat spacing was unusually liberal, with wide cushions, high backs, and arm rests. Interior finish was of hand-rubbed mahogany with pilas-

ter panels bordered in a neat inlay of contrasting wood. The baggage racks were of oxidized bronze trim as were the brackets for individual reading lamps. The ceiling was the vaulted full Empire style finished in pale green with a chain pattern in gold leaf. The floors were covered with an attractive pattern of inlaid linoleum. Even the vestibules were heated. "The Electric Pullmans" became a byword of the early publicity; as well it might have in a day when gracious affluence was its own excuse, and the expression of it made each ride "An Affair to Remember."

The builder's contract had specified twenty-five cars, including nineteen of the big high-speed Limiteds: four combination passenger/baggage types designed for the local schedules; and two box car type freight motors which would serve as locomotives for interline freight and as work cars. The local cars were of slightly smaller dimensions and were fitted with only two motors geared for lower speed. In October 1907, the cars began arriving at the company's shops where electrical equipment was installed by technicians from General Electric. The complete system was opened to

Number 23 when it was new. Note the complex insulators at the trolley bases and trolley hooks. King collection.

Motorman's compartment of one of the original local cars. King collection.

the public on April 3, 1908.

On rare occasions, a two-car consist might be scheduled. But considering the tortuous curves through the streets of Baltimore, it would leave as separate sections as far as Scott Street where the train was then coupled for the interurban run.

But experimental technology in alternating current, as applied to traction motors, was beset with numerous problems*. While the Limiteds were very fast on open track, there was a tendency of the motors to overheat, a problem further aggravated by the high torque demands of frequent stops on city streets. Nor were these troubles limited only to the cars, whose operations often induced heavy line surges, causing damage at the substations. The need for constant maintenance and excessive power demands would soon demonstrate weaknesses of the system as a whole.

The decision to convert to a 1200 volt DC system would entail an onerous list of additional costs, among them:

Cleveland Construction Co., for design and construction and (eventually) two additional substations
Aluminum Company of America, for new transmission lines
General Electric Company, to equip substations and cars

---

* see Chapter 15: The Electrical System

Combination car 67 at Washington in 1933. William Lichtenstern photograph.

Washington Railway & Electric Company, for rebuilding the tracks in Washington
Niles Car & Manufacturing Co., to provide new cars.

At first there were to be 28 cars, comprising one freight motor (number 3); 17 straight passenger types (40-56); and 10 combination passenger/baggage cars (67-76) ordered in 1909. In exterior appearance, the new cars embodied the same attractive features carried over from the first series, and except for somewhat smaller dimensions and a reduced rating of their top speed, offered the same appeal from the passenger's viewpoint.

Eighteen of the original Limited cars were returned to the builder for credit against the new order which, again, was negotiated by the Baltimore Terminal Company. But its affiliate (the WB&A Company) being then in receivership, had required that each delivery be covered by a separate draft with bill of lading to be paid on the spot. This process, as well as coordinating the supply of parts for trucks and equipment, had so slowed the arrival of new cars that only twenty of them were ready by January 14, 1910, barely 30 days from the deadline when all phases, including testing for the changeover, would take effect. But compromise prevailed, and twenty-eight cars were available for the new operation which began on February 15, 1910.

Experience under the new system was encouraging, and before long the monthly performance averages were tabulated to reflect significant improvement in every aspect of operations. In power costs alone, comparisons indicated a saving of approximately 40 percent in the company's monthly bill. Not least of those to applaud the new results were the engineering staff at General Electric, who published several detailed reviews of their work.

Comfortable interior of parlor car 100. John B. Yeabower photograph

Parlor car 100 at Naval Academy Junction in 1934. For a view of the other side of this car, see page 42. George E. Votava photograph.

The freight motors (1&2) and three of the original combines (20-22-23) were also refitted with new motors. Because the smaller cars would now operate in trains, more would be needed. In October, 1910, a second order was placed for ten additional cars (57-65 and 100), bringing the total to forty-three cars equipped for the new service.

On April 18, 1911, President Taft traveled to Annapolis for a ceremony at St. John's College. It was the first trip of the company's newest car. Shortly thereafter, a bit of' bombast appeared in a local advertisement, that read:

"Those fastidious persons who are a bit more exacting in their demands than the average sort of traveler will find that their every whim can be gratified by 'The Electric Line'. With this in mind the company has added to their abundance of excellent passenger equipment a most luxurious and completely furnished private car for the use of their patrons on special occasions"

This, of course, referred to the parlor car. Number 100 was easily recognized by its exceptionally large side windows, each surmounted by an upper sash of Gothic design that extended in seven graceful arches, each glazed with cathedral glass mounted in zinc frames. The interior furnishings included twenty-six wicker arm chairs, with green window drapes and matching carpet. A lavatory, fitted with all amenities including running water, occupied the length of two standard windows. Usually carrying white markers, any appearance of the majestic parlor car was heralded as a special event. The Conductor selected to take out car 100 was even required to keep a new uniform always in reserve.

Over the years, newer and rebuilt cars would be added; however, time would prove the Niles series to be the mainstay under all conditions. On special occasions such as crowds attending the Democratic National Convention of 1912; presidential inaugurations; or wartime parades in Washington, some trains clocked a daily average of over 600 miles, without a single failure.

But scars on their safety record were unfortunately as serious as they were fortunately few. Back in June, 1908, two of the original Niles cars had been demolished in a head-on collision. In January, 1922, a fire completely destroyed car 63. On March 27, 1923, a dramatic fire at the Junction had enveloped car 64 until the body was burned right down to the frame. But the age of stern ingenuity and grass roots challenge was then slightly different from a later generation where everything is simply returned to the factory. Number 64 would be rebuilt! From the blacksmith to the upholsterer, from the electrician to the painter, this building of a completely new car was a tribute to shop men in the most revered sense of the word. Fourteen months later, a new 64 emerged as a steel arch-roof type patterned after the later Cincinnati series. This incident would always distinguish 64 as something of an oddity; and, because of its more durable construction, it was to survive (on the B&A Railroad) for many years beyond the abandonment.

At the end of the line, the Niles cars were assigned to the ironmongers.. Although the modern idea of many another interurban, meanwhile, had evolved as something that was a lightweight single unit one-man operation, the Niles cars had continued in regular service essentially unchanged. In all that time (with but one exception) they were neither remodeled, nor renumbered, nor sold to any other owners.

So, while The Interurban Legend may, indeed, be differently portrayed according to its separate observers, yet a certain consensus might still prevail that if ever THE CARS FROM NILES typified a *classic interurban*—they were these!

Above: Car 54, one of the original DC cars, in Baltimore, October 29, 1934. M. D. McCarte
collection. **Below**: Car 51 at Baltimore on March 3, 1935. This view shows the opposite side of
car of the same series as 54 above. R. D. Horton photograph, George Krambles collection.

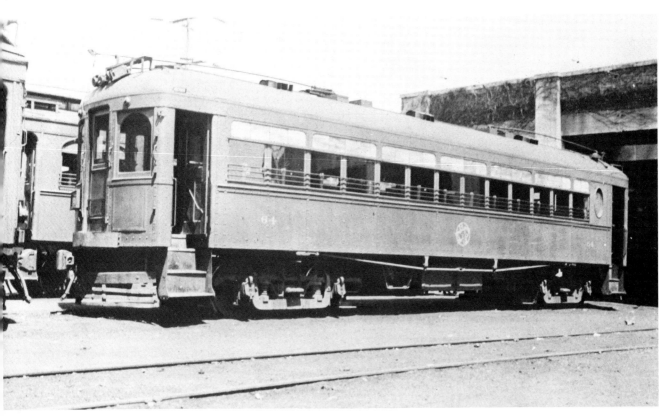

After a fire in 1923, car 64 was rebuilt in the WB&A shops to resemble the newer Cincinnati cars. Author's collection.

Number 77, shown at Naval Academy Junction August 18, 1935, was one of the original cars retained after the DC conversion. James P. Shuman photograph.

Eight of the original Niles cars were sold to the Rock Island Southern in Illinois. Number 300 is shown here on the Westinghouse Interworks Railway at East Pittsburgh, Pa. George Krambles collection.

The Bamberger Railroad of Utah acquired three of the original WB&A Niles cars. Number 450 is shown here, derelict, in 1937, at North Salt Lake. William C. Janssen photograph.

Oregon Electric trailer 109, in storage, was one of four ex WB&A cars. No explanation has been discovered for the deliberate black stripe on the photograph at the letterboard. King collection.

Union Traction of Indiana car number 280, Mt. Summit, in a photo copied from the November 1919 issue of the company magazine "Safety". Though rebuilt to a single end car by the Union Traction, the appearance of the car body suggests that it was one of the original WB&A cars. The same suggestion fits UT of I number 279. However, no proof has been found. George Krambles collection.

Car 39 at Naval Academy Junction about 1934. King collection.

THE CINCINNATI CARS

In 1913, when the mixed concept of wooden railroad cars and those built of steel still overlapped, the newer notion found favor for convincing reasons of safety; so it was not surprising that the Company had ordered its first all-steel passenger cars at a time when new freight motors of wooden construction (numbers 8 and 9) were still on order.

That December, the Company had received proposals for three combination passenger/baggage steel cars to be built according to specifications 807-A prepared by the Cincinnati Car Company. Except for the simplified arch roof and a slightly longer baggage compartment, their overall dimensions closely followed those of the previous Niles cars. Somewhat unusual for that day, however, was the welded side sheathing which presented a smooth exterior devoid of rivets. The interiors were handsomely finished in oil-rubbed mahogany woodwork, with floors of inlaid rubber tile, and reversible seats upholstered in dark green leather.

The new car bodies were delivered to Naval Academy Junction where the brake and electrical equipment was installed in the Company shops. Each car carried four trolley poles. Unlike the Washington streetcars, whose dual trolleys were mounted side by side on a swivel base, the negative trolley base in the case of the interurban cars, was placed off center with a pole that was 3 feet shorter than the main trolley.

Two cars had Baldwin 78-25AA trucks, and the third one had 78-25A trucks. All three cars were equipped with 4 GE 205 motors and multiple-unit type M controls. At a completed cost of $11,459 each, the new cars entered service in June, 1914, as combination cars 80, 81, and 82.

1914 marked the opening of Prince George's Race Track at Bowie Road, and among the novel assignments for any one of the new combines was an extra run known as the "money car". This trip was always the last car to leave Bowie, and with total proceeds from the day's betting, required an

Number 82, shown here in 1935, was the only Cincinnati car with this type of Baldwin 78-25A trucks. George Krambles collection.

Chicago Aurora & Elgin 702, ex WB&A 82 on a CERA fan trip August 6, 1939.. Note the narrower front platform. LaMar M. Kelley photograph, King collection.

augmented crew of the Road Superintendent or the Master Mechanic, in addition to the cashiers and an armed escort.

The following year, a second order was placed with the Cincinnati Car Company for ten straight passenger car bodies of similar design, which were intended for use as control trailers. However, in April, the plans were amended to specify only five cars to be fully equipped as passenger motors numbered 35 through 39. Like those of the previous order, they embodied the attractive flat-arch upper window sash which was to become a hallmark of the Cincinnati builders. This second group, though, were of riveted steel construction more typical of the builders' methods of that period.

In 1937 and early 1938, the eight Cincinnati cars were sold in separate increments to the Chicago Aurora & Elgin Railroad. After considerable modification in the shops at Wheaton, Illinois, they entered service as control trailers numbers 600-604 and 700-702. In their new appearance, most notable was the loss of the stained glass window sash and the conversion of the baggage compartments for added seating. The platforms were tapered for greater clearance at the elevated stations. Under the heavy demands of wartime traffic, complete trains of Aurora & Elgin cars were lent, on occasion, to the Chicago North Shore Line, at which times the former WB&A cars could be found as far away as Milwaukee.

For another twenty years, the Cincinnati cars served Chicago's western suburbs along "The Great Third Rail" until 1957, when it too surrendered to the ways of change.

THE CARS FROM HAZLETON

In 1902 the J. G. Brill Company built six interurban cars for the Keystone Improvement Company. Although delivered in April, the new cars were held over a year awaiting completion of the Wilkes-Barre & Hazleton Railway. They were wooden combination car bodies mounted on the builder's type 27-E-2 trucks equipped with third rail shoes and General Electric type 66-B motors. Because of heavy grades along the Nescopeck Valley, each car had four separate braking devices, which included Westinghouse automatic air and magnetic appliances, each supplemented by hand brakes,

Although designed for double-end operations, loading steps were provided on just one side of each vestibule, so that the motorman's cab had only a side window in place of a door. The car interiors were finished in solid mahogany inlaid with contrasting marquetry. Upper window sash were glazed in etched glass of decorative patterns. Ceiling lights were augmented by oil lamps mounted in brackets on either bulkhead.

After fourteen years the original cars were replaced by newer all-steel equipment; and in May, 1917, were advertised for sale. Almost at once, one car was acquired by the Kankakee & Urbana Traction Company, where it continued in service essentially unchanged. Next year the remaining five were acquired by the Washington Baltimore & Annapolis Electric Railroad at a cost of $4,007 each. But purchase of the cars and trucks was a relatively modest outlay compared to the installation of new Westinghouse motors and controls at a cost of $10,704 per set, which, with shipping and labor, came to a total investment of $98,336 for the five cars fully equipped.

At the company shops, extensive body work included removal of all side accessories, which still left the Hazleton cars the widest of any on the system,

On each blind side (or cab corner), the motorman's side window was remodeled into a door; while the passenger smoking compartment was extended by two windows on either side which increased the total seating capacity from 38 to 43. At the same time, the original seats of rattan were reupholstered in leather; while the car exteriors were painted in the standard dark green, striped

As originally built, electric lighting was supplemented by oil lamps mounted on brackets on either bulkhead. When rebuilt by the WB&A, the baggage section, shown here, was converted to passenger use. Author's collection.

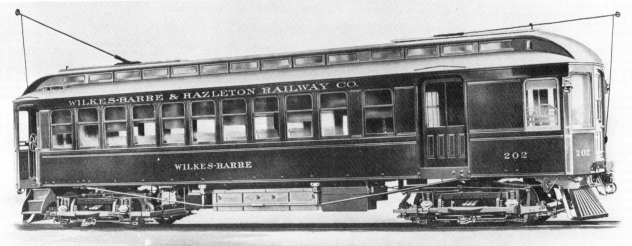

One of the new cars built for the Wilkes Barre & Hazleton Railway as completed by the J. G. Brill Company in April, 1902. Note the third rail shoes and the dual hand brake wheels at each side of the front platform.. Top, George Krambles collection, bottom, King collection.

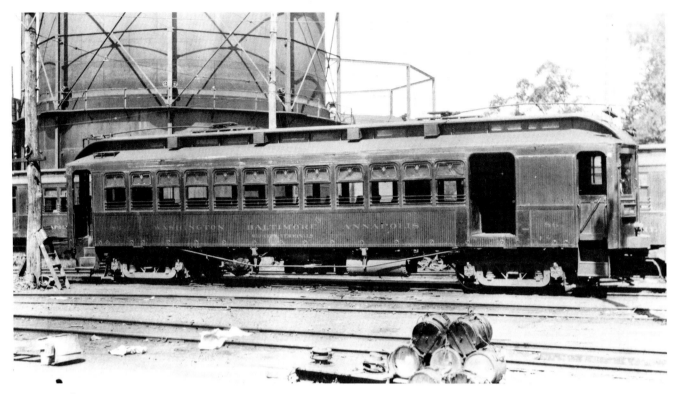

Number 86 at Bladen Street, Annapolis in the mid-twenties. Note the American Locomotive Company trucks which came from one of the freight motors. King collection

in gold, and numbered as cars 83 through 87.

In time, at least three of this series were mounted on the heavier American Locomotive type B-380 trucks which had been exchanged with the former Short Line cars. With an identical gear ratio and all new electrical equipment, which had increased their total weight by some two tons, the Hazleton cars were equal in performance to the freight motors. In this category, they frequently served interchangeably with the so-called locomotives in hauling the troop trains to and from Camp Meade.

Following the merger of 1921, various changes were required to adapt the former Short Line cars for joint operations. Pending the remodeling of those cars, the Hazleton series was the mainstay of service on the Annapolis North Shore Division. In fact, for another eight years, the 83 - 87 Hazleton cars were to handle all trailer operations for rush-hour schedules.

In 1934, five complete sets of Westinghouse equipment from these cars, among others, were reinstalled in the newer 200 series; but, unlike their previous service geared for slower train operation with frequent stops, a revised gear reduction (2.08:1) would demonstrate these motors as the fastest and most versatile* of the entire system.

_____

* Requirements for quick acceleration of heavy trains on city streets, in combination with the fastest schedules imposed on the main line, were to pose a severe test of these motors.

Number 86 at Naval Academy Junction in May, 1934. George E. Votava photograph.

Brill 27 E 2 truck built for the Wilkes Barre & Hazleton cars. The wooden beam between the journals was for support of the third rail shoe. Author's collection.

THE ST. LOUIS CARS

The necessities of wartime have often produced innovations, substitutes, or other aberrant practices which have survived long after the crisis that caused them. In the case of transportation, the Emergency Maritime Fleet or the excise tax on rail travel were relics that lasted years beyond the armistice. In the case of the Electric Line, the wartime cars from St. Louis turned out to be rather durable assets, two of which were to last another thirty years.

During the summer of 1918, the WB&A Company set out in search of more equipment to alleviate a shortage of passenger motor cars for use with their newly-acquired trailers from Long Island. Some measure of the urgency to find additional cars is revealed in the sequence of this project where complete sets of Westinghouse motors and brake equipment had been ordered even before they had confirmed a source of car bodies and trucks. At the St. Louis Car Company, they located five partially completed interurban car bodies which had been in storage for nearly ten years. In the design of their founding days, these were heavy wooden cars of timber-beam truss-rod construction, fifty-seven feet over buffers.

The original builder's order, back in 1908, had specified eight of these cars for the St. Louis Monte Sano & Southern Railroad, but was cancelled shortly

thereafter. For years the skeletal cars sat around the builder's yards until the exigencies of wartime produced a buyer. Early in 1916, they were consigned to the Imperial Bank of Canada under a car trust agreement for the newly-electrified London & Port Stanley Railway. However, only three cars were actually delivered, May 22, 1916. Two years later, under a transfer agreement (Contract 1185 dated September 25, 1918), the remaining five were taken (as they were) for the WB&A Electric Railroad.

Upon arrival at Naval Academy Junction, these units presented a somewhat austere sight, painted only in dull grey primer, without windows, without trucks, and devoid of all accessories requisite to the normal notion of an operating car. An expenditure averaging $2840 per car was first authorized to finish the bodies, in addition to the cost of new Westinghouse 557-W-8 motors which were mounted in Baldwin type 8435-AA trucks, The braking and control equipment would conform to a standard plan used on some twenty different cars that were rebuilt by the Company between 1917 and 1921.

The body work involved a large sliding door in the baggage compartment which served as both passenger and cargo entrance for that end. Fully equipped, the new cars were perhaps as

Eight car bodies were stored at the plant of the St. Louis Car Co. from 1908 to 1916. Three were then sold to the London (Ontario) & Port Stanley Railway and, in 1918, the remaining five were acquired by the WB&A. King collection.

92 at Baltimore, November 30. 1933. James P. Shuman photograph.

much the pride of WB&A Shops as they were products of the St. Louis Car Company, which had started the woodwork ten years before. In a shining new livery of dark green, striped and lettered in gold leaf, they were assigned numbers 88 through 92, and entered service in June 1919.

For train operation with all other WB&A Cars, the St. Louis combines were equipped with regular Janney MCB couplers until 1929. The new Brill trailers which arrived that summer, came with a much larger type of Tomlinson Automatic Tightlock coupler, whereupon the 88-92 series were similarly equipped. At the same time, new leather seats were installed which, together with the modern style couplers and other improvements, represented an outlay of some $16,000. In this decision the company had chosen to upgrade their St. Louis cars in preference to the older Hazleton cars which theretofore had been the principal motive power for trailer operations. In 1934, the motors and controls were removed from cars 89-90; two (among others) whose electrical equipment was then installed in the 200 series steel cars.

When the railroad was sold in 1935, one item of the vendue specified that the new Baltimore & Annapolis Railroad was to retain the fifteen cars that had originally belonged to the former Maryland Electric Railways Company. This included the three Jewett Cars which had since been renumbered as 18, 106, and 107; but since the latter two had been stripped of their electrical equipment, an agreement was reached whereby they would be replaced by two serviceable cars (91-92). In that service, number 92 survived another fifteen years to the end of electric operations on the Baltimore & Annapolis Railroad.

In the lengthening shadow of fifty-five years, the identity and inventory of cars so long gone is never fully finished, nor is that quest for one more detail of the roster ever quite ended. Among the 236 cars which comprised the Company's final listing, the obscure origin of these five (88-92), more than any others, has posed a poser whose answer at times seemed farther away than miles or years. Indeed, the persistent curiosity aroused by such a challenge has lent a certain added luster to the completion of this brief account of the CARS FOR MONTE SANO.

Car 89 at Bladen Street, Annapolis, May 30, 1934. George Votava photograph.

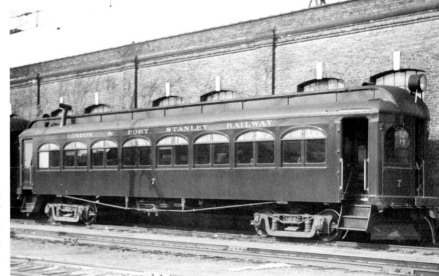

London & Port Stanley number 7. Note that L&PS narrowed the wide front door of the original carbody by enlarging the corner post. Compare with photograph above. See also illustration on page 206. George Krambles collection.

WB&A 89 as a trailer at Bladen Street, Annapolis in April, 1935. 89 was one of two of the St. Louis cars which lost motors and electrical equipment to motorize the 200 series trailers. Alfred E. Seibel photograph.

THE WASON CARS

The years immediately preceding World War I might be called the age of the center-entrance car. A new trend in car design would break with the age-old notion that a car's platforms were not integral to the body proper. Early engineers had often described the size of a "box" car measured only between bulkheads, placing the coachman or driver someplace outside, fully exposed to wind and rain. Indeed the primitive stagecoach, the urban hansom, even the first limousines had all envisioned the chauffeur perched behind, above, or out front, quite apart from the vehicle's interior. In 1897, a Baltimore motorman froze to death at the controls of his open-front car, which led to a public outcry for cars to have a windshield. In time the driver's position became part of the car, and the motorman came in from the cold.

To incorporate the whole car as a single entity had several advantages. A center vestibule required only half the space of two end platforms and therefore increased the seating capacity. A center well in the floor line could be designed closer to the ground, thereby reducing the number of steps, and thus lessen the possibility for accidents. Moreover, the distinct halves either side of the entrance, would isolate the malodorous smoking section from that occupied by ladies. And, as everyone knows, the conductor conducts from a middle point of van-

tage. Additionally, the ends of a center door car, unencumbered by stairwells, enabled a greater spacing between truck centers, thereby reducing the overhang on sharp curves. Of course, such a car did not lend itself to one-man operation, but that was an idea still in the future.

So, as the electric car evolved from wood to steel, from a lantern-roof to an arch-roof, and later from PCC to LRV, it was at this juncture of the center-entrance vogue, that Maryland Electric Railways installed a new 1200 volt electrical system with a new set of cars.

During July of 1913, they ordered twelve all-steel center-door combination cars to be built by the Wason Manufacturing Company of Springfield, Massachusetts, with Brill MCB 2X trucks and Westinghouse electrical equipment. Brill order 19075 for the trucks was cross referenced to Wason order 14250 for the completed cars which were delivered that December. They entered service on January 4, 1914, as Short Line numbers 50 through 61. Local news accounts were lavish in their praise of the new cars, describing them as a radical departure from conventional cars and an advance in safety, comfort, and convenience.

With pardonable oversight, the newspapers of course had failed to mention that little bench at the front window where every boy scrambled for a place beside the motorman's cab; or the motorman's

The carbody of a Wason car takes shape. This 1913 photograph was taken at the builder's Springfield, Massachusetts plant. For other pictures of this series, before rebuilding, see Chapter 9. King collection.

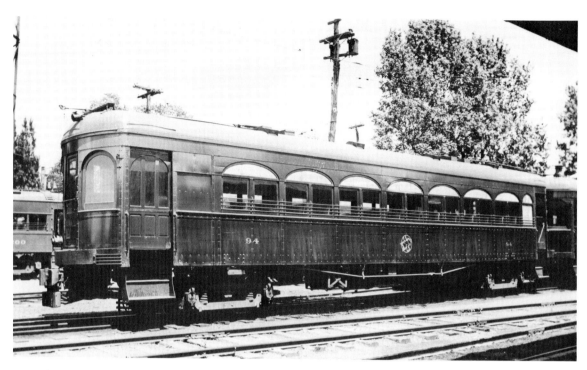

Number 93, taken in April, 1935, and number 94, taken in May, 1934, are shown here together to point out the asymmetric door arrangement of the baggage ends when viewed from different sides. Both photographs at Annapolis by George E. Votava.

adjustable seat that more nearly resembled a motorcycle saddle; or, next to the whistle cord, a valve which emitted a long hiss for the air-operated pantograph. Then in the smoker, for striking matches, there were knurled brass plates on every window post, and spittoons were on the floor, which was covered with a beautiful pattern of inlaid rubber tile. Beyond the conductor's position, the main compartment had rows of green plush seats, with a ceiling striped in gold, and bordered by lights fitted with scallop-edged shades of opalescent glass. Another minor distinction was that electro-pneumatic conductor's signal which activated a faint "beep-beep" indicator in place of the standard cord and bell signal. Trivia, you say? Well—yes. But then, a small boy's wide-eyed wonderment was made of things like these.

For seven years the Short Line cars provided a brisk competition for the South Shore schedules to Annapolis; until 1921 when they were acquired by the Washington Baltimore and Annapolis Electric Railroad as part of fourteen passenger cars included in the merger. In the new roster they became WB&A numbers 93-99 and 101-105. To make them compatible with operating features of their new route into Baltimore, the Wason cars were remodeled to include standard MCB couplers; the MU connections mounted beside the couplers were replaced by jumper receptacles on the roof; and the pantographs were replaced by trolleys. Alteration of the car bodies (to eliminate the center doors) followed in two distinct phases that would last another three years. It can only be assumed that

part of the work was prolonged because they were meanwhile required in service. Owing to this successive conversion, an asymmetric door arrangement resulted that was always apparent when the baggage end was compared from opposite sides.

In 1929 all cars of the North Shore Division were equipped with automatic tightlock couplers at a cost averaging some $2,000 per car. Perhaps the biggest couplers ever seen on an interurban car, each of these assemblies carried a large fiber block of electrical contacts and self-aligning air-line connections. By including air and electrical features as part of the coupler, a heavier draft rigging was required to support a massive pin and socket casting for the lock designed to eliminate lost motion (friction) between electrical faces of the coupling. Whereas lightweight radial couplers had originally been adopted to reduce weight, the heavy tightlock devices had now added some 2400 pounds per pair which, with new 90 HP motors, increased the car's overall weight to 88,700 pounds, or about 4.5 tons heavier than when new.

The car trust agreement that had financed the rolling stock inherited from the Maryland Electric Railways was retired in 1931. The 90 series cars were thus among the newer equipment free of debt; an important consideration four years later when disposition of the Company's assets enabled the bondholders to repurchase them under a special option. In service of the Baltimore & Annapolis Railroad, the Wason cars were to run for another fifteen years.

Unlike all previous cars which had been assembled in the company's shops, the articulateds were delivered as complete units. Here their innovative features are being explained by the builder's representative in March , 1927. Author's collection

THE ARTICULATED CARS

The concept of an articulated railroad car was not new. Around the turn of the century, Great Britain had employed a type of jointed railway coach in mainline service. But it was a far cry from their operation over gentle curves of solidly-built roadbed to the sharp turns and, too often, decrepit state of city streetcar tracks. Hence, later adaptations of a hinged, or jointed, car body to more severe operating conditions were to prove more ingenious than the original design.

Nearly every system of city fare collection required that people be allowed to pass freely from one car body to the other, and that this be accomplished safely with a minimum of displacement at the point of connection. And from variations on this theme, there followed an accordion bellows-type gangway between car sections as found in the early types of Milwaukee; the cylinder, or drum vestibule, as was seen in the streetcars of Baltimore, Cleveland, and Detroit; and later the hinged diaphragm, a feature of the Chicago North Shore *Electroliners*. In any consideration of articulated

cars the greatest advantage was economy—of less equipment per car, reduction in weight, maintenance, wear and tear on track, power consumed, and, finally, fewer trainmen.

At first, this idea of articulated units in streetcar service had been accepted somewhat tentatively; and, with few exceptions, city traction companies had ventured their experiments with home-made units remodeled from older cars. But compared to many streetcar lines where a larger high-capacity articulated car was justified only during periods of peak traffic, it was now suggested that high-speed interurban schedules which regularly required two-car trains in all-day service presented the ideal opportunity for the savings claimed with this type of unit.

In the probative technology of that day, such claims were as yet largely theoretical when the WB&A's Board of Directors met on April 21, 1925 to consider proposals from the General Electric Company, together with a set of plans from the Cincinnati Car Company, listing data on design, and cost of a two-section articulated interurban car. The meeting ended with an authorization for the President to proceed with negotiations for the purchase of ten units. For the next year, meetings and correspondence with the Cincinnati engineers discussed modifications to their blueprints which had specified:

"The combination of two adjacent cars and a supporting truck, common to both cars and to which they are articulated, with an enclosed vestibule unit adapted to ride on the adjacent platforms of both cars, though supported on said truck through the intermediary of said platforms, the vestibule being structurally independent of the cars"

This unique design was the invention of Thomas Elliott whose US Patent number 1,499,510 (July 1, 1924) had been assigned to the Cincinnati Car Company.

On July 21, 1926, the WB&A Board met again to hear the President's report, though for reasons not explained, he now recommended that the new cars be built by the J. G. Brill Company. The project was unanimously approved, and the order was placed the same day. It is, however, of note that the builder's Order 22449 for the twenty car bodies and their end trucks was entered separate from the Orders 22450-52 which specified the center trucks, the vestibule units, and connecting assemblies to be constructed according to patent rights leased from the Cincinnati Car Company. Although work started at once, the patent agreement was not confirmed in writing until December 24, 1926. These plans included a number of interesting features.

At the facing ends of each car body, center sills of the steel underframe were bolted to a substantial buffer casting having a vertical nose or stud, hemispherical in shape, and cored out to form a chamber of oil and waste packing. These adjacent ends were carried on the center truck in separate bearing plates positioned one in advance of the other, being thus capable of rocking fore or aft to compensate for vertical breaks in grade, or laterally to accommodate possible rolling movement when passing over uneven track. Any tendency to sway

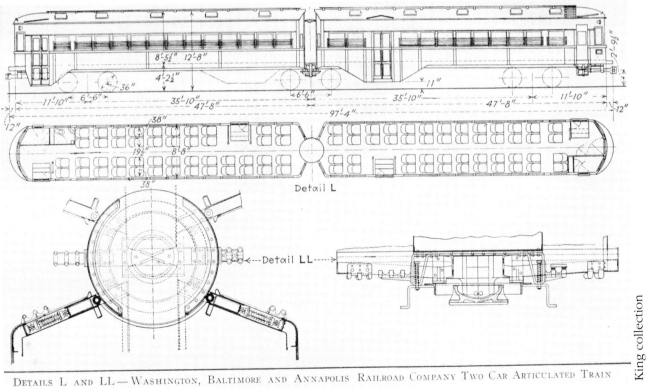

Detail L

Detail LL

King collection

DETAILS L AND LL — WASHINGTON, BALTIMORE AND ANNAPOLIS RAILROAD COMPANY TWO CAR ARTICULATED TRAIN

This construction view shows relative widths of a twenty inch passageway through the forty inch (diameter) vestibule drum. The five openings at the top will channel the bus jumpers while the spring mechanisms on either side are to exert lateral force against full length rubber guards to insure a weathertight connection. Historical Society of Pennsylvania.

or roll on curves was dampened by a large circular bearing plate mounted atop the truck bolster. It served mainly to support the vestibule drum and to resist side motion, but did not share the weight of either car body. Unlike articulated units which rotate about a common center, this arrangement of twin center plates posed a slight disadvantage in that the point of wear was not the true center of the truck. Though the plan did afford better access for lubrication and for disengaging the bodies when in the shop.

The center vestibule consisted of a cylinder forty inches in diameter, which was rigidly secured to the truck in such a way as to allow each car body to rotate around the cylinder. The facing ends of each car body were angular, sufficient to accommodate a close apposition when negotiating a curve of forty-nine foot radius, while at the same time permitting a passageway (twenty inches wide) through the cylinder. These adjacent ends were fitted, top and bottom, with heavy spring-mounted guards which held long vertical rollers that engaged the outer surface of the drum to insure a weathertight coupling. All electrical connections were carried in jumpers mounted above the center drum, while air lines for the straight and automatic braking passed through special couplings on either side of the drum. To facilitate repairs to the center truck, there were latches which allowed for the entire vestibule unit to be readily disconnected from the truck

One of the several tests conducted at the Brill plant in September, 1926 to demonstrate vertical stress as well as radial range of this relatively new design of articulated car. Historical Society of Pennsylvania.

bolster; and couplings that enabled either car section to be quickly disengaged from the truck without interfering with the other. Although the cars were never operated as half units, the facing ends of each section were equipped with grab rails and lantern brackets for such a contingency.

To accommodate vertical stress, the center bearings as well as the vestibule drum arrangement were to allow for the opposite end of either car body to be raised for removal of a front or rear truck without causing binding in the center device. The accompanying photo shows tests being conducted at the Brill plant to demonstrate this vertical tolerance.

Fully equipped, the completed unit tipped the scales at fifty-eight and a third tons, or slightly less than the total weight first projected by the designers. Though more to the point, they had achieved a reduction of twenty-seven percent under the combined tonnage of two MU cars—one of the more convincing arguments for an articulated car. In analyzing the braking forces of this odd plan, pressure from a cylinder mounted under each body had to be distributed to two pairs of wheels on

the end truck, as against only one pair of the adjacent center truck. Nor was the weight exactly balanced between one end equipped with a lavatory and the opposite end which provided for a plow hanger and minor accessories for conduit operations. And because of the load variation between both motorized end trucks and the lighter-weight center truck, braking ratio for the heavier trucks was adjusted to exert some ninety-seven percent greater leverage than that for the middle truck, in order to equalize the application when slowing from high speed. Indeed, that smooth and comfortable starting and stopping was more of an attainment than any passenger realized.

Application for government concurrence in the use of this new type equipment was submitted July 16, 1926.*

---

* This proposal was treated as two separate cases before the Maryland Public Service Commission. Case 2502 subsequently approved as PSC Order 10452 dated July 20, 1926 covered actual design and safety of the cars themselves; while Case 2503 later approved as PSC Order 10470 dated August 3, 1926 discussed the financing of their purchase.

Attached to the car specifications there were alternate bills of material from both the Westinghouse and General Electric Companies. The Westinghouse equipment finally selected included:

Electrical :   Westinghouse Electric & Mfg. Co.

      Four WH 333-VV-8 Traction motors of 125 HP rating
      Two Master controllers, HL Type 15-D modified
      Two Trolleys. Type 20-A complete with 14-ft 6-in pole, harp and wheel
      Two Trolley rope insulators
      One Trolley-plow shoe changeover, Type 284-C4 modified
      Two Train-line receptacles, Type 460-A mounted on roof
      Train-line jumpers, Type 461-A

Air Brake: Westinghouse Traction Brake Co.

      Two 1200-volt Compressors, Type D-2-K complete with 8-inch suction strainers
      Two motorman's brake valves, Type M-24-C, with one handle
      Two 12-in x 12-in Brake cylinders, Type E
      Two Trombone air whistles

The J. G. Brill Company's Specifications 509-B, revised to June 28, 1926, were a part of their order entered July 21, 1926 which had promised completion within six months. The essential statistics included:

Overall length of two-car unit 97-ft 4-in
Extreme width 8-ft 11-in
Height, rail to top of roof 12-ft 8-in
Truck centers, each section 35-ft 10-in
Two end trucks ....Brill 27 MCB-2 6-ft 6-in wheelbase
The center truck ....Brill 27 MCB-3 7-ft wheelbase
Total weight of two-car unit ....116,770 lbs
Seats ....Hale & Kilburn Type 900 double rotating chairs
 Seating Capacity:

Smoking compartment	Section A		16	Genuine leather
Passenger "	" A		32	Gray frieze velour
Passenger "	" B		46	Gray frieze velour
Total			94	

As completed, all seats were upholstered in gray striped frieze velour, Chase pattern 188

In accordance with a lease agreement between the J. G. Brill Company and the Railroad dated July 26, 1926, the ten units were to be built for a contract price of $483,053; of which $123,053 was to be paid at time of delivery, with the balance secured by an assignment to the Fidelity-Philadelphia Trust Company, which issued 120 monthly lease warrants to run for ten years at six percent interest. Regular installments of $3,000 were payable on the 12th of each month under a formula wherein the agreed

Passenger entry on the right side of the front section. The small plate to the right of the door notes that Brill is the owner and lessor. Historical Society of Pennsylvania

price plus interest on the outstanding principal for the life of the trust, would have reached a total cost of well over a half million dollars.

The lease agreement further specified that each car would carry a cast nameplate on each side showing the lessor's name and a reference to the trust agreement. For identification, it stipulated that the cars were to be numbered 20 to 29 inclusive, painted Tuscan Red and lettered with the railroad company's standard monogram. However, as delivered they were, in fact, painted Forest Green and lettered with the company's full name, omitting the emblem.

Toward the end of February 1927, as the first unit passed its final testing, number 20 was posed outside the Philadelphia plant for one last builder's photo shortly before a B&O freight brought her to Clifford Junction.

It was Friday morning, March 11, 1927, and a distinguished party had gathered at the Washington terminal. There was the President of Cleveland Railways Company with most of his operating staff; from Baltimore came the General Manager and Master Mechanic of United Railways; from Pittsburgh, Mr. A. S. Wentworth, representing the Westinghouse Electric Company; the Utility Commissioners of Cleveland and Washington were there; as were the press; and ,of course, top officials of the WB&A as hosts for the occasion. As they waited along the station concourse, there was a moment of high anticipation as number 20, resplendent in highly varnished livery of green and gold, with that sibilant blast of her air gong, rounded the curve into Track 2. Mr. Samuel Sole of the J. G. Brill Company was on hand to point out such innovative features as the fully-enclosed low-slung stairwells and pneumatic door controls, the rotating bucket-style seats, the rich decor of polished mahogany contrasting with seats upholstered in gray striped frieze velour, and, of course, the mechanics of the articulated center coupling. The ride to Baltimore demonstrated all that was claimed as number 20, with minimum noise or vibration, was clocked at 63 miles per hour. Particularly impressive was the absence of surge or side-sway as passengers passed freely between the two sections. Next day, the usual assemblage of leading businessmen from each city, politicians and wives were also given a demonstration ride, but it would be several more weeks until at least six of the new units were tested and ready for regular schedules.

On another railroad at about this time, the "President Washington" came to Washington. Number 5300 was a magnificent Pacific-type locomotive, splendrous and regal in its glistening livery of olive green trimmed in maroon and gold. As first of the twenty new president series, the President Washington was soon to become a main attraction at "The Fair of the Iron Horse"; the star of "The Capitol Limited"; and something of a long tradition among B&O's finest and fastest. According to *The Evening Star* (March 31, 1927), the other star would appear the following Sunday for public inspection at the Eckington freight yards. It was announced in a little

A NEW ERA
in Luxurious
TRANSPORTATION

Travel in Comfort, at High Speed on the New Articulated Trains of the W. B. & A.

WASHINGTON, BALTIMORE & ANNAPOLIS
ELECTRIC RAILROAD COMPANY

Baltimore Terminal: HOWARD AND LOMBARD STS.
Washington Terminal: 12TH ST. AND NEW YORK AVE.

Five panels of an eight panel brochure issued by the WB&A describing the virtues of the new trains. Displayed half size. Author's collection

A NEW ERA
in Luxurious
TRANSPORTATION

WE ARE very proud of our big, new steel articulated cars, not because it cost a half million dollars to build them, but because in offering them to our passengers, we offer the utmost contribution to comfortable travel at high speed. We want you to be proud to be among the first to ride in them. Nothing like them has ever been used on any inter-city electric railroad in this country, and in the past few weeks railroad officials have come here from all over the United States to inspect and admire them.

You will notice many out-of-the-ordinary things about these cars. Almost everything about them

A NEW ERA IN TRANSPORTATION

is pleasantly different from all that you have been accustomed to in electric railway transportation.

For instance, you will notice the singular fact that each train is really only one car, mounted on three trucks, though quite as large as two ordinary cars mounted on four trucks. This is called "articulation" and though, at first, it may not seem as impressive to the passenger as some other things, it is really very important since it serves to make you vastly more comfortable.

If you think it over you will readily see what it means to be able to put two car bodies on three trucks instead of four. It means that the noise and vibration of one truck is entirely eliminated. But it means much more than that. It means that the two car bodies are rigidly supported at the middle and that side-sway is thereby "dampened", that is, reduced to almost nothing.

The cylindrical steel passage-way between the two sections of the car is called "the drum"—a remarkable invention which, no matter how steep the curve, how fast the motion, or how angry the weather outside, allows you to pass from one division to the other with complete safety, freedom and comfort.

And the seats! We dare say that never have you ever encountered in a railway car seats to which your body has yielded more readily and gratefully than it will to these. Between

A NEW ERA IN TRANSPORTATION

one seat and the next are 35 full inches—room and to spare for your knees and legs. Beneath each seat there are *two* sets of springs, a deep one in the base of the seat and one in the very cushion. The backs of the seats are curved no less and no more than enough to meet exactly the outline of your own back as it sinks against the cushion. The upholstery is *Frieze velour*. Probably it will not surprise you to be told that each of these seats cost $125 to build. Yet isn't that rather more than you would spend for a chair for your living room or library at home?

The windows are of *plate glass* and much wider than car windows usually are, affording abundant light for reading in daytime.

There is abundant light at night time, too, because one of the many soft shaded lights overhead has been nicely adjusted so that a glow falls without shadow or reflection across every seat.

How fast do these new cars go? Probably, because there is scarcely any vibration or swaying, you haven't been conscious of it; but the free-running speed of the cars is more than 60 miles an hour. And when we come to Naval Academy Junction (the only stop between Baltimore and Washington) observe how smoothly the car will come to the halt, and how quickly and with what little creaking and lunging it will get under way again.

There is more—very much more!—that we could tell you about these cars, but we shall take another time to tell it. Still, if anything else about the cars, mechanical or otherwise, has

A NEW ERA IN TRANSPORTATION

aroused your interest or curiosity, write to us, and we shall be glad to describe and explain it in full.

The new articulated express cars leave Baltimore and Washington every thirty minutes, on the hour and half hour.

All New Trains--Parlor Car Comforts

THE LAST WORD IN LUXURIOUS HIGH-SPEED TRANSPORTATION

Now, on the Washington-Baltimore Division of the W. B. & A., the First Articulated, All-steel Interurban Electric Trains in America—Every 30 Minutes on the Hour and Half-hour

SINK into one of the richly up-holstered chairs of the new W. B. & A. trains, open your book or paper or your favorite magazine and you are prepared for the quickest, the cleanest and the most comfortable trip you can make from downtown Washington to the heart of Baltimore—on the railroad that is electrified all the way.

At no increase in fare—the round trip is still $2.37*—the W. B. & A. now gives you the finest inter-city electric railroad trains in America; every train entirely new, de-signed and built for the W. B. & A., with the smooth riding comfort of "articulated" bodies, and the expensive appointments ordinarily found only in parlor cars.

What Articulation Means

From the outside, each of these new articu-lated trains looks like two long cars. Ac-tually, each train is one very long unit, con-sisting of two car bodies mounted on three trucks instead of four. This means that noise, vibration, and the tendency of trains to sway when in rapid motion, are reduced to an absolute minimum. It means, also, that you can walk from one car to another in complete safety, steadiness and comfort, with no doors to open and no drafty, dusty vestibules to lurch through.

Each Double Seat Cost $125

At such a price, of course, you have truly

"the comforts of home"—individual seats, arranged in pairs; tastefully finished in two-tone Frieze velours; deep springs in the base of every seat to absorb vibration; springs in the overstuffed cushions; easy backs—and room enough in front of you for the longest and weariest of legs.

There are wide, curtained windows of plate glass to give you abundant reading light by day, and shaded individual lights above each seat by night, thus giving you, day or night, freedom from glare or shadow.

Half the Train for Smokers

In each of these two-car trains, one car is for those who smoke and one for those who do not. And the smoking car is furnished with exactly the same luxurious appoint-ments as the other car.

Another feature, which applies to each car, is the electric heating system, encased in steel, running the full length on each side of every car, with a thermostat control that keeps the cars, throughout the winter, from being either cold or uncomfortably warm.

In summer, the swift movement of the trains and more than 30 broad windows and 20 ventilators in each train will keep you cool even on the most humid of days.

Speed, Smoothness, Safety

The new Westinghouse 500 horse-power motors give the trains a free rolling speed

of 60 miles an hour. So smooth is the accel-eration, however, and so steady and rigid are the articulated bodies, that you do not realize the rate of speed at which you are traveling.

The steel frame construction of the cars, and the Westinghouse double airbrake system, which operates on all twelve wheels at once—"twelve-wheel brakes" they are—give you the utmost in modern railroad safety.

The First in America

Naturally, we take some pride in the fact that the W. B. & A. is the first interurban electric railroad in America to give its pas-sengers the remarkable comforts and con-veniences of these high-speed, all-steel, articulated trains. It cost half a million dollars to build them and to provide them with these extraordinary facilities.

Now they are all in service—and every 30 minutes, on the hour and half hour, one of them leaves on an express schedule from Washington for Baltimore, and from Balti-more for Washington. We can truly say, therefore, to everyone who travels between these two cities—and particularly to those who, driving their automobiles, encounter parking troubles, traffic congestion and occasional breakdowns—that you can save both time and money—and ride in vastly greater comfort—by using these new trains of the W. B. & A.

The full running time from downtown Washington to downtown Baltimore on the W. B. & A. is only 85 minutes - - - the quickest, the most direct and the most economical way to make the trip. Street car lines at the Baltimore Terminal will take you or transfer you to any part of the city or suburbs. Taxicab stands maintained at terminals in both cities.

Ten, twenty and fifty trip tickets at still lower rates

Washington, Baltimore & Annapolis Electric Railroad Co.

Washington Terminal: 12th St. & New York Ave.   *Baltimore Terminal:* Howard and Lombard Sts.

One of several newspaper ads placed by the WB&A to promote their new and distinctive articulated cars. King collection

four inch squib on page twenty-eight.

As against a later age of electronic news report-ing that seems never to exhaust a capacity for endless minutiae about any and every sports event or political personality, the printed news accounts of truly important happenings were once treated with a casualness bordering on indifference. So a spokesman for the WB&A had determined that the arrival of their new cars was newswor-thy, and should be accorded the prominence it deserved. After all, these were the first articu-lated interurban cars anywhere, and among the first electric railway cars so designed as completely new units. *Electric Railway Jour-nal* commented editorially that: "Here is a specific example of the faith that large financial interests have in the future of the (traction) industry". Representing a half million uninflated dollars, it marked a turning point of some moment. In addition to a brochure which extolled the various improvements, a press release called them: "WB&A's Answer to Busses". Taking that a step further, *The Star* (March 12, 1927) even had it: "New Cars to Wage Bus War"; though whatever the bally-hoo, everyone agreed that their luxurious com-fort and speed was sure to restore a degree of prosperity—the interurban lines were making a comeback!

On June 20, 1928, barely a year after the new cars had entered service, number 22 was involved in an unusual accident at the trestle over Cabin Branch near Springman's curve. Running at high speed late at night, the southbound limited hit a stray horse, then jack-knifed in such a way that it landed with both ends facing in the same direction. The impact tore up several hundred feet of track and sev-ered a transmission line, causing Annapolis to be plunged into darkness temporarily. Num-ber 22 was eventually returned to service, but it was many months before specially-fabri-cated parts for the center coupling were obtained from the Brill Company.

Early in 1935, the main line schedules were greatly accelerated (36 minutes District Line to Baltimore Terminal) with the assignment of even faster cars of the 200-series; whereupon some of the articulated units were transferred to local service on the Annapolis South Shore Division.

The spacious interior of the articulated cars is well illustrated in this view. Historical Society of Pennsylvania

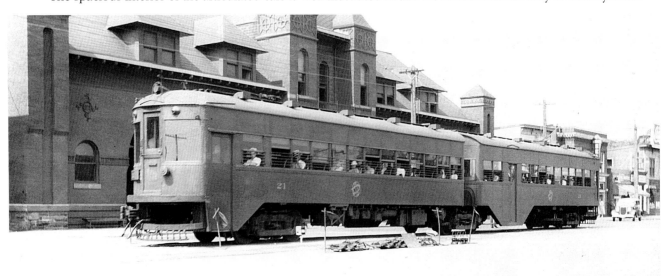

Number 21, bound for Baltimore, at the plow pit July 14, 1935. Capital Transit's Columbia barn is in the background. James P. Shuman photograph.

On June 20, 1928, number 22 hit a stray horse whose legs had become jammed in the trestle over Cabin Branch. The impact caused the articulated unit to jack-knife in such a way that it landed with both ends facing in the same direction. Author's collection.

When the railroad was sold on June 14, 1935, the ten twin-car trains were less than 58 percent paid for, there having been no payments toward the principal outstanding since date of the receivership. In the final accounting, numbers 20 - 29 were listed separately, subject to a lien of the J. G. Brill Company in respect of which, there was due the sum of $205,079 plus interest. While the other rolling stock was bid in by the Boston Iron & Metal Company, the articulated units, which were not auctioned, reverted to their owners through default on the equipment notes still outstanding. The cars were subsequently offered for sale by the United Iron & Metal Company, as agents for the owners, but were never sold.

As an aside, the United Iron & Metal Company's scrap yards were located along the north side of the Baltimore & Ohio's Mount Clare branch, extending from Catherine Street to Millington Avenue. There, the articulated cars were stored on four makeshift tracks improvised on the spot where the founding fathers of the Baltimore & Ohio Railroad had laid their cornerstone 108 years before. Thus, by an artful twist of semantics, might it not be said that the WB&A ended where the B&O began?

Much has been told and retold about these unusual cars, whose period of actual service (with possible allowance for the 300 series of the Illinois Terminal Railroad) was the shortest of any order of new cars ever made for an electric interurban. In the mere telling we have, perhaps, magnified their phenomenal speed, their luxurious comfort, and their unusual appearance. But withal, the legendary "articulateds" left an indelible mark in the annals of the WB&A. And while their memory may, at times, be blurred by the mists of sentiment, they will remain ever huge and poignant in that treasure-house we call nostalgia!

The articulated trains at the United Iron & Metal company's yard at Wilkens Avenue and Millington Street, Baltimore, April 2, 1939. Author photograph.

Trailer 200 at the Brill plant in 1929. King collection.

THE BRILL CARS

After the publicity surrounding the arrival of the new articulated trains, the prospect of even more new cars just then came as something of an anticlimax; though, from the standpoint of modern equipment, 1927, it seemed, was a year of decision in which everything happened to happen.

The articulated series were introduced in April, and four months later the company adopted plans for twenty-four additional cars whose general description followed a return to the more conventional type of interurban car. Accordingly, on September 28, 1927 the Cincinnati Car Company submitted detailed specifications covering eight 56-foot steel arch-roof combination passenger and baggage motor cars, and sixteen straight passenger trailers of similar body design.

Meanwhile, controlling interests in the railroad had passed from the original management in Cleveland to a new directorate in Baltimore. Whether this change influenced the plans for major expenditures is not clear. In any event, the project for additional cars was temporarily deferred, to be revived some two years later.

In April 1929, a modified version was approved for nine 58-foot straight passenger trailers, to be ordered this time from the J. G. Brill Company.

Specifications were furnished by the builders describing car bodies which in many respects resembled construction details and appearance of their recent articulated trains. Notable exceptions, however, specified the older reversible type leather seats instead of the plush upholstered rotating bucket seats; and a return to standard vestibules having open stair wells in place of the enclosed steps with air-operated folding doors furnished in the previous order.

From a mechanical viewpoint, the most novel accessory of these cars was a new coupler which held a large fiber block of electrical contacts and self-aligning air-line connections mounted below the coupler itself in such a way that all features of the train line would be coupled automatically upon impact. Known as a Tomlinson Tightlock, this unusually wide device included (either side of the knuckle) a heavy pin and pocket casting designed to prevent vertical movement between the electrical contacts. Further specified were Brill 27 MCB-3 trucks to be equipped with "nose piece for motor supports, so arranged for possible future conversion into motor trucks". And on each vestibule "provisions were to be made for later installation of a motorman's cab, if desired". Thus, even at that early date, the contract revealed items

The front view of one of the Brill trailers shows the detail of the imposing automatic Tomlinson Tightlock coupler. Unlike many so-called automatic couplers, this one truly was: all electrical and air connections were made on contact. The air hose to the left allowed coupling with cars equipped with standard knuckle type couplers. The destination shown is prophetic of their later service as motor cars. Historical Society of Pennsylvania.

The interior of the new trailers was utilitarian. Note the fire extinguisher and emergency tool box on the compartment wall. Historical Society of Pennsylvania.

Trailer 207 at Annapolis, 1934. Note revised paint scheme. William Lichtenstern photograph.

which foretold eventual plans for the new trailers.

They were painted and lettered in the standard green and gold, and assigned the numbers 200 - 208. On September 6, 1929, the new cars entered service on the Annapolis North Shore Division, replacing an equal number of the older 300 series wooden trailers. The next five years marked a rather uneventful routine for the 200 class cars until a celebrated, albeit brief, interlude was to distinguish them as the principal "Limited" entries in a timetable already renowned for high-speed schedules. Within the span of those five years, the nation had entered the Great Depression, the Company had entered receivership, and much of its accounting resulted in red ink. Among other obligations, payments toward the articulated cars were long in arrears. If the Company was to keep its competitive edge over the rival steam roads, some aggressive move was essential. Since, fortunately, the 200 class trailers were designed for eventual use as motors, they could be converted with equipment already on hand. During the fall of 1934, a full complement of Westinghouse brake and electrical equipment was installed in each car. Though by far their most outstanding feature was a gear ratio (2.08:1) which enabled them to reach speeds of almost 80 miles per hour. One had field taps that could be cut in to exceed even that performance.

In contrast with the air whistles of all other cars, the 200's were outfitted with dual-bell pneumatic horns which seemed to accentuate the current concept of modern styling and speed. Horns and sirens were a curious symbol of that day; for everywhere, on rivers, roads, and rails, the charm of older machines that once *tooted and clanged* had surrendered to the urgency of faster machines that *honked and screamed*. And to further enhance their new image, the rebuilt cars were refinished in a striking livery of Tuscan Red, lettered in gold.

At the same time, improvements to track and roadbed with the assignment of faster cars had enabled a drastic reduction in running time, as reflected in the new schedules effective January 20, 1935.* But this emphasis on speed was soon eclipsed by the sobering effect of an incident that was hardly an accident in the strictest sense. One of the new cars, running at high speed, was suddenly derailed then rerailed before it could stop. Although the event was never formally investigated, it was explained as the impact of the wheel climbing a trailing-point switch. Later evidence at the site and damage to the car's truck would confirm that a near miracle had occurred on that day that fate rode the WB&A.

---

*   Transit Journal, July 1934 and January 1935.

208 at Naval Academy Junction July 29, 1935 in its finest configuration as a Main Line Limited. George Krambles collection. For a picture of these cars in service as Washington Limiteds see page 106.

As a result, the company's newest and fastest cars were withdrawn from service, to remain idle until the line was abandoned.

At the auction of June 14th, the 200's were subject to certain legal conditions wherein the cars themselves, owned by the Baltimore Corporation of Maryland, had been equipped with motors and controls owned by the WB&A then subject to foreclosure. Recognizing the need for additional equipment to maintain their proposed schedules, the new Baltimore & Annapolis Railroad on November 29, 1935 arranged for purchase of the nine 200's as complete cars which were modified** for continued service on the North Shore Line.

** For service on the new B&A, the 200's were modified by having window guards removed, destination sign boxes blocked out, regeared for lower speed and repainted.

Car numbers 42 and 40 in the short lived orange and cream livery at Naval Academy Junction in 1925. King collection.

CAR COLORS

For the greater part of their existence, cars of the Washington Baltimore & Annapolis Electric Railroad were identified by the conservative colors of dark green, striped and lettered in gold. During the first years, the names of the three cities, without further adornment, appeared midway of the car body. Though by February 1910 the line in Washington had been extended over city streets all the way to the US Treasury Building; whereupon an additional caption MID-CITY TERMINALS was painted below the name to underscore this convenience as a unique advantage over the competing steam roads.

In keeping with exceptionally high standards of maintenance, each car was sent to the Paint Shop on an average of every eighteen to twenty-four months, where the new finish was applied either by "cutting-in" around existing gold work, or, depending upon its condition, the entire exterior would be burned-off to remove everything down to the bare wood. Then followed a painstaking procedure of "knifing" or glazing all cracks and openings, four coats of rough primer, and an application of lampblack which was carefully rubbed down with pumice and water. Next came three coats of the basic dark green to be followed by lettering and trim which glistened in 14 karat gold foil. All doorways and window outlines were then chamfered in fine-line black to accentuate the three-dimentional character of the moldings and arches. And two coats of final varnish lent an artistry to the completed car, which emerged from the scaffolding as the cynosure of all eyes.

Painting methods of those years followed the meticulous practices used in fine carriage and coach building that could achieve a porcelain-like finish. Only after a rigorous apprenticeship could these craftsmen qualify as professional "Coach Painters" who, alone, could paint, varnish, and trim a car completely. Such thorough-going technique in time became quite expensive, resulting in certain compromises being adopted. About 1925, the painted reference to terminal facilities was dropped, and a simple caption that denoted merely WASHINGTON BALTIMORE ANNAPOLIS was standardized along the letterboards. The new articulated units, however, carried a very complete masthead which was printed in large extended block lettering: WASHINGTON BALTIMORE & ANNAPOLIS ELECTRIC RAILROAD COMPANY, running the full length of the ninety-seven foot car bodies.

All of the original cars presented a handsome interior of inlaid mahogany with clerestory transoms of stained glass which lined either side of the full Empire ceiling finished in pale green decorated with a chain pattern in gold-leaf. On either bulkhead, the car number as well as a sketch of the US Capitol, the Maryland State House, or landmarks of the Naval Academy were stenciled in gold on mahogany. Though, following arrival of the newer arch-roof cars, that featured a simplified headlining, all ceilings were thereafter done in ivory with a gold border.

With a determination to retain most of the rich interiors, the management held to the more costly course of removing the brass fixtures, then polishing all wood-work to an oil-rubbed patina, as befits genuine mahogany. They had thus resisted the cheaper routine of many another paint shop, where transom glass, seats and woodwork were often drenched in one amorphous melange of pastel mediocrity.

Although never actually used on the equipment, the Company's first monogram, adopted in 1908 for timetables and other literature, and continued in their advertising until about 1924, was a set of three initials (lettered green on white) encompassed by a circular band with inscription THE ELECTRIC LINE printed white on green.

On May 18, 1925, a striking departure from the conservative green was the appearance of car number 53 painted a bright traction orange and ivory, striped and lettered in black; and further decorated by a new emblem which comprised a white capitol dome against a sky-blue background, broken by a heraldic scroll inscribed THE CAPITAL LINE. This new combination had resulted from a change to the "krackno" method, a proprietary enamel technique that would eliminate most of the preparatory work involved with the old procedure. No less than thirty-three cars, representing at least one from each series, were refinished in this vivid new styling before it was discontinued exactly six months later.

But the brief venture in orange enamel wasn't quite over. In February 1926, car number 38, one of the steel body cars, after careful preparation was sprayed in three coats of orange lacquer, and trimmed in black. This was a sample car chosen for a test of appearance and durability. And, indeed, it proved both! But the technique was costly, and not entirely practical when used on the majority of the cars which were of wooden construction. As an interesting footnote, the Cincinnati steel cars (first WB&A; later Chicago Aurora & Elgin Ry cars) in the course of their history, had been finished in green, orange, green, blue, gray and red livery.

In 1925, all way stations and maintenance build-

One of the Hazleton cars in orange and ivory at Naval Academy Junction about June 1925. Michael H. Ford photograph.

82 in orange and ivory as interpreted by George Krambles.

ings throughout the system were likewise redone in orange and black. Even the Washington Railway & Electric Company adopted identical colors for its 1600 series open cars.

By 1923, a new contract with Southeastern Express Company had specified that the agency's emblem appear on the freight motors and baggage trailers. That trade mark was a gammadion in gold on a scarlet square which included the letters S E C O in the four angles of the cross. (see page 91)

In 1925, the railroad introduced its fourth, and probably best remembered, emblem which consisted of a gold circle bounding a stripe of symbolic electricity, intercepted by a broad arrow bearing the three initials of its name. For a time this design was used on all cars, exclusively in lieu of any lettering; but toward the middle thirties, the last years witnessed a return to the former letterboard captions.

Unlike the standard dark green previously used, the new articulated trains delivered by the J.G.Brill Company in 1927 had been painted a color variously described as forest green, which thereafter was applied, without striping, as regular finish for all cars. Three new busses obtained in 1927 were gray with a broad green band.

As an increasingly serious loss of revenue made itself felt, the management turned to a program of publicity emphasizing outstanding features of the places it served, such as:

Pageantry of the Naval Academy
Convenience of Mid-City Terminals
Most Direct Route to Eastern Shore
Historic Sights of Nations Capital
Special Service Direct to Bowie Races
Development of Shore Front Communities
Interesting Points of Colonial Annapolis

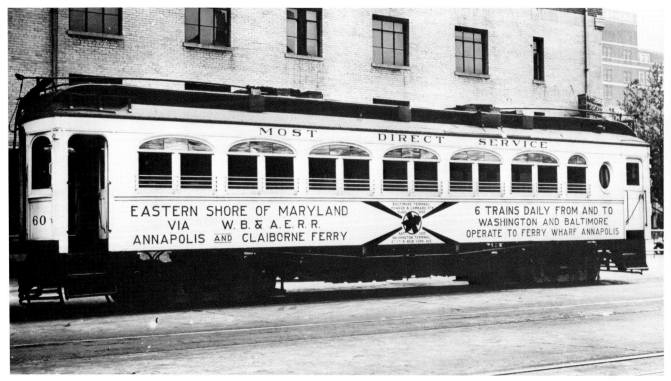

60 in white advertising scheme at Washington, May 22, 1933. William Lichtenstern photograph.

51 in light blue advertising colors at Naval Academy Junction in 1934. George Votava photograph.

Number 26 at Naval Academy Junction July 29, 1935. Note the plow hanger at the rear of the front truck. George Krambles collection.

In keeping with this program, three cars were selected for special advertising. On June 30, 1932, the Niles Car number 60 was painted in solid white, trimmed with emblem and lettered in black, to announce convenient ferry connections for Eastern Shore, Maryland. This was followed in August by two more, when number 51 was turned out in a shiny coat of bright blue and white, while number 57 appeared in a new livery of brilliant red & white. The blue car proclaimed things to see in historic Annapolis, while the red car featured a placard of bargain excursion fares between Baltimore and Washington. The red white and blue publicity cars were but another example of the initiative and inventiveness that marked the Company's consistent bid for increased passenger business.

When the 200 class trailers were rebuilt as motor cars in 1934, their inauguration distinguished them as the fastest and most modern of the fleet, resplendent in Tuscan red with large gold lettering, and new two-tone bell pneumatic horns instead of whistles. Unfortunately, their splendor was short-lived, for although the successor Baltimore & Annapolis Railroad gradually returned to the traditional maroon of the earlier Short Line, its equipment in the latter years was all too often characterized by a lack of any color.

Throughout its history, the WB&A Railroad was singularly a paragon of excellent rolling stock well maintained. To the very end, its continued efforts toward efficient high-speed service with attractive cars played a significant part in the esteem it has earned among those who knew it.

A Baltimore and Annapolis train is at Bancroft Hall in the Naval Academy grounds in this May, 1940 photograph. It is, of course, after the abandonment of the WB&A but it is the only known photograph of an electric train in the Academy grounds and the 200 class cars are in the same Tuscan red color that was used by the WB&A in 1934. Bruce Meulendyke photograph.

Page 233: Here are the front and rear covers of the sixteen page folder which was issued when service began on the new line in 1908. It illustrated the elegant rolling stock, features of the railroad, its terminals and places of interest in the terminal cities. The actual size of each panel is four by nine inches. Tom Underwood collection.

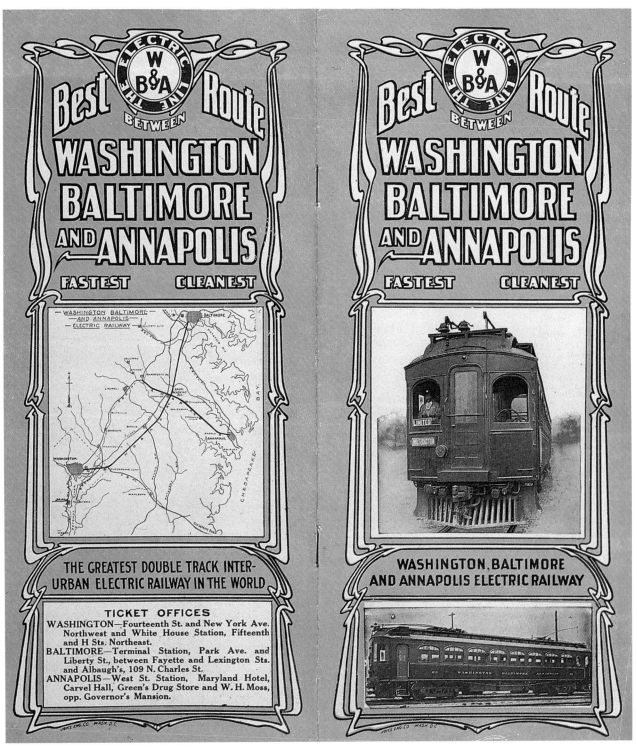

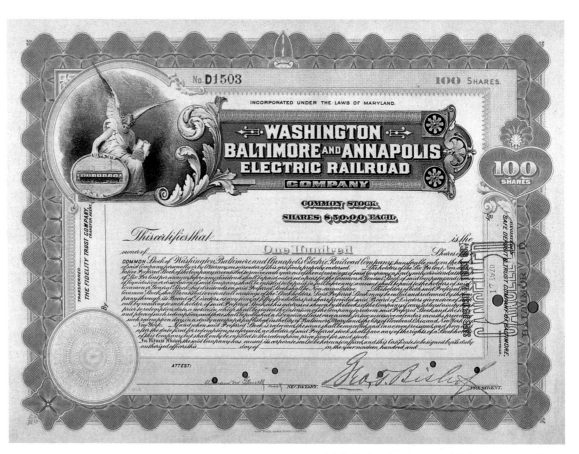

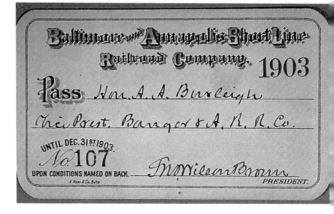

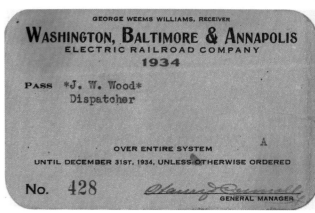

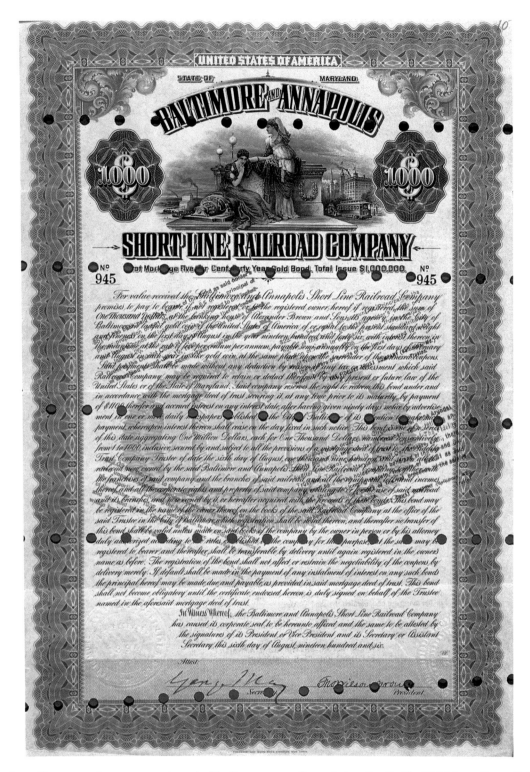

The two stock certificates are shown approximately fifty-five percent of actual size. Credit: The WB&A certificate, Robert A. Truax collection; the Annapolis Short Line certificate, Norman Nelson collection.

The four annual passes are shown at eighty-three percent of actual size. Credit: The 1876 and 1903 passes, Tom Underwood collection; the 1927 and 1934 examples are from the Author's collection.

Many interurban railroads issued postcards but few did in as much variety as the WB&A. Many of the cards issued announced Navy Football games, others commemorated visits by notables and quite a few simply displayed the historic features of the three major cities served. Three cards, Robert A. Truax collection; bottom right, King collection.

TOURISTS LEAVING ANNAPOLIS.

Souvenir of The Electric Line
Tuberculosis Congress
Washington, Sept. 21 to Oct. 12, 1908.

DR. ROBERT KOCH
THE NOTED DISCOVERER OF
THE TUBERCULOSIS BACILLUS

WASHINGTON BALTIMORE ANNAPOLIS

TYPE OF 55-TON CARS USED ON THE GREATEST DOUBLE TRACK
CARS EVERY HALF HOUR   INTERURBAN ELECTRIC RAILWAY IN THE WORLD
WASHINGTON BALTIMORE AND ANNAPOLIS ELECTRIC RAILWAY

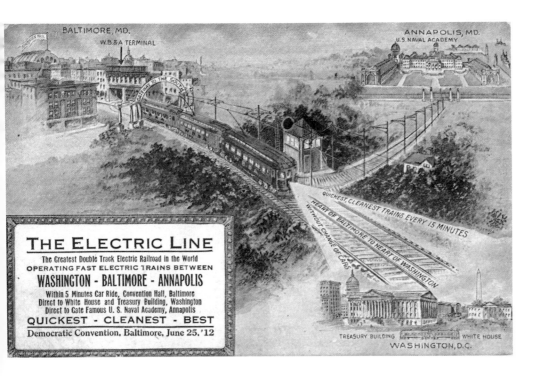

NEW TERMINAL STATION AND YARD, W. B. & A. ELECTRIC RAILROAD, BALTIMORE, MD.

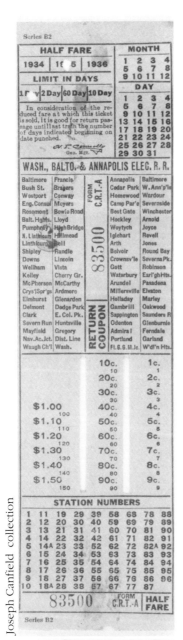

Joseph Canfield collection

Author's collection

Joseph Canfield collection

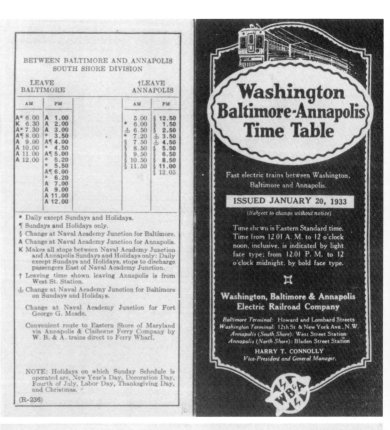

King collection

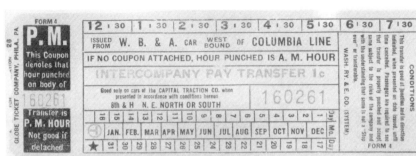

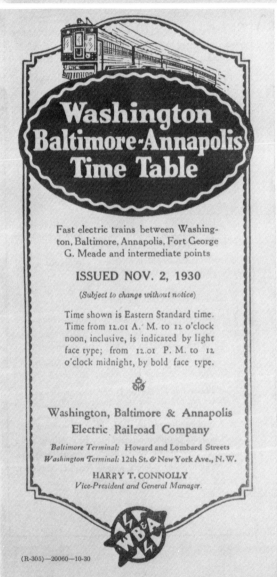

King collection

King collection

Note: All illustrations on this and the facing page are seventy-five percent actual size.

GEORGE WEEMS WILLIAMS
Receiver.

WASHINGTON, BALTIMORE and ANNAPOLIS ELECTRIC RAILROAD COMPANY

MAIN LINE

NORTH SHORE DIVISION

and

SOUTH SHORE DIVISION

TIME TABLE No. 27

EFFECTIVE 4.00 A. M., EASTERN STANDARD TIME

SUNDAY, JANUARY 8, 1933

CARSON SCHUMACHER,
Superintendent Transportation.

H. T. CONNOLLY,
Gen'l Manager.

Employee Timetable one-half size. George Krambles collection.

R-422-12-32

SPECIAL INSTRUCTIONS

RIGHTS OF TRAINS

Trains in either direction have no superior right over trains of the same class in opposite direction, but will meet trains as per time table unless otherwise ordered by the despatcher.

All trains becoming ten minutes late must report to the despatcher.

Scheduled meeting points are indicated in full faced type. The numbers of trains that are to be met are shown by small red figures above time of meeting.

Extra trains must clear all regular trains five minutes. See Rules 208, 209 and 219 Book of Rules.

When a train arrives at a meeting point and train to be met has not arrived, conductor will notify the despatcher.

When an extra train has cleared the main track the conductor will notify the despatcher, stating at what point he is clearing and for what train.

On single track, regular trains after they become one hour late will lose time card rights, until after they have become 12 hours late.

On double track, regular trains will not lose their time card rights.

On double track only, trains not representing a schedule, will proceed as an extra upon receiving from the despatcher or station master a blank X.

Rule No. 212 does not apply on double track.

REGISTER AND BULLETIN BOARDS

Baltimore Terminal.
Shipley (North Shore Division).
Naval Academy Junction.
West St. Station, Annapolis.
Bladen St. Station, Annapolis.
12th St., Washington.

SPEED RESTRICTIONS

All trains will come to a DEAD STOP at rapid transit crossings in Baltimore City, approaching all other street crossings under control.

Trains will not exceed:

20 miles per hour between Viaduct and Westport Station.

15 miles per hour at B. & O. Bridge south of Westport.

15 miles per hour through interlocking territory at Linthicum.

15 miles per hour through yard limits at Naval Academy Jct.

10 miles per hour between District Line and No. 1 overhead bridge.

6 miles per hour approaching Scott and Ostend Streets when flagman is on duty. When flagman is not on duty, Dead Stop must be made.

Trains will come to a DEAD STOP at all rapid transit crossings in Washington, D. C., approaching all other street crossings under full control.

Over the tracks of the Washington Railway & Electric Co. all trains will be governed by the Washington Railway & Electric Co.'s "Stop" and "Slow" boards.

North Shore Division

Trains will not exceed:

15 miles per hour over College Creek Bridge.

6 miles per hour over draw sections of College Creek and Severn River Bridges.

6 miles per hour over spring switches.

15 miles per hour in Annapolis yard limits.

15 miles per hour over Severn River Bridge except draw sections.

Trains will come to Dead Stop at Shipley and Glen Burnie Road Crossings.

South Shore Division

All trains operating through Annapolis will approach all crossings under full control.

Trains will not exceed:

15 miles per hour in Annapolis Yard limits.

6 miles per hour over Murrays, Silvers, Laundry, Admiral, Ice House Road, Midway Road, and Loop Road crossings.

Approach Hockley Road Crossing under Full Control.

6 miles per hour over spring switches.

Trains will come to Dead Stop at Crownsville, Iglehart, Cedar Park and Fairall Road Crossings.

UNCLASSIFIED

All trains will approach ends of double track sections under control.

Trains approaching each other at meeting points will reduce speed to six miles per hour when opposite each other. This to insure a thorough understanding of signals in event that one or the other is carrying signals for a following section.

Motormen will observe and comply fully with indications of whistle posts, stop and slow boards.

AUTOMATIC BLOCK SIGNALS

Main Line

When Block Signal No. 11 at foot of Scott Street does not show "Proceed" indication, southbound trains will stop at Near Side of Ostend Street if signal does not assume "Proceed" indication after five (5) seconds, train may proceed.

On double track between Baltimore and Washington, when an Automatic Block Signal is imperfectly displayed or displaying "Red," trains will stop at signal; if signal does not assume "Proceed" indication after five (5) seconds, train will proceed under caution, looking for obstruction in the block.

North Shore Division

Special Instructions Governing Train Operation Between Jones and Arnold

The territory between Jones and Arnold consists of two pieces of double track, with about 3,000 feet of single track intervening. This territory is equipped with Automatic Block Signals of the Preliminary type, which normal indication is "Red," and when approached in either direction will indicate whether or not the 3,000 feet of single track is occupied.

SOUTHBOUND motormen upon arrival at Jones will be governed first by the "P" signal No. "C-63". If this signal shows RED it indicates that a train running in the same direction is between the "P" signal and the next signal in advance. If the signal shows YELLOW it indicates that the southbound track is unoccupied.

SPECIAL INSTRUCTIONS—Continued

Upon arrival at Signal No. C-59 motormen will make a positive stop. After stopping, both motorman and conductor will observe the signal and have an understanding as to the signal indication. If the signal shows YELLOW you will proceed over the single track to the Arnold double track. If the signal shows RED or is imperfectly displayed you will call the despatcher for authority to proceed.

NORTHBOUND motormen upon arrival at Arnold will first be governed by the "P" signal No. C-46. If this signal shows RED it indicates that a train running in the same direction is between the "P" signal and the next signal in advance. If the signal shows YELLOW it indicates the northbound track is unoccupied.

Upon arrival at Signal C-50 motorman will make a positive stop. After stopping, both motorman and conductor will observe the signal and have an understanding as to the signal indication. If the signal shows YELLOW you will proceed over the single track to the Jones double track. If the signal shows RED or is imperfectly displayed you will call the despatcher for authority to proceed.

Special Instructions Governing Train Operation Over Severn River Draw

An interlocking system is provided at Severn River Draw to permit the movement of trains only when the drawbridge is locked in proper position. Southbound signal C-21 and northbound Signal C-14 govern movements over the draw and are controlled by the interlocking system. These signals also are a part of and connected with Automatic Signals on either side of the draw. These two signals are marked with the letter "S" illuminated by day and night to differentiate them from others wholly automatic, used only for spacing of trains. Derails have been installed at these signals. Trains will approach Signals C-21 and C-14 under full control.

A train stopped by Signal C-21 or C-14 displaying "STOP" will stay until authorized to proceed: or in case of failure of means of communication it may proceed when preceeded by a flagman to the next signal displaying proceed indication.

When a train is moved under such condition trainmen will see that derailer is locked for the main track and train may pass over draw only after receiving proper signal from Bridge attendant.

Special Instructions Governing Train Operations Over College Creek Draw

The block system at College Creek is designed to assure that the draw is locked in proper position before signals can be cleared for trains to move over the bridge.

Home Signal No. CO-2 will govern the movement of Northbound trains over College Creek Draw.

Home Signal No. CO-5 will govern movement of Southbound trains over College Creek Draw.

Trains will approach Signals No. CO-2 and CO-5 under full control. A train stopped by Signals CO-2 and CO-5 displaying "STOP" will stay until authorized to proceed: or in case of failure of means of communication it may proceed when preceeded by a flagman to the next signal displaying a proceed indication, being sure to observe that the rail joints at the draw are in proper position.

COMPANY'S PHYSICIANS:

Dr. Reid Edwards, University Hospital, Baltimore, Md.
(Telephone PLaza 6320)

Dr. J. Willis Martin, 185 Prince George, St., Annapolis, Md.
(Telephone Annapolis 96)

Dr. Walton H. Hopkins, 15 Maryland Ave., Annapolis, Md.
(Telephone Annapolis 98)

Dr. J. Oliver Purvis, 40 Franklin St., Annapolis, Md.
(Telephone Annapolis 1050)

Dr. J. W. Mankin, 2030 16th St., N. W., Washington, D. C.
(Telephone Potomac 0071)

In all cases of injuries to passengers or employees requiring medical aid, the despatcher in turn will immediately notify the Physician of the Company who can reach the point the quickest and the case put in his exclusive control. If impossible to secure the immediate attendance of the Company's Physician other medical aid should be promptly secured to attend until the arrival of the Company's Physician.

CARSON SCHUMACHER,
Supt. Transportation

2

3

SOUTH BOUND — MAIN LINE

Dis-tance	TRAIN NUMBERS / TIME POINTS	Daily Local 1 A.M.	Daily Ex. Sun. Local 3 A.M.	Daily 5 A.M.	Daily Ex. Sun. Local 7 A.M.	Daily Ex. Sun. Local 301 A.M.	Daily 9 A.M.	Daily 203 A.M.	Daily 11 A.M.	Daily 303 A.M.	Daily 13 A.M.	Daily Ex. Sun. Local 15 A.M.	Daily Ex. Sun. Local 305 A.M.
0.0	Baltimore	5.00	....	6.00	....	6.05	6.25	6.30	6.32	6.35	7.00	....	7.05
1.44	Viaduct Crossover	5.09	....	6.09	....	6.14	6.34	6.39	6.41	6.44	7.09	....	7.14
4.22	Brian "	5.14	....	6.14	....	6.20	6.39	6.44	6.46	6.50	7.14	....	7.20
6.56	Linthicum	5.18	....	6.17	....	6.26	6.42	6.47	6.49	6.56	7.17	....	7.26
9.40	McPherson Crossover	5.23	....	6.21	....	....	6.46	6.51	6.54	....	7.21	....	....
12.19	Craig "	5.27	....	6.24	....	....	6.49	6.55	6.59	....	7.24	....	....
15.24	Naval Academy Jct.	5.32	6.05	6.28	6.35	....	6.53	7.00	7.05	....	7.28	7.35	....
18.30	Bragers Crossover	5.37	6.10	6.32	6.40	....	6.57	....	7.10	....	7.32	7.40	....
21.24	Bowie Rd. "	5.41	6.14	6.35	6.44	....	7.00	....	7.14	....	7.35	7.44	....
23.93	Cooks "	5.45	6.19	6.38	6.49	....	7.03	....	7.19	....	7.38	7.49	....
26.65	Buena Vista "	5.51	6.25	6.41	6.55	....	7.06	....	7.25	....	7.41	7.55	....
29.12	Ardmore "	5.57	6.31	6.44	7.01	....	7.09	....	7.31	....	7.44	8.01	....
31.25	Whites "	6.03	6.37	6.47	7.07	....	7.12	....	7.37	....	7.47	8.07	....
33.18	District "	6.09	6.42	6.50	7.12	....	7.15	....	7.42	....	7.50	8.17	....
37.38	White House Sta.	6.24	6.57	7.05	7.27	....	7.30	....	7.57	....	8.05	8.27	....
39.94	Washington	6.40	7.15	7.20	7.44	....	7.45	....	8.15	....	8.20	8.45	....
	TRAIN NUMBERS	1	3	5	7	301	9	203	11	303	13	15	305

NORTH BOUND — MAIN LINE

Dis-tance	TRAIN NUMBERS / TIME POINTS	Daily Local 202 A.M.	Daily Ex. Sun. Local 302 A.M.	Daily Local 2 A.M.	Daily Ex. Sun. Local 304 A.M.	Daily Ex. Sun. Local 204 A.M.	Daily Local 306 A.M.	Daily Local 4 A.M.	Daily Ex. Sun. Local 308 A.M.	Daily Local 206 A.M.	Daily 6 A.M.	Daily Local 310 A.M.	Daily Ex. Sun. 8 A.M.
0.0	Washington	....	....	5.00	....	....	....	5.50	....	....	6.30	....	7.00
2.56	White House Sta.	....	....	5.15	....	....	....	6.05	....	....	6.45	....	7.15
6.56	District Crossover	....	....	5.29	....	....	....	6.19	....	....	6.59	....	7.29
8.69	Whites "	....	....	5.33	....	....	....	6.23	....	....	7.03	....	7.32
10.82	Ardmore "	....	....	5.37	....	....	....	6.28	....	....	7.08	....	7.35
13.29	Buena Vista "	....	....	5.41	....	....	....	6.32	....	....	7.12	....	7.38
16.01	Cooks "	....	....	5.45	....	....	....	6.37	....	....	7.17	....	7.41
18.70	Bowie Rd. "	....	....	5.49	....	....	....	6.43	....	....	7.23	....	7.44
21.64	Bragers "	....	....	5.54	....	....	....	6.48	....	....	7.28	....	7.47
24.68	Naval Academy Jct.	5.30	....	6.00	....	6.30	....	6.54	....	7.20	7.34	....	7.51
27.75	Craig Crossover	5.36	....	6.06	....	6.36	....	7.00	....	7.26	7.40	....	7.55
30.54	McPherson "	5.41	....	6.11	....	6.41	....	7.05	....	7.31	7.45	....	7.58
33.38	Linthicum	5.46	5.54	6.17	6.24	6.46	6.54	7.11	7.24	7.36	7.51	7.54	8.02
35.72	Brian Crossover	5.50	5.59	6.22	6.29	6.50	6.59	7.16	7.29	7.40	7.56	7.59	8.05
38.50	Viaduct "	5.56	6.05	6.28	6.35	6.56	7.05	7.22	7.35	7.46	8.02	8.05	8.11
39.94	Baltimore	6.05	6.15	6.36	6.45	7.05	7.15	7.31	7.45	7.55	8.11	8.15	8.20
	TRAIN NUMBERS	202	302	2	304	204	306	4	308	206	6	310	8

SPECIAL INSTRUCTIONS

All Limited trains will stop at Linthicum to receive passengers for Washington.
All Limited trains will stop at Linthicum to Discharge passengers from Washington.
Nos. 11, 21, 27, 33, 39 and 45 will stop between Baltimore and Linthicum to receive Only, for points south of Linthicum.
Nos. 17, 23, 29, 35, 41, 51 and 55 will stop at McPherson, Elmhurst, Delmont, Clark, Severn Run and Mayfield to receive and discharge.

SOUTH BOUND — MAIN LINE

Dis-tance	TRAIN NUMBERS / TIME POINTS	Daily Ex. Sun. 17 A.M.	Daily Local 307 A.M.	Daily 19 A.M.	Daily Ex. Sun. Local 309 A.M.	Daily Local 21 A.M.	Daily 311 A.M.	Daily Local 23 A.M.	Daily Local 313 A.M.	Daily Local 25 A.M.	Daily Local 27 A.M.	Daily Local 315 A.M.	Daily 29 A.M.
0.0	Baltimore	7.30	7.35	8.00	8.05	8.30	8.35	9.00	9.35	10.00	10.30	10.35	11.00
1.44	Viaduct Crossover	7.39	7.44	8.09	8.14	8.39	8.44	9.09	9.44	10.09	10.39	10.44	11.09
4.22	Brian "	7.44	7.50	8.14	8.20	8.44	8.50	9.14	9.50	10.14	10.44	10.50	11.14
6.56	Linthicum	7.47	7.56	8.17	8.26	8.47	8.56	9.17	9.56	10.17	10.47	10.56	11.17
9.40	McPherson Crossover	7.51	....	8.21	....	8.52	....	9.21	....	10.21	10.52	....	11.21
12.19	Craig "	7.54	....	8.24	....	8.56	....	9.24	....	10.24	10.56	....	11.24
15.24	Naval Academy Jct.	7.58	....	8.28	....	9.02	....	9.28	....	10.28	11.02	....	11.28
18.30	Bragers Crossover	8.02	....	8.32	....	9.08	....	9.32	....	10.32	11.08	....	11.32
21.24	Bowie Rd. "	8.05	....	8.35	....	9.12	....	9.35	....	10.35	11.12	....	11.35
23.93	Cooks "	8.08	....	8.38	....	9.17	....	9.38	....	10.38	11.17	....	11.38
26.65	Buena Vista "	8.11	....	8.41	....	9.22	....	9.41	....	10.41	11.22	....	11.44
29.12	Ardmore "	8.14	....	8.44	....	9.28	....	9.44	....	10.44	11.28	....	11.44
31.25	Whites "	8.17	....	8.47	....	9.33	....	9.47	....	10.47	11.33	....	11.47
33.18	District "	8.20	....	8.50	....	9.38	....	9.50	....	10.50	11.38	....	11.50
37.38	White House Sta.	8.35	....	9.05	....	9.53	....	10.05	....	11.05	11.53	....	12.05
39.94	Washington	8.50	....	9.20	....	10.08	....	10.20	....	11.20	12.08	....	12.20
	TRAIN NUMBERS	17	307	19	309	21	311	23	313	25	27 P.M.	315	29 P.M.

NORTH BOUND — MAIN LINE

Dis-tance	TRAIN NUMBERS / TIME POINTS	Daily Ex. Sun. 208 A.M.	Daily Ex. Sun. Local 312 A.M.	Daily Local 10 A.M.	Daily Local 314 A.M.	Daily Local 12 A.M.	Daily Local 316 A.M.	Daily Local 14 A.M.	Daily 16 A.M.	Daily Local 318 A.M.	Daily 18 A.M.	Daily Local 320 A.M.	Daily Local 20 A.M.
0.0	Washington	....	....	7.30	....	8.30	....	9.00	9.30	....	10.30	....	11.00
2.56	White House Sta.	....	....	7.45	....	8.45	....	9.15	9.45	....	10.45	....	11.15
6.16	District Crossover	....	....	7.59	....	8.59	....	9.29	9.59	....	10.59	....	11.29
8.69	Whites "	....	....	8.03	....	9.02	....	9.33	10.02	....	11.02	....	11.33
10.82	Ardmore "	....	....	8.07	....	9.05	....	9.38	10.05	....	11.05	....	11.38
13.29	Buena Vista "	....	....	8.11	....	9.08	....	9.43	10.08	....	11.09	....	11.43
16.01	Cooks "	....	....	8.15	....	9.11	....	9.48	10.11	....	11.11	....	11.48
18.70	Bowie Rd. "	....	....	8.19	....	9.14	....	9.53	10.14	....	11.14	....	11.53
21.64	Bragers "	....	....	8.23	....	9.17	....	9.57	10.17	....	11.17	....	11.57
24.68	Naval Academy Jct.	7.52	....	8.29	....	9.21	....	10.03	10.21	....	11.21	....	12.03
27.75	Craig Crossover	7.58	....	8.34	....	9.25	....	10.09	10.25	....	11.25	....	12.09
30.54	McPherson "	8.03	....	8.38	....	9.28	....	10.14	10.28	....	11.28	....	12.14
33.38	Linthicum	8.09	8.24	8.42	8.54	9.32	9.54	10.20	10.32	10.54	11.32	11.54	12.20
35.72	Brian Crossover	8.12	8.29	8.45	8.59	9.35	9.59	10.23	10.35	10.59	11.35	11.59	12.23
38.50	Viaduct "	8.18	8.35	8.51	9.05	9.41	10.05	10.29	10.41	11.05	11.41	12.05	12.29
39.94	Baltimore	8.27	8.45	9.00	9.15	9.50	10.15	10.38	10.50	11.15	11.50	12.15	12.38
	TRAIN NUMBERS	208	312	10	314	12	316	14	16	318	18 P.M.	320	20 P.M.

SPECIAL INSTRUCTIONS—Continued

No. 221 will stop between Downs and Naval Academy Jct. to receive and discharge.
No. 49 will stop between Downs and Naval Academy Jct. to receive and discharge, Sundays Only.
Nos. 223, 225, 227 and 229 will make all stops between Linthicum and Naval Academy Jct. to receive and discharge.
Nos. 10 and 32 will stop between Linthicum and Baltimore to discharge Only.
No. 32 will make all stops on Sundays Only.

Page 6

SOUTH BOUND — MAIN LINE

Distance	Train Numbers / Time Points	317 Daily Local A.M.	31 Daily NOON	501 Sat. Only Local P.M.	33 Daily Local P.M.	319 Daily Local P.M.	35 Daily P.M.	503 Sat. Only Local P.M.	321 Daily Local P.M.	37 Daily P.M.	505 Sat. Only Local P.M.	39 Daily Local P.M.	323 Daily Local P.M.
0.0	Baltimore	11.35	12.00	12.05	12.30	12.35	1.00	1.05	1.35	2.00	2.05	2.30	2.35
1.44	Viaduct Crossover	11.44	12.09	12.14	12.39	12.44	1.09	1.14	1.44	2.09	2.14	2.39	2.44
4.22	Brian "	11.50	12.14	12.20	12.44	12.50	1.14	1.20	1.50	2.14	2.20	2.44	2.50
6.56	Linthicum	11.56	12.17	12.26	12.47	12.56	1.17	1.26	1.56	2.17	2.26	2.47	2.56
9.40	McPherson Crossover		12.21			12.52	1.21			2.21			2.52
12.19	Craig "		12.24			12.56	1.24			2.24			2.56
15.24	Naval Academy Jct.		12.28			1.02	1.28			2.28			3.02
18.30	Bragers Crossover		12.32			1.08	1.32			2.32			3.08
21.24	Bowie Rd. "		12.35			1.12	1.35			2.35			3.12
23.93	Cooks "		12.38			1.17	1.38			2.38			3.17
26.65	Buena Vista "		12.41			1.22	1.41			2.41			3.22
29.12	Ardmore "		12.44			1.28	1.44			2.44			3.28
31.25	Whites "		12.47			1.33	1.47			2.47			3.33
33.18	District "		12.50			1.38	1.50			2.50			3.38
37.38	White House Sta.		1.05			1.53	2.05			3.05			3.53
39.94	Washington		1.20			2.08	2.20			3.20			4.08
	Train Numbers	317	31	501	33	319	35	503	321	37	505	39	323

NORTH BOUND — MAIN LINE

Distance	Train Numbers / Time Points	22 Daily A.M.	322 Daily Local P.M.	24 Daily P.M.	324 Daily Local P.M.	26 Daily Local P.M.	28 Daily P.M.	326 Daily Local P.M.	30 Daily P.M.	328 Daily Local P.M.	32 Daily P.M.	330 Daily Ex. Sun. Local P.M.	34 Daily P.M.
0.0	Washington	11.30		12.30		1.00	1.30		2.30		3.00		3.30
2.56	White House Sta.	11.45		12.45		1.15	1.45		2.45		3.15		3.45
6.16	District Crossover	11.59		12.59		1.29	1.59		2.59		3.29		3.59
8.69	Whites "	12.02		1.02		1.33	2.02		3.02		3.33		4.02
10.82	Ardmore "	12.05		1.05		1.38	2.05		3.05		3.38		4.05
13.29	Buena Vista "	12.08		1.08		1.43	2.08		3.08		3.43		4.08
16.01	Cooks "	12.11		1.11		1.48	2.11		3.11		3.48		4.11
18.70	Bowie Rd. "	12.14		1.14		1.53	2.14		3.14		3.53		4.14
21.64	Bragers "	12.17		1.17		1.57	2.17		3.17		3.57		4.17
24.68	Naval Academy Jct.	12.21		1.21		2.03	2.21		3.21		4.03		4.21
27.75	Craig Crossover	12.25		1.25		2.09	2.25		3.25		4.09		4.25
30.54	McPherson "	12.28		1.28		2.14	2.28		3.28		4.14		4.28
33.38	Linthicum	12.32	12.54	1.32	1.54	2.20	2.32	2.54	3.32	3.54	4.20	4.24	4.32
35.72	Brian Crossover	12.35	12.59	1.35	1.59	2.23	2.35	2.59	3.35	3.59	4.23	4.29	4.35
38.50	Viaduct "	12.41	1.05	1.41	2.05	2.29	2.41	3.05	3.41	4.05	4.29	4.35	4.41
39.94	Baltimore	12.50	1.15	1.50	2.15	2.38	2.50	3.15	3.50	4.15	4.38	4.45	4.50
	Train Numbers	22	322	24	324	26	28	326	30	328	32	330	34

SPECIAL INSTRUCTIONS—Continued

No. 47 will stop at Mayfield, Severn Run, Clark, Delmont, Elmhurst, McPherson, Shipley and Linthicum to receive and discharge, Sundays Only.

Nos. 12, 18, 24, 30, 46 and 52 will stop at Mayfield, Severn Run, Clark, Delmont, Elmhurst, McPherson, Shipley and Linthicum to receive and discharge.

Page 7

SOUTH BOUND — MAIN LINE

Distance	Train Numbers / Time Points	41 Daily P.M.	507 Sat. Only Local P.M.	325 Daily Local P.M.	221 Daily Ex. Sun. P.M.	43 Daily P.M.	327 Daily Ex. Sun. Local P.M.	45 Daily Local P.M.	329 Daily Local P.M.	223 Daily Ex. Sun. P.M.	47 Daily P.M.	331 Daily Ex. Sun. Local P.M.	225 Daily Local P.M.
0.0	Baltimore	3.00	3.05	3.35	3.50	4.00	4.05	4.30	4.35	4.50	5.00	5.05	5.20
1.44	Viaduct Crossover	3.09	3.14	3.44	3.59	4.09	4.14	4.39	4.44	4.59	5.09	5.14	5.29
4.22	Brian "	3.14	3.20	3.50	4.04	4.14	4.20	4.44	4.50	5.04	5.14	5.20	5.34
6.50	Linthicum	3.17	3.26	3.56	4.08	4.17	4.26	4.47	4.56	5.08	5.17	5.26	5.38
9.40	McPherson Crossover	3.21			4.13				4.52	5.14	5.21		5.44
12.19	Craig "	3.24			4.17	4.24			4.56	5.19	5.24		5.49
15.24	Naval Academy Jct.	3.28			4.23	4.28			5.02	5.26	5.28		5.56
18.30	Bragers Crossover	3.32				4.32			5.08		5.32		
21.24	Bowie Rd. "	3.35				4.35			5.12		5.35		
23.93	Cooks "	3.38				4.38			5.17		5.38		
26.65	Buena Vista "	3.41				4.41			5.22		5.41		
29.12	Ardmore "	3.44				4.44			5.28		5.44		
31.25	Whites "	3.47				4.47			5.33		5.47		
33.18	District "	3.50				4.50			5.38		5.50		
37.38	White House Sta.	4.05				5.05			5.53		6.05		
39.94	Washington	4.20				5.20			6.08		6.20		
	Train Numbers	41	507	325	221	43	327	45	329	223	47	331	225

NORTH BOUND — MAIN LINE

Distance	Train Numbers / Time Points	226 Daily Ex. Sun. P.M.	332 Daily Local P.M.	36 Daily Ex. Sun. Local Wash.-N.A.J. P.M.	334 Daily Local P.M.	38 Daily P.M.	228 Daily Ex. Sun. P.M.	40 Daily Ex. Sat. & Sun. Local P.M.	336 Daily Local P.M.	42 Daily Ex. Sun. P.M.	44 Daily Local P.M.	46 Daily P.M.	48 Daily Ex. Sun. Local P.M.
0.0	Washington			4.00		4.30		4.32		5.00	5.02	5.30	5.32
2.56	White House Sta.			4.15		4.45		4.47		5.15	5.17	5.45	5.47
6.16	District Crossover			4.29		4.59		5.01		5.29	5.31	5.59	6.01
8.69	Whites "			4.33		5.02		5.06		5.32	5.36	6.02	6.06
10.82	Ardmore "			4.38		5.05		5.12		5.35	5.42	6.05	6.12
13.29	Buena Vista "			4.43		5.08		5.18		5.38	5.48	6.08	6.18
16.01	Cooks "			4.48		5.11		5.24		5.41	5.54	6.11	6.24
18.70	Bowie Rd. "			4.53		5.14		5.30		5.44	6.00	6.14	6.30
21.64	Bragers "			4.57		5.17		5.34		5.47	6.04	6.17	6.34
24.68	Naval Academy Jct.	4.22		5.02		5.21	5.22	5.40		5.51	6.10	6.21	6.40
27.75	Craig Crossover	4.26				5.25	5.28	5.44		5.55	6.14	6.25	
30.54	McPherson "	4.30				5.28	5.33	5.48		5.58	6.19	6.28	
33.38	Linthicum	4.39	4.54		5.13	5.32	5.39	5.54	5.24	6.02	6.24	6.32	
35.72	Brian Crossover	4.42	4.59		5.16	5.35	5.42	5.59	5.29	6.05	6.29	6.35	
38.50	Viaduct "	4.48	5.05		5.22	5.41	5.48	6.05	5.35	6.11	6.35	6.41	
39.94	Baltimore	4.57	5.15		5.30	5.50	5.57	6.15	5.45	6.20	6.45	6.50	
	Train Numbers	226	332	36	334	38	228	40	336	42	44	46	48

SPECIAL INSTRUCTIONS—Continued

Nos. 34 and 38 will make all stops between Naval Academy Jct. and Linthicum to receive and discharge, Sundays Only.

Nos. 206, 208, 226 and 228 will make all stops between Naval Academy Jct. and Linthicum to receive and discharge.

EAST BOUND — SOUTH SHORE DIVISION

Distance	Time Points	201 Daily Ex. Sun. Local A.M.	203 Daily A.M.	205 Daily Ex. Sun. Local A.M.	401 Sun. Only Local A.M.	207 Daily Local A.M.	209 Daily Local A.M.	211 Daily Local A.M.	213 Daily Local P.M.	215 Daily Local P.M.	217 Daily Local P.M.	219 Daily Local P.M.	221 Daily Ex. Sun. Local P.M.
0.0	Fort Meade Jct.												
4.25	Admiral												
6.25	Naval Academy Jct.	6.40	7.00	8.00	8.30	9.30	10.30	11.30	12.30	1.30	2.30	3.30	4.23
8.33	Gambrills	6.45	7.04	8.04	8.34	9.34	10.34	11.34	12.34	1.34	2.34	3.34	4.27
9.64	Millersville	6.47	7.06	8.06	8.36	9.36	10.36	11.36	12.36	1.36	2.36	3.36	4.29
11.60	Waterbury (Double Track) [206] [210]	6.51	7.10	8.10	8.40	9.40	10.40	11.40	12.40	1.40	2.40	3.40	4.33
13.23	Crownsville	6.55	7.14	8.14	8.44	9.44	10.44	11.44	12.44	1.44	2.44	3.44	4.36
15.37	Iglehart [206]	7.01	7.19	8.19	8.49	9.49	10.49	11.49	12.49	1.49	2.49	3.49	4.40
17.11	Best Gate	7.05	7.23	8.23	8.53	9.53	10.53	11.53	12.53	1.53	2.53	3.53	4.44
18.13	Camp Parole [208] [212] [214] [216] [220] [222] [224] [226]	7.07	7.25	8.25	8.55	9.55	10.55	11.55	12.55	1.55	2.55	3.55	4.46
20.13	Annapolis [228]	7.13	7.30	8.30	9.00	10.00	11.00	12.00	1.00	2.00	3.00	4.00	4.50
	Train Numbers	201 A.M.	203 A.M.	205 A.M.	401 A.M.	207 A.M.	209 A.M.	211 NOON	213 P.M.	215 P.M.	217 P.M.	219 P.M.	221 P.M.

WEST BOUND — SOUTH SHORE DIVISION

Distance	Time Points	202 Daily Local A.M.	204 Daily Ex. Sun. Local A.M.	206 Daily Local A.M.	208 Daily Ex. Sun. Local A.M.	210 Daily Local A.M.	212 Daily Local A.M.	214 Daily Local A.M.	216 Daily Local A.M.	218 Daily Local A.M.	220 Daily Local P.M.	222 Daily Local P.M.	224 Daily Local P.M.
0.0	Annapolis	5.00	6.00	6.50	7.20	7.50	8.50	9.50	10.50	11.50	12.50	1.50	2.50
2.00	Camp Parole [203] [401] [207] [209] [211] [213] [215] [217]	5.04	6.04	6.55	7.25	7.55	8.55	9.55	10.55	11.55	12.55	1.55	2.55
3.02	Best Gate	5.06	6.06	6.57	7.27	7.57	8.57	9.57	10.57	11.57	12.57	1.57	2.57
4.76	Iglehart [201]	5.10	6.10	7.01	7.31	8.01	9.01	10.01	11.01	12.01	1.01	2.01	3.01
6.90	Crownsville	5.14	6.14	7.06	7.36	8.06	9.06	10.06	11.06	12.06	1.06	2.06	3.06
8.53	Waterbury (Double Track) [203] [205]	5.18	6.18	7.10	7.40	8.10	9.10	10.10	11.10	12.10	1.10	2.10	3.10
10.49	Millersville	5.22	6.22	7.14	7.44	8.14	9.14	10.14	11.14	12.14	1.14	2.14	3.14
11.80	Gambrills	5.24	6.24	7.16	7.46	8.16	9.16	10.16	11.16	12.16	1.16	2.16	3.16
13.88	Naval Academy Jct.	5.28	6.28	7.20	7.50	8.20	9.20	10.20	11.20	12.20	1.20	2.20	3.20
15.88	Admiral												
20.13	Fort Meade Jct.												
	Train Numbers	202 A.M.	204 A.M.	206 A.M.	208 A.M.	210 A.M.	212 A.M.	214 A.M.	216 A.M.	218 P.M.	220 P.M.	222 P.M.	224 P.M.

SPECIAL INSTRUCTIONS—Continued

No. 201 will take siding at Iglehart, when meeting as per time table, unless otherwise directed.

No. 201 has right over No. 208 to Annapolis.
No. 204 has right over No. 201 to Naval Academy Jct.
No. 208 has right over No. 205 to Naval Academy Jct.
No. 210 has right over No. 401 to Naval Academy Jct.
No. 212 has right over No. 207 to Naval Academy Jct.
No. 214 has right over No. 209 to Naval Academy Jct.
No. 216 has right over No. 211 to Naval Academy Jct.
No. 218 has right over No. 213 to Naval Academy Jct.
No. 220 has right over No. 215 to Naval Academy Jct.
No. 222 has right over No. 217 to Naval Academy Jct.
No. 224 has right over No. 219 to Naval Academy Jct.
No. 226 has right over No. 221 to Naval Academy Jct.

EAST BOUND — SOUTH SHORE DIVISION

Distance	Time Points	403 Sun. Only Local P.M.	223 Daily Local P.M.	225 Daily Ex. Sun. Local P.M.	227 Daily Local P.M.	229 Daily Ex. Sun. Local P.M.	231 Daily Local P.M.	233 Daily Local P.M.	235 Daily Local A.M.	237 Daily Local A.M.
0.0	Fort Meade Jct.									
4.25	Admiral									
6.25	Naval Academy Jct.	4.30	5.26	5.56	6.26	6.56	7.30	9.35	11.35	12.35
8.33	Gambrills	4.34	5.32	6.02	6.32	7.02	7.34	9.39	11.39	12.39
9.64	Millersville	4.36	5.35	6 05	6 35	7.05	7.36	9.41	11.41	12.41
11.60	Waterbury (Double Track) [230] [232]	4.40	5.40	6.10	6.40	7.10	7.40	9.45	11 45	12.45
13.23	Crownsville	4.44	5.44	6.14	6.44	7.14	7.44	9.49	11 48	12.48
15.37	Iglehart	4.49	5.49	6.19	6.49	7.19	7.49	9.54	11.52	12.52
17.11	Best Gate	4.53	5.53	6.23	6.53	7.23	7.53	9.58	11.56	12.56
18.13	Camp Parole [228] [230] [232]	4.55	5.55	6.25	6.55	7.25	7.55	10.00	11.58	12.58
20.13	Annapolis	5.00	6.00	6.30	7.00	7.30	8.00	10.05	12.02	1.02
	Train Numbers	403 P.M.	223 P.M.	225 P.M.	227 P.M.	229 P.M.	231 P.M.	233 P.M.	235 A.M.	237 A.M.

WEST BOUND — SOUTH SHORE DIVISION

Distance	Time Points	226 Daily Local P.M.	228 Daily Local P.M.	230 Daily Local P.M.	232 Daily Local P.M.	234 Daily Local P.M.	236 Daily Local P.M.	238 Daily Local A.M.
0.0	Annapolis [221]	3.50	4.50	5.50	6.50	8.50	11.00	12.05
2.00	Camp Parole [219] [403] [223] [227]	3.55	4.55	5.55	6.55	8.55	11.05	12.09
3.02	Best Gate	3.57	4.57	5.57	6.57	8.57	11.07	12.11
4.76	Iglehart	4.01	5.01	6.01	7.01	9.01	11.11	12.14
6.90	Crownsville	4.06	5.06	6.06	7.06	9.06	11.16	12.18
8.53	Waterbury (Double Track) [225] [229]	4.10	5.10	6.10	7.10	9.10	11.20	12.21
10.49	Millersville	4.14	5.14	6.14	7.14	9.14	11.24	12.25
11.80	Gambrills	4.16	5.16	6.16	7.16	9.16	11.26	12.27
13.88	Naval Academy Jct.	4.20	5.20	6.20	7.20	9.20	11.30	12.30
15.88	Admiral							
20.13	Fort Meade Jct.							
	Train Numbers	226 P.M.	228 P.M.	230 P.M.	232 P.M.	234 P.M.	236 P.M.	238 A.M.

SPECIAL INSTRUCTIONS—Continued

No. 226 has right over No. 403 to Naval Academy Jct.
No. 228 has right over No. 223 to Naval Academy Jct.
No. 230 has right over No. 227 to Naval Academy Jct.
No. 232 has right over No. 231 to Naval Academy Jct.
No. 234 has right over No. 233 to Naval Academy Jct.
No. 236 has right over No. 235 to Naval Academy Jct.
No. 238 has right over No. 237 to Naval Academy Jct.

No. 235 has right over No. 238 to Annapolis.
No. 203 will stop east of Naval Academy Jct. to discharge, Daily except Sunday.
No. 203 will make all stops East of Naval Academy Jct. to receive and discharge, Sundays Only.
No. 203 will stop at Millersville, Waterbury, Iglehart, Best Gate, Camp Parole, and Homewood to receive passengers.

IMPORTANT DATES

Potomac & Severn Electric Railway chartered	May 22, 1899
AW&B (Elkridge) steam railroad acquired	Feb. 26,1903
George T. Bishop elected President of WB&A	May 2, 1905
Baltimore Terminal Company organized	June 5, 1905
Line from Washington to Annapolis opened	Feb. 7, 1908
First Car ran in Annapolis	March 25, 1908
Baltimore Division opened for service	April 3, 1908
First Electric Car on Annapolis Short Line	April 13, 1908
AC Electrical system converted to DC	Feb. 15,1910
Through service to the Treasury in Washington	March 1, 1910
Annapolis city service abandoned	June 8, 1914
Branch line to Camp Meade completed	Sept., 1917
Peak year of traffic included 5,946,697 revenue passengers and construction materials for Camp Meade	1918
New Washington Terminal opened	January 31, 1921
Annapolis Short Line acquired	Feb. 18,1921
Tracks joined at Linthicum Junction	March 16, 1921
New Baltimore Terminal opened	October 30, 1921
First articulated interurban train in US placed in service	April 6, 1927
Railroad sold at auction	June 14, 1935
WB&A System abandoned	August 20, 1935
B&A Railroad abandoned passenger service	Feb. 5, 1950

CORPORATE NAMES

Annapolis & Baltimore Short Line Railroad	1880-1894
Annapolis & Chesapeake Bay Power Company	1923-1933
Annapolis & Chesapeake Railroad	1899-1921
Annapolis & Elk Ridge Rail Road	1836-1886
Annapolis Short Line Railroad	February, 1921
Annapolis Washington & Baltimore Railroad	1886-1908
Anne Arundel Electric Railroad	March 31,1911
Baltimore & Annapolis Short Line Railroad	1894-1906
Baltimore & Annapolis Railroad	1935-
Baltimore Corporation of Maryland	1927-1935
Baltimore Terminal Company Inc.	1905-1911
Bay Ridge & Annapolis Railroad	1886-1907
Consolidated Gas Electric Light & Power Co.	1927-
Electric Express Company	1909-1910
Maryland Electric Railways	1906-1921
Maryland Development & Realty Co. of Anne Arundel County	
Potomac & Severn Electric Railway	1899-1900
Severn Light & Power Company	1923
Southeastern Express Company	1920-1938
Terminal Real Estate Company	1905-1929
Traction Construction Company Inc.	1905-1908
Washington & Annapolis Electric Railway	1900-1902
Washington Baltimore & Annapolis Electric RY.	1902-1911
Washington Baltimore & Annapolis Electric RR.	1911-1935
Washington Baltimore & Annapolis Realty Corp.	1935-1946
Washington Berwyn & Laurel Electric Railroad	1901-1910

POWER DISRIBUTION

	1908 AC Single Phase	1910 1921 600 - 1200-Volt DC	
Benning:	7 x 800 kw Transformers (1 as spare) local direct from WRY&ECo	Station Number 5 87,000 kw (System) 9660 kw 12 Transformers	
Ardmore:		Station Number 1 1200 kw 4 x 300 kw Converters	1200 kw 4 x 300 kw Converters
N.A.Junction:	4 x 800 kw Transformers 2 x 300 kw Motor Gen. Sets (Yards & Shop)	Station Number 2 1500 kw 5 x 300 kw Converters	1950 kw 4 Rotary converters 1 Synchronous conv
Linthicum:		- - -	600 kw 2 x 300 kw Converters
Scott Street: Baltimore	2 x 300 kw Motor Gen. Sets (City)	Station Number 3 1200 kw 4x300 kw Converters	2200 kw 4 x 300 kw 2 x 500 kw Converters
West Street: Annapolis	2 x 300 kw Motor Gen. Sets (City)	Station Number 4 600 kw 2 x 300 kw Converters	2040 kw 4 Converters
Admiral: Camp Meade		- - -	3750 kw not for railway operation
Jones Number 1:	3 x 300 kw Transforners Tied into Westport	Abandoned	
Jones Number 2 :		3 x 300 kva Converters Tied into Westport	Closed

Details on the never-completed Hyattsville Power Station and the Ammendale Station which was sold with the Washington Berwyn & Laurel have been omitted for reasons of space.

UNDERGROUND CONDUIT NOTES

In both of the major cities, trackage (in the streets and at the terminals) was maintained by the local streetcar companies. Beginning in 1910, when the service was extended into downtown Washington, the interurban would operate over an underground conduit system of current collection. This system employed a device, called a "plow", attached to an extended hanger on one of the car's trucks.

Conductor bars, which carried current through the conduits, were necessarily interrupted by a complete break at specialwork and section insulators, requiring the train to drift across the "cut out". Since WB&A trains operated at only half-voltage on city streets, acceleration was sluggish, or even interrupted by traffic, causing a sudden stop in the cut out. In such an emergency, there were electric leads attached to jump-start the train.

All track switches were manually operated;

this to preclude the case of a train approaching the magnetic relay of an automatic switch where successive plows could reverse the solenoid to cause a derailment.

The map on page 123 illustrates the situation of a train leaving the Washington Terminal, where it encountered two, or even four, breaks in close succession. The motorman had to shut off while the plow was crossing each of these dead spots, while at the same time gain momentum to avoid stalling on the next break; a deft maneuver to say the least.

The conductor then held a chain of the spring switch for his train to negotiate two more dead spots in the curve into New York Avenue. While all loading at the terminal was from the left side, regular practice (before starting) was to raise the trap of the right rear doorway, which enabled the conductor to catch his train without delay.

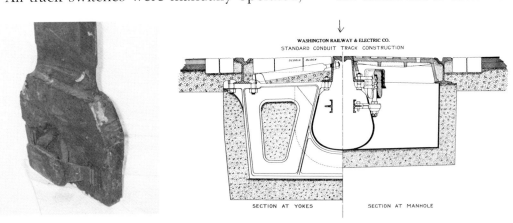

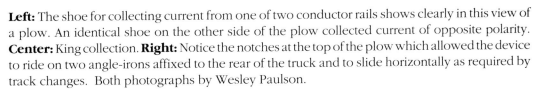

Left: The shoe for collecting current from one of two conductor rails shows clearly in this view of a plow. An identical shoe on the other side of the plow collected current of opposite polarity. **Center:** King collection. **Right:** Notice the notches at the top of the plow which allowed the device to ride on two angle-irons affixed to the rear of the truck and to slide horizontally as required by track changes. Both photographs by Wesley Paulson.

WASHINGTON BALTIMORE AND ANNAPOLIS ELECTRIC RAILROAD ROSTER

PASSENGER CARS:

CAR NUMBER	TYPE	BUILDER/DATE	TRUCKS	MOTORS	CONTROL	GROSS WEIGHT	SEATS	LENGTH O/ALL	WIDTH O/ALL	HEIGHT O/ROOF
10	DECK ROOF CITY CLOSED	BRILL '94	BRILL 21E	2 GE 217A	R-200A	-	24	27'5"	7'11"	10'8"
	Wood single truck car. Originally Baltimore City Passenger Railway 303 purchased 3/26/08 from URys&ECo for Annapolis local service. Scrapped in 1912.									
11	DECK ROOF OPEN MOTOR	BROWNELL 1895	BRILL 21E	2 GE217A(?)	(?)	-	8 BENCH	28'	8'7"	10'11"
	Originally Baltimore Traction Co. 857 purchased 3/26/08 from URys&ECo. Annapolis local service. Withdrawn from service and scrapped after 2/15/10 when Annapolis converted to 1200V.									
19	DECK ROOF CITY CLOSED	LACONIA '96	PECKHAM 14-D-3	2 GE 205	GE K-40	-	-	-	-	-
	Double truck wood car. Ex WRy&ECo 301. Acquired in 1912. Scrapped 1928.									
20-23	RR ROOF WOOD COMBINATION	NILES '07	BALDWIN 90-40MCB	4 GE 603	GE-M C-57	87,600	42	54'11"	9'1"	13'1"
	Original 6600V AC local cars. 21 wrecked at Parole 6/5/08. Remaining three converted to 1200V DC with new trucks, motors and controls 2/15/10 and renumbered 77-79 which see.									
50-68	RR ROOF WOOD PASSENGER	NILES '07	BALDWIN 90-40MCB	4 GE 603	GE-M C-57	109,000	66	62'3"	9'1"	13'1"
	Original 6600V AC Limited cars, known as "Electric Pullmans". 64 wrecked at Parole 6/5/08. Others sold in 1910 to Bamberger Railroad (Utah) (3) 450-452. Rock Island Southern (IL) (8) 300-305 & 425-426 and Oregon Electric (4) 106-109.. One may have become Union Traction of Indiana 279 and one 280. No information on the remaining one.									
20-29	ARCH ROOF STEEL 2 SECTION ARTICULATED	BRILL '26	BRILL 2-27MCB2 1-27MCB3	4 WH 333-VV-8	WH-HL 15-D-12	116,770	94	97'4"	8'11"	12'8"
	Builder spec 509B dated 6/28/26. In service 4/7/27. Unit 22 wrecked 6/20/28 and rebuilt. All reverted to Equipment Trust Cert. holder in 1935.									
35-39	ARCH ROOF STEEL	CINC '15	BALDWIN 78-25AA	4 GE 205	GE-M C-80-A	83,780	54	51'6"	8'10"	13'1"
	Original order for ten trailers amended to five motors. Sold in 1937 to Chicago Aurora and Elgin - their 600-604.									
40-56	RR ROOF WOOD	NILES '09	BALDWIN 78-25A	4 GE 205	GE-M C-80-A	80,000	54	50'	8'9"	13'3"
	New for 1200V system 2/15/10. 44 burned 12/3/22 and rebuilt. It was wrecked in 1933.									

CAR NUMBER	TYPE	BUILDER/ DATE	TRUCKS	MOTORS	CONTROL	GROSS WEIGHT	SEATS	LENGTH O/ALL	WIDTH O/ALL	HEIGHT O/ROOF
57-65	RR ROOF WOOD	NILES '10	BALDWIN 78-25A	4 GE 205 or 4 GE 233	GE-M C-80-A	78,900	54	50'	8'9"	13'3"

In service April, 1911. 63 destroyed by fire 1/2/22. and never rebuilt. 64 burned 3/27/23 and rebuilt. See under 64.

CAR NUMBER	TYPE	BUILDER/ DATE	TRUCKS	MOTORS	CONTROL	GROSS WEIGHT	SEATS	LENGTH O/ALL	WIDTH O/ALL	HEIGHT O/ROOF
64	ARCH ROOF STEEL	WB&A '24	BALDWIN 78-25A	4 GE 205	GE-M C-80-A	78,900	54	49'7"	8'8"	13'

Rebuilt in company shops 5/19/24. Sold 1935 to Boston Iron & Metal. Sold 1944 to B&ARR (trailer).

CAR NUMBER	TYPE	BUILDER/ DATE	TRUCKS	MOTORS	CONTROL	GROSS WEIGHT	SEATS	LENGTH O/ALL	WIDTH O/ALL	HEIGHT O/ROOF
67-76	RR ROOF WOOD COMBINATION	NILES '09	BALDWIN 78-25A	4 GE 233	GE-M C-80-A	78,900	46	50'	8'9"	13'3"

New for 1200 V system 2/15/10.

CAR NUMBER	TYPE	BUILDER/ DATE	TRUCKS	MOTORS	CONTROL	GROSS WEIGHT	SEATS	LENGTH O/ALL	WIDTH O/ALL	HEIGHT O/ROOF
77-79	RR ROOF WOOD COMBINATION	NILES '07	BALDWIN 78-25A	4 GE 205	GE-M C-80-A	84,000	42	55'	9'2"	13'1"

Rebuilt from 6600V AC cars 20, 22 &23.

CAR NUMBER	TYPE	BUILDER/ DATE	TRUCKS	MOTORS	CONTROL	GROSS WEIGHT	SEATS	LENGTH O/ALL	WIDTH O/ALL	HEIGHT O/ROOF
80-82	ARCH ROOF STEEL COMB.	CINC '14	BALDWIN 78-25A 78-25AA	4 GE 205	GE-M C-80-A	80,000	42	51'3"	8'9"	13'1"

Baldwin 78-25AA trucks had a crescent shaped equalizing beam. There was one set of 78-25A with straight equalizing beam which were at different times used under 80 or 82. Builder specs 807A dated 2/11/14. Welded steel body construction. Sold 1938 to CA&ERR. Their 700-702

CAR NUMBER	TYPE	BUILDER/ DATE	TRUCKS	MOTORS	CONTROL	GROSS WEIGHT	SEATS	LENGTH O/ALL	WIDTH O/ALL	HEIGHT O/ROOF
83-87	RR ROOF WOOD COMBINATION	BRILL '02	BRILL 27E2	4 WH 557 W8	WH-HLF 15 D 9	88,000	46	53'	9'8"	13'9"

Purchased in 1918 from WB&HRy. Rebuilt in 1919 with new motors and controls. Originally had Brill 27E2 trucks. These were exchanged from time to time for Alco B 380's from 601 & 602.

CAR NUMBER	TYPE	BUILDER/ DATE	TRUCKS	MOTORS	CONTROL	GROSS WEIGHT	SEATS	LENGTH O/ALL	WIDTH O/ALL	HEIGHT O/ROOF
88-92	RR ROOF WOOD COMBINATION	ST. LOUIS '08 BALDWIN (WB&A)	BALDWIN 84 35A	4 WH 557 W8	WH-HLF 15 D 9	97,300	54	58'	9'7"	13'9"

Originally ordered for but never delivered to St. Louis Monte Sano and Southern. Bodies only acquired 1918 from builder. New trucks, motors and controls installed by WB&A by 1919. Tightlock couplers installed in 1929. 89-90 converted to trailers. 91-92 sold to B&ARR 1935.

CAR NUMBER	TYPE	BUILDER/ DATE	TRUCKS	MOTORS	CONTROL	GROSS WEIGHT	SEATS	LENGTH O/ALL	WIDTH O/ALL	HEIGHT O/ROOF
100	RR ROOF WOOD PRIVATE CAR	NILES '10	BALDWIN 78 25A	4 GE 205	GE-M C 80 A	78,000	26	51'	8'11"	12'11"

In service April 1911. Furnished with movable parlor chairs, carpets, and draperies for special charter service.

CAR NUMBER	TYPE	BUILDER/ DATE	TRUCKS	MOTORS	CONTROL	GROSS WEIGHT	SEATS	LENGTH O/ALL	WIDTH O/ALL	HEIGHT O/ROOF
93-99, 101-105	ARCH ROOF STEEL COMB.	WASON '13	BRILL MCB 2X	WH 317 A4	WH-HLF 25 B	80,300 88,700	52	55'	9'	13'3"

Originally center door combination cars for 50-61 of MERys. Acquired in 1921 merger. Bodies rebuilt eliminating center-doors and increasing seating capacity to 58 1921-1924. Tightlock couplers added 1929. The larger weight figure is after rebuilding and addition of Tightlock couplers . 96, 99, 101 & 104 converted to trailers. All sold to B&ARR in 1935.

CAR NUMBER	TYPE	BUILDER/ DATE	TRUCKS	MOTORS	CONTROL	GROSS WEIGHT	SEATS	LENGTH O/ALL	WIDTH O/ALL	HEIGHT O/ROOF
106	RR ROOF WOOD PASSENGER	JEWETT '09	ALCO	WH 557 W8	WH-HLF 15 D 9		62	56'4"	9'1"	13'7"

Originally 6600V AC combination car of MERys. Acquired by merger 1921.

CAR NUMBER	TYPE	BUILDER/ DATE	TRUCKS	MOTORS	CONTROL	GROSS WEIGHT	SEATS	LENGTH O/ALL	WIDTH O/ALL	HEIGHT O/ROOF
107	RR ROOF WOOD COMBINATION	JEWETT '09	ALCO	WH 557 W8	WH-HLF 15 D 9		54	56'3"	9'2"	13'4"

Originally 6600V AC combination car of MERys. Acquired in 1921 merger

CAR NUMBER	TYPE	BUILDER/ DATE	TRUCKS	MOTORS	CONTROL	GROSS WEIGHT	SEATS	LENGTH O/ALL	WIDTH O/ALL	HEIGHT O/ROOF
200-208	ARCH ROOF STEEL TRAILER	BRILL '29	BRILL 27MCB3	NONE	NONE	76,400	58	58'1"	8'10"	12'8"

Builder spec 562 E dated 4/17/29. Equipped with Tightlock couplers. Rebuilt to motor cars with WH 557 A8 motors and WH- HLF 15 D 9 controls in 1934. Weight increased to 93,400 lbs. Experimental speed runs 1935. Sold to B&ARR in 1935

CAR NUMBER	TYPE	BUILDER/ DATE	TRUCKS	MOTORS	CONTROL	GROSS WEIGHT	SEATS	LENGTH O/ALL	WIDTH O/ALL	HEIGHT O/ROOF
301-354	RR ROOF WOOD OPEN PLATFORM CENTER DOOR TRAIL	PULLMAN '98 WASON '99	-	NONE	NONE	-	54	46'	8'6"	12'4"

Purchased 1917 from the Long Island RR. 24, (LI 852-875) built by Pullman; 30, (LI 877-906) by Wason. MCB Couplers added by WB&A. 345, 352 & 354 rebuilt without center doors. 321, 323 & 325 converted to mail cars; 305 converted to line car and 310 & 314 converted to box and flat cars respectively.

CAR NUMBER	TYPE	BUILDER/ DATE	TRUCKS	MOTORS	CONTROL	GROSS WEIGHT	SEATS	LENGTH O/ALL	WIDTH O/ALL	HEIGHT O/ROOF
355-356	RR ROOF WOOD	WASON '07	TAYLOR MCB	NONE	NONE	-	58	53'6"	-	-

Purchased 1918 from the Albany Southern RR their 30 & 32. Electric equipment removed and rebuilt as trailers with end train doors.

CAR NUMBER	TYPE	BUILDER/ DATE	TRUCKS	MOTORS	CONTROL	GROSS WEIGHT	SEATS	LENGTH O/ALL	WIDTH O/ALL	HEIGHT O/ROOF
357-358	RR ROOF WOOD OPEN PLATFORM COACH	-	-	NONE	NONE	-	62	54'	-	-

Original B&A Short Line RR 14 & 16. Acquired in 1921 Merger.

FREIGHT CARS:

CAR NUMBER	TYPE	BUILDER/DATE	TRUCKS	MOTORS	CONTROL	GROSS WEIGHT	LENGTH O/ALL	WIDTH O/ALL	HEIGHT O/ROOF
1-2	WOOD RR ROOF FREIGHT MOTOR	NILES '07	BALDWIN 90-40 MCB	GE 603	GE-M C 57	86,000	54'	9'6"	14'1"
	Original 6600V AC cars converted to 1200V DC 2/15/10 with GE 207 motors and GE 74A control. Weight increased to 92,000 lbs. Number 1 burned 6/6/29.								
2ND 1	STEEL ARCH ROOF FREIGHT MOTOR	BRILL '29	BALDWIN 90-40	GE 207	GE-M C 74 A	94,000	54'8"	9'2"	13'11"
	Builder specs 616A. Trucks, motors and control from 1st number 1. Sold 1936 to CCTCo. and became their 7. Acquired from a Stockton, CA scrap dealer in 1967 by the Bay Area Electric RR Assn. Museum, Rio Vista, California.								
3	WOOD RR ROOF FREIGHT MOTOR	NILES '09	BALDWIN 78 56 A	GE 207	GE-M C 74 A	83,000	50'	8'8"	14'1"
	New for 1200V DC SYSTEM 2/15/10. Burned 12/16/13 and rebuilt with arch roof.								
4-6	WOOD ARCH ROOF EXPRESS TRAILERS	NILES '12	BALDWIN 78 25 A	NONE	GE-M C 74	-	51'	9'4"	13'7"
	Originally had controls which were later removed. End windows paneled in 1921. 4 dropped from records 1921.								
7	WOOD ARCH ROOF EXPRESS MOTOR	NILES '12	BALDWIN 78 25 A	GE 205	GE-M C 80 A	-	51'	9'4"	13'7"
	Same order as trailers 4-6.								
8-9	WOOD ARCH ROOF EXPRESS MOTORS	NILES '14	BALDWIN 78 25 A	-	-	-	51'	9'4"	13'7"
	Number 8 equipped with end train doors.								
10-17	WOOD RR ROOF FREIGHT MOTORS	SOUTHERN '08	ALCO B 380	WH 557 W8	WH-HL 15 D 9	91,400	56'9"	9'2"	13'11"
	Rebuilt by WB&A from passenger cars purchased from MERys: 2 in 1916 and 6 in 1917. Number 12 rebuilt with arch roof. 15 burned 8/20/22 and rebuilt to 602. 16 & 17 sold to Capital Transit Company in 1935.								
18	WOOD RR ROOF LOCOMOTIVE	JEWETT '09	ALCO	WH 562X5	WH-HLF 572 D2	119,000	56'	9'5"	13'11"
	Originally 6600V AC combination car 37 of MERys converted 3/27/14 to locomotive 300. Acquired by merger 1921. Sold to B&ARR 1935.								
200-202	REFRIGERATOR TRAILERS	-	-	NONE	NONE	5 TON ICE CAPACITY	37'4"	9'4"	13'2"
	Purchased 1914, 15 & 17 from Swift and Company. Out of service 1923, scrapped 1926.								
401	REFRIG. TRAILER	-	-	NONE	NONE	-	-	-	-
	Acquired 1918, dropped 1924.								

CAR NUMBER	TYPE	BUILDER/ DATE	TRUCKS	MOTORS	CONTROL	GROSS WEIGHT	LENGTH O/ALL	WIDTH O/ALL	HEIGHT O/ROOF
601	WOOD RR ROOF EXPRESS TRAILER	SOUTHERN '08	ALCO B380	NONE		48,000	56'9"	9'2"	13'5"

Original MERys combination car 31. Rebuilt 10/14 to baggage trailer 211. Acquired by merger 1921 and renumbered to WB&A 20. Again renumbered to 601 in 1924. Alco trucks exchanged for Brill 27 E2 trucks from Hazleton car 86 or 87. Sold to B&ARR in 1935.

| 602 | WOOD RR ROOF FREIGHT TRAILER | SOUTHERN '08 | ALCO B380 | NONE | | 48,000 | 56'9" | 9'2" | 13'5" |

Rebuilt in 1924 from freight motor 15. Alco trucks exchanged for Brill 27 E2 trucks from Hazleton car 86 or 87. Sold to B&A RR in 1935.

| 900-949 | STEEL DROP BOTTOM HOPPER CARS | - | | NONE | | 100,000 | 31'8" | 10'4" | 10'8" |

Two basic types. 30 acquired in 1928; 20 aquired in 1929.

ANNAPOLIS SHORT LINE - MARYLAND ELECTRIC RAILWAYS
ROSTER OF ELECTRIC CARS

CAR NUMBER	TYPE	BUILDER/ DATE	TRUCKS	MOTORS	CONTROL	GROSS WEIGHT	LENGTH O/ALL	WIDTH O/ALL	HEIGHT O/ROOF
29-35 (odd #'s only)	RR ROOF COMBINATION	SOUTHERN '08	ALCO B380	4-WH 132-A 100 HP	?	88,000	56'	9'2"	13'11"
30-38 (even #s only)	RR ROOF PASSENGER	SOUTHERN '08	ALCO B380	4-WH 132-A 100 HP	?	88,000	56'	9'2"	13'11"

29-38 were 6600V AC single phase cars also equipped for 600V DC operation over the Baltimore city system with trolley poles, but that never came to pass. 31 converted to baggage trailer 211 in 1914 - see WB&A 601. The remaining eight were converted to trailers which were sold to the WB&A in 1916.

| 37-41(odd #sonly) | RR ROOF COMBINATION | JEWETT '09 | ALCO B380 | 4-WH132-A | ? | ? | ? | ? | ? |

37 rewired for 1200V DC in 1914 and converted to locomotive 300 - weight increased to 119,000 lbs. To WB&A 18 . 39 converted to 1200V DC and to Package Express motor 70. To WB&A 107. In 1919, 41 rebuilt by MERys to straight passenger car 100. It was also rewired for 1200 V DC with 4 140 HP motors and designated a passenger locomotive. To WB&A 106.

| 50-61 | ARCH ROOF STEEL COMB. | WASON '13 | BRILL MCB 2X | 4 WH 75HP | ? | 80,300 | | | |

These twelve center door cars ordered for the conversion of the road to 1200V DC. 75hp motors were replaced by 90hp motors by ASL.. To WB&A 93-99 & 101-105 which see.

ABBREVIATIONS:

ASL	Annapolis Short Line
ALCO	American Locomotive Company, Schenectady, New York
B&ARR	Baltimore and Annapolis Railroad
BALDWIN	Baldwin Locomotive Works, Eddystone, Pennsylvania
BRILL	J. G. Brill Company, Philadelphia
BROWNELL	Brownell Car Company, St Louis
CA&E RR	Chicago Aurora and Elgin Railroad
CCTCO	Central California Traction Company, Stockton
CINC	Cincinnati Car Company
CTCO	Capital Transit Company, Washington
GE	General Electric Company
JEWETT	Jewett Car Company, Newark, Ohio

MERys	Maryland Electric Railways
NILES	Niles Car Co., Niles, Ohio
PECKHAM	Peckham Manufacturing Company
PULLMAN	Pullman's Palace Car Company
ST LOUIS	St Louis Car Company
SOUTHERN	Southern Car Company, High Point, N Carolina
WASON	Wason Manufacturing Co., Springfield, Mass
WB&HRy	Wilkes Barre and Hazleton Railway
WRy&ECo	Washington Railway and Electric Company
WH	Westinghouse Electric and Manufacturing Co
URys&ECo	United Railways and Electric Company, Baltimore

Figures below show the greatest inventory of any one type of freight equipment owned :

Caboose	1	1911-1917
Mail cars	3	1928-1935
Line cars	4	1924-1935
Box cars	7	1921-1930
Flat cars	25	1924-1928
Gondolas	10	1911

The company owned three busses numbered 1, 2 & 3 from 1927-1935. They were type "Y" Yellow Coaches with 29 seats. In 1935, they were acquired by the B&ARR.

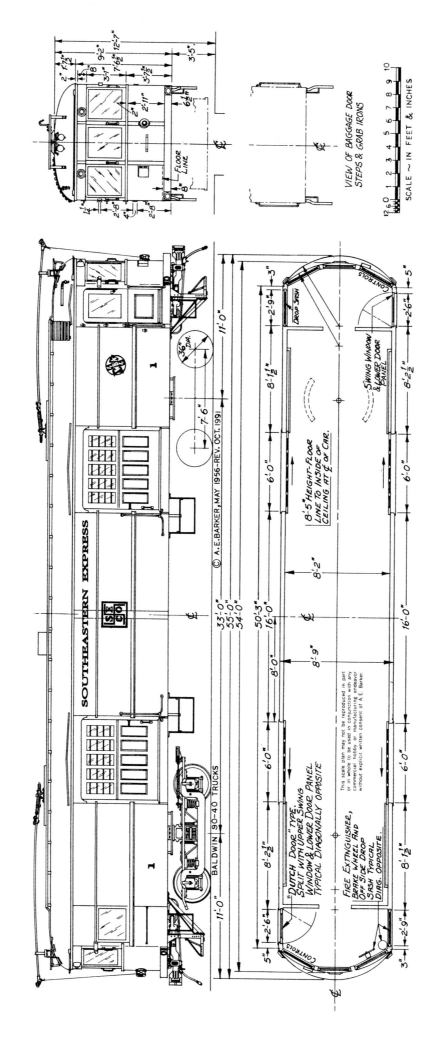

VIEW OF BAGGAGE DOOR
STEPS & GRAB IRONS

SCALE ~ IN FEET & INCHES

SOUTHEASTERN EXPRESS

SE CO

BALDWIN 90-40 TRUCKS

© A.E.BARKER, MAY 1956-REV. OCT. 1991

This scale plan may not be reproduced in part or in whole to be used in conjunction with any commercial hobby or manufacturing endeavor without explicit written consent of A. E. Barker.

"DUTCH DOOR" TYPE, SPLIT WITH UPPER SWING WINDOW & LOWER DOOR PANEL TYPICAL DIAGONALLY OPPOSITE

FIRE EXTINGUISHER, BRAKE WHEEL AND OFF SIDE DROP SASH TYPICAL DIAG. OPPOSITE.

8'-5" HEIGHT-FLOOR LINE TO INSIDE OF CEILING AT ₵ OF CAR.

DROP SASH

SWING WINDOW & LOWER DOOR PANEL

CONTROLS

WASHINGTON BALTIMORE & ANNAPOLIS FREIGHT MOTOR NUMBER ONE - J. G. BRILL COMPANY, PHILADELPHIA, 1929.
DRAWING BY A. E. BARKER

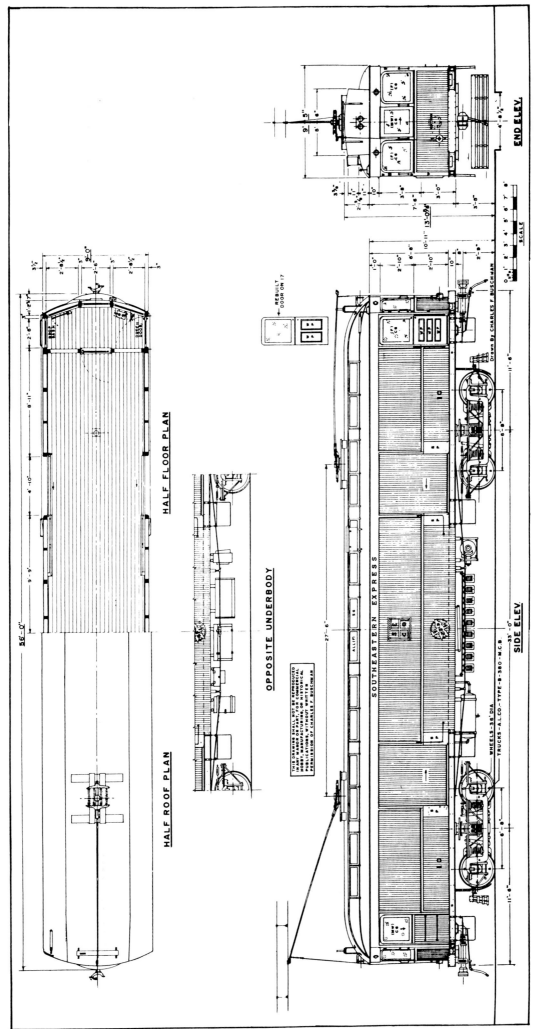

HALF ROOF PLAN

HALF FLOOR PLAN

OPPOSITE UNDERBODY

REBUILT
DOOR ON 17

THIS DRAWING SHALL NOT BE REPRODUCED
IN PART, MANOR OR PART, 'OB COMMERCIAL
HOBS/ MANUFACTURING, OR HISTORICAL
PUBLICATIONS, WITHOUT WRITTEN
PERMISSION OF CHARLES F. BUSCHMAN

SOUTHEASTERN EXPRESS

WHEELS—36" DIA
TRUCKS—ALCO—TYPE—B—380—M.C.B.

SIDE ELEV.

END ELEV.

SCALE

Drawn By CHARLES F. BUSCHMAN

WASHINGTON BALTIMORE & ANNAPOLIS FREIGHT MOTOR SERIES 10-17 - SOUTHERN CAR COMPANY, HIGH POINT, NORTH CAROLINA, 1908
DRAWING BY CHARLES F. BUSCHMAN, COURTESY OF THE BALTIMORE STREETCAR MUSEUM, INC.

Washington, Baltimore and Annapolis Rwy.
Niles Car and Mfg. Co. 1907.

DRAWING BY A. E. BARKER

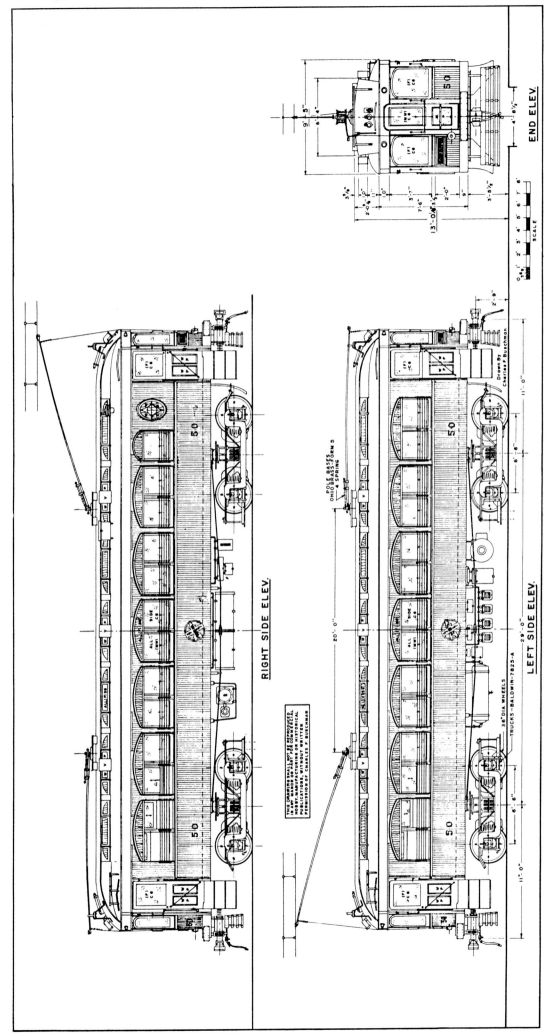

END ELEV.

RIGHT SIDE ELEV.

LEFT SIDE ELEV.

WASHINGTON BALTIMORE & ANNAPOLIS PASSENGER MOTORS 40-65 – NILES CAR AND MANUFACTURING COMPANY, NILES, OHIO, 1909-10. DRAWING BY CHARLES F. BUSCHMAN, COURTESY OF THE BALTIMORE STREETCAR MUSEUM, INC.

259

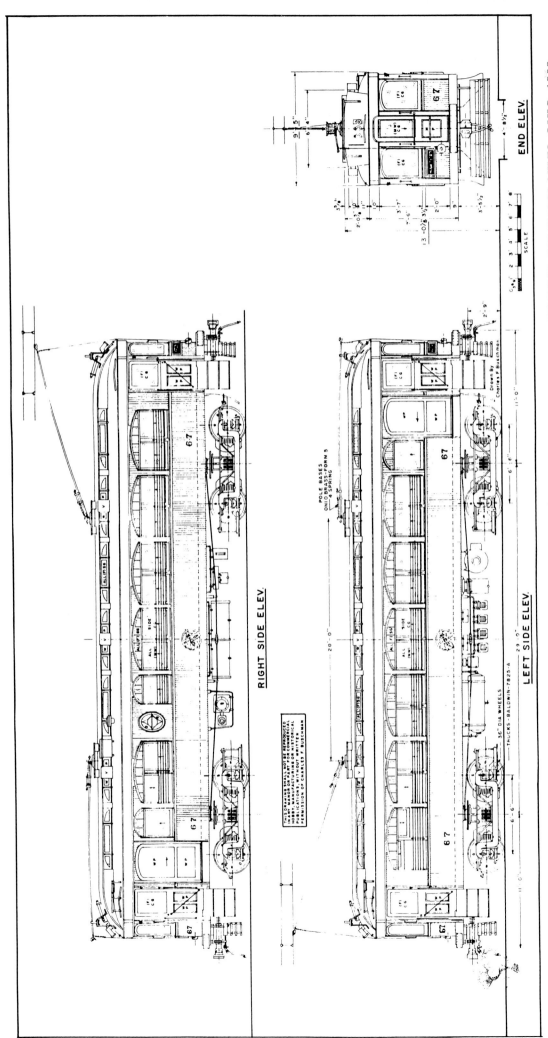

WASHINGTON BALTIMORE & ANNAPOLIS PASSENGER MOTORS 67-76 - NILES CAR AND MANUFACTURING COMPANY, NILES, OHIO, 1909.
DRAWING BY CHARLES F. BUSCHMAN, COURTESY OF THE BALTIMORE STREETCAR MUSEUM, INC.

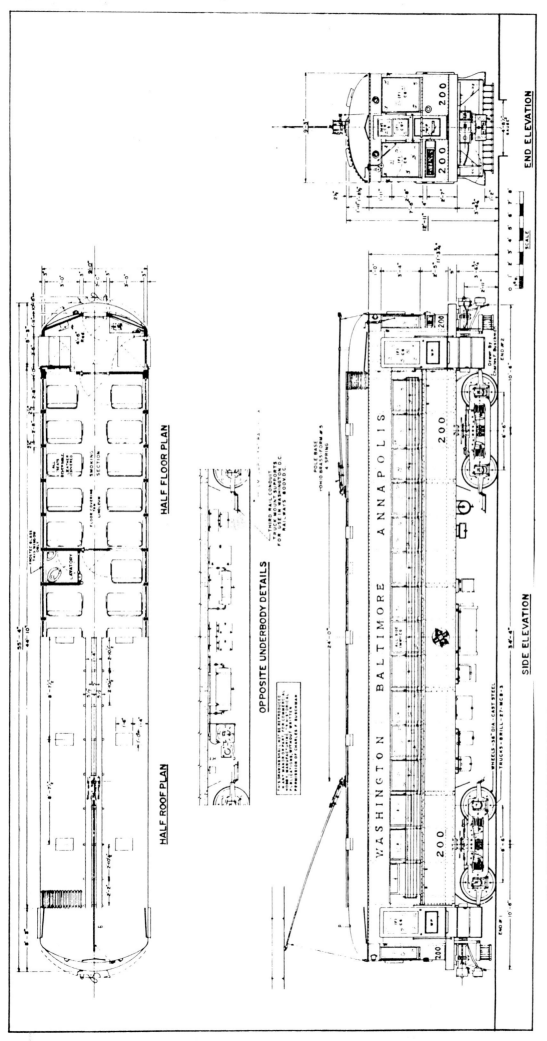

HALF ROOF PLAN

HALF FLOOR PLAN

OPPOSITE UNDERBODY DETAILS

END ELEVATION

SIDE ELEVATION

WASHINGTON BALTIMORE ANNAPOLIS

WASHINGTON BALTIMORE & ANNAPOLIS PASSENGER MOTORS 200-208 - J. G. BRILL COMPANY, PHILADELPHIA, 1929.
DRAWING BY CHARLES F. BUSCHMAN, COURTESY OF THE BALTIMORE STREETCAR MUSEUM, INC.

Note: 200 series motor cars were lettered with the terminal cities on the letter board or with the company emblem centered on the car side below the windows. Both were not used at the same time.

$1,400,000

Washington, Baltimore and Annapolis Electric Railroad Company

Two-Year Seven Per Cent. Mortgage and Collateral Trust Notes

Dated March 1, 1921   Due March 1, 1923

Interest payable—March 1st and September 1st

Coupon notes in denominations of $1,000 and $500

Redeemable in whole or in part on any interest date prior to maturity at 100 and interest upon 30 days' notice.

Exempt from Federal Normal Income Tax up to 2%

THE FIDELITY TRUST COMPANY (BALTIMORE, MD.), Trustee

The following summary is from a letter of Mr. George T. Bishop, President of the Company:

PROPERTIES

The Company owns and operates a high speed electric interurban railroad from Baltimore, Maryland, to Washington, D. C. with passenger and freight terminals in both cities, together with a line of railroad beginning at Camp Meade Junction where it connects with the Baltimore and Ohio Railroad, through Camp Meade, connecting with the Pennsylvania Lines at Odenton, and extending on the south side of the Severn River to Annapolis, the Capitol of the State of Maryland, and the location of the United States Naval Academy; also a line of railroad formerly known as the Annapolis Short Line, to be connected with the Baltimore and Washington line at Shipley, Md., running on the north side of the Severn River to Annapolis, both lines to use same passenger and freight terminals at Annapolis and Baltimore.

The total trackage to be operated is equivalent to 130 miles of single track, of which all but 1.37 miles in the streets of Annapolis and 2.92 miles in the city of Baltimore are on private right of way.

The Company owns 149 cars of various kinds, and in addition operates 15 cars leased under car trust agreement by the Annapolis Short Line Railroad Company.

It also owns the capital stock of the Annapolis Public Utilities Company which supplies all the gas and electric energy consumed in the city of Annapolis (except electric energy consumed by U. S. Naval Academy), and has a contract with the United States Government for furnishing electric energy for the Government Radio Station at Greenbury Point near Annapolis, and it likewise furnishes electric energy for Camp Meade and the State Hospital for Colored Insane at Crownsville.

The Company owns complete modern machine shops and car barns at Naval Academy Junction as well as its own substations and transmission system in duplicate. It obtains its electric energy from the plant of the Potomac Electric Power Company at Bennings, D. C.

The railroad serves a population of more than 1,300,000.

An increase in passenger fares became effective on the Annapolis Short Line Railroad July 1, 1920, and on the W. B. & A. Electric Railroad July 11, 1920.

FRANCHISES

The provisions of the franchises under which the Company operates in Baltimore and Annapolis are favorable, and extend beyond the maturity of the W. B. & A. 1st Mortgage 5s. In Washington it operates under a contract with the Washington Railway and Electric Company which is co-extensive with the latter's franchises.

SECURITY

These notes are a direct obligation of the Company, and will be secured by the deposit with The Fidelity Trust Company, Baltimore, Md., Trustee, under a collateral trust indenture of $1,600,000 par value W. B. & A. Electric Railroad First Mortgage 5% Bonds, by a first mortgage on real estate properties in Washington, D. C., costing $668,000, and by a first mortgage on about seven miles of railroad between the city of Baltimore and Shipley, Md., valued at $150,000. The two latter properties may be severally withdrawn from this mortgage by payment of 54% of the above recited figures, or by depositing with the Trustee additional W. B. & A. 1st Mortgage 5% bonds, at a par value equal to 166⅔% of the cash amount for which said properties may be withdrawn.

EARNINGS

Washington, Baltimore & Annapolis Electric Railroad Company:

	1919	1920
Gross Earnings	$2,368,025	$2,324,839
Operating Expenses and Taxes	1,753,424	1,737,934
	$614,601	$586,905
Fixed Charges	295,202	*299,899
Net Income	$319,399	$287,006

*This item includes $29,269 interest charges on obligations which will be retired by the proceeds of these notes.

ESTIMATED EARNINGS

Combined Railroad Properties:

	1921
Gross Earnings	$2,887,000
Operating Expenses and Taxes	1,980,300
	$906,700
Fixed Charges, including interest on these notes	471,090
Net Income	$435,610

Sinking Fund requirements on obligations guaranteed by the Company amount to $38,600 annually.

PURPOSE OF ISSUE

Proceeds from the sale of these notes are to be used for the completion of terminals at Baltimore and Washington made necessary by the increased passenger and freight traffic, to retire obligations therefor and for other corporate purposes.

LEGALITY

All legal matters in connection with this issue have been approved by Marbury, Gosnell and Williams, for the Company, and Henry D. Harlan, Esquire, for the bankers.

The notes are issued subject to approval by the Public Service Commission of Maryland.

Price 98.19 and interest, to yield 8%

If, as and when issued and received by us.

THE FIDELITY TRUST COMPANY

ROBERT GARRETT & SONS   W. W. LANAHAN & CO.

NELSON, COOK & CO.   COLSTON & CO.

CRANE, PARRIS & CO., Washington, D. C.

The above statements were obtained from sources we consider reliable, and, while not guaranteed, we believe them to be correct.

Statioin List- Main Line- Baltimore Division

1	Baltimore	23	Conway
3	Westport	24	Meyers
4	English Consul	25	Bowie Road
5	Rosemont	26	Lloyd
6	Baltimore Highlands	27	High Bridge
7	Pumphrey	28	Hillmeade
8	North Linthicum	29	Bell
9	Linthicum	30	Randle
11	Downs	31	Lincoln
12	Wellham	32	Vista
13	Kelly	33	Cherry Grove
14	McPherson	34	McCarthy
15	Elmhurst	35	Ardmore
16	Delmont	36	Glenarden
11	Clark	37	Dodge Park
18	Severn Run	38	East Columbia Park
19	Naval Academy Junction	39	Huntsville
20	Waugh Chapel	40	Gregory
21	Francis	41	District Line
22	Bragers		

Station List North Shore Division

68	Shipley
69	Woodlawn Heights
70	Garland
71	Ferndale
72	Glen Burnie
73	Saunders Range
74	Oakwood
75	Marley
76	Elvaton
77	Pasadena
78	Earleigh Heights
79	Robinson
80	Severna Park
81	Round Bay
82	Jones
83	Revell
84	Jones
85	Arnold
86	Winchester
87	Severnside (Manresa)
88	Wardour
89	West Annapolis
90	Annapolis - Bladen Street

Station List - South Shore Division

44	Camp Meade Junction
45	Portland
46	Disney
47	Admiral
48	Fairall
49	Odenton
50	Naval Academy Junction
51	Sappington
52	Gambrills
53	Millersville
54	Waterbury
55	Gotts
56	Crownsville
57	Belvoir
58	Arth
59	Iglehart
60	Weytych
61	Hockley
62	Best Gate
63	Camp Parole
64	Homewood
65	Cedar Park
66	Bay Ridge Junction
67	Annapolis - West Street

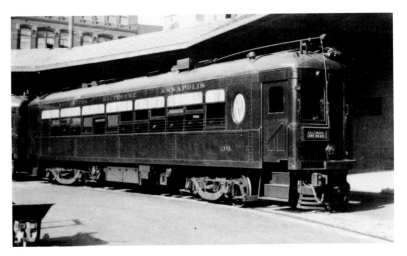

Number 36 at the Baltimore terminal March 16, 1935. George Krambles collection.

ACKNOWLEDGEMENTS

The author wishes to acknowledge the kindness of those who, through interviews, photographs, or critical review of his research, have contributed to the finished work:

Chris Andreae
A. E. Barker
Charles F. Bindeman
Charles G. Britton
Charles F. Buschman
Gerald F. Cunningham
Wylie L. Donaldson
Henry L. Erb
William A. Ernst
Michael H. Ford
Edward A. Gannon
William M. Garrett
William D. Gray
Herbert H. Harwood, Jr.
William C. Janssen
Elmer Jubb
Mrs. Earl H. Keese
Jacques Kelly
LeRoy O. King, Sr.
LeRoy O. King, Jr.
George Krambles
William Lichtenstern

James A. Mellor
Richard C. Meyer
Mrs. W. J. Muchow
Norman Nelson
Barney Neuberger
George F. Nixon
Arnold S. Osbelt
Henry F. Rinn
Gary W. Schlerf
Emil J. Schlueter
Alfred E. Seibel
James P. Shuman
Alonzo Smith
George E. Taylor
Francis B. Tosh
Robert A. Truax
Eugene Van Dusen
George E. Votava
George D. Watts
William Welden
Frank White
Miss Evelyn C. Wood

And to David McCullough for his words of encouragement

The following institutions, through their library facilities, have graciously aided in specific research in ways too numerous to recount:

Andrew Carnegie Public Library
National Archives
Washington National Records Center
Maryland Hall of Records
Interstate Commerce Commission
Historical Society of Pennsylvania
Circuit Court of Baltimore City
Circuit Court of Anne Arundel County
Circuit Court of Prince George's County
McKeldin Library, University of Maryland

Enoch Pratt Free Library
Library of Congress
Baltimore Streetcar Museum, Inc.
Maryland Public Service Commission
Columbia Historical Society
Western Reserve Historical Society
Barker Library, School of Engineering, M.I.T.
Hayden Memorial Library of M.I.T.
Baker Library, Business School, Harvard University

And the following publications:

Street Railway Journal
Electric Railway Journal
Electric Railway Review
Electric Traction Weekly
Railroad Gazette
Electric Railway Gazette
Electrical World
Railway & Engineering Review
Official Railway Equipment Register
Moody's Investment Manual
Poor's Investment Manual

Report on the Washington Traffic Situation to the Public Utilities Commission by John A. Beeler, 1918 Section Three

Minutes of the Board of Directors of the WB&A
Minutes of the Executive Committee of the WB&A
Minutes of Annapolis Town Council
Minutes or the Maryland State Senate
Minutes of Hearings, Maryland PSC

Annapolis Evening Capital
Baltimore News
Baltimore American
Baltimore Sun
Brunswick Herald
Cleveland Plain Dealer
Cleveland Press
National Cyclopedia of American Biography
Washington Times-Herald
Washington Evening Star
Washington Post
Laurel Leader

Electric Railway Handbook (1915)
   by Albert B. Richey
General Electric Bulletin Number 4950 (May 1912)

EDITOR'S NOTE

Acknowledgments for research help appear above; photograph credits appear with the pictures. In addition, a number of friends helped in the production phase. George Krambles enthusiastically granted me complete access to his collection and, as seen in the book, shared his considerable artistic talent; Jim Shuman sent his entire negative collection, and Norman Nelson sent records of employee interviews which were useful in many ways. Bob Truax generously used his time and superb skill to copy rare photographs, stock certificates, postcards and other advertising material, and Jack Leming contributed artwork of the company's two symbols.

My interest in this long project was sustained by fond memories of excursions with my father on the majestic dark green interurbans.

As has happened before, my wife, Helen, has been helpful almost daily, and my son, James, volunteered many hours of his uncanny proof-reading ability.

LeRoy O. King, Jr.
Dallas, Texas

INDEX

Symbols